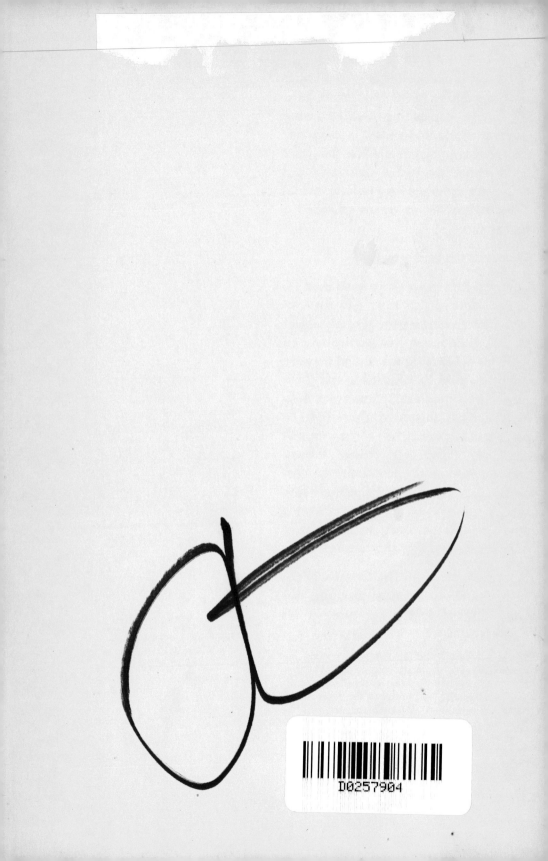

THE UNIVERSITY OF CHICAGO PRESS · CHICAGO

THE BAKER & TAYLOR COMPANY, NEW YORK; THE CAMBRIDGE UNIVERSITY
PRESS, LONDON; THE MARUZEN-KABUSHIKI-KAISHA, TOKYO, OSAKA,
KYOTO, FUKUOKA, SENDAI; THE COMMERCIAL PRESS, LIMITED, SHANGHAI

MILK DISTRIBUTION AS A PUBLIC UTILITY

By

W. P. MORTENSON, Ph.D.

*Associate Professor in the Department of Agricultural Economics
University of Wisconsin*

THE UNIVERSITY OF CHICAGO PRESS
CHICAGO · ILLINOIS

To
PETER AND PAUL

FOREWORD

MORE than any other farm product milk has won recognition as a food vital to the health of our people. Each day the milk must reach the hospitals and the homes where little children are—in spite of storms and regardless of strikes or other civil disturbances. Widespread is the realization that milk production and distribution are industries that bear directly on the welfare of nearly all urban people as consumers.

Rural people, too, have a special interest in milk and dairy products. Dairying is much the largest enterprise of America's farmers, for it furnishes a fifth of the national farm income.

For more than a generation there has been more or less dissatisfaction with the system of milk distribution in our larger cities. While it is admitted that the sanitary protection and quality of our urban milk supplies have given America world-leadership in this field, the cost of distributing milk has seemed to consumers and producers alike to be out of proportion. Farmers and city people both have questioned the economic justification of making urban consumers pay as much for distributing milk as for producing and delivering it to the city.

Many investigations have been made of milk-distribution costs in cities in various parts of the United States. Scores of proposals have been made as to ways in which these costs might be reduced and still retain the present competitive system of milk distribution. Some of these have been tried out in certain distribution areas. The fact remains, however, that in none of the large city markets are consumers or producers satisfied that the present arrangements are as efficient as they should be.

A few years ago the suggestion was made that milk, because of its special importance in protecting and promoting the public welfare, should be made a public utility like water, gas, and electricity. The Agricultural Experiment Station at the University of Wisconsin, in its capacity as a publicly supported research agency, inaugurated a study of this proposal. Professor Mortenson was made leader of the research project which was carried on over a period of some four years.

Because no city has actually had experience in handling milk as a monopoly product under the conditions we associate with a public utility, Professor Mortenson has had to make his analysis largely on an abstract basis. It is our belief that he has covered his assignment thoroughly and objectively. We are certain that the material he presents will be interesting and useful to the general public as well as to those directly associated with the production and distribution of milk.

The University of Wisconsin long has stood for academic freedom for its staff. The institution does not censor the books written by its faculty. Professor Mortenson's findings and conclusions are his own, not the University's, but we shall be surprised if they do not win wide attention and exert considerable influence on public thinking as regards this controversial subject of milk distribution.

NOBLE CLARK
Associate Director
Agricultural Experiment Station
University of Wisconsin

PREFACE

ROUGHLY one half of the dollar paid by city consumers for fluid milk goes for processing and distributing it, leaving only the other half for the farmer who produces it. This condition has prompted much discussion and in many quarters has aroused deep public concern. The high cost of distribution is being criticized by scores and studied by many; but, while facts have been gathered and revealed as to what makes for the high costs, no one has found a way of greatly reducing the charge. The wide margin between what the consumer pays at his doorstep and what the farmer receives at his gate is common everywhere in our cities and continues to be one of the important, unsolved, and vexing problems in milk distribution. The general welfare of the urban population is dependent in no small way upon the opportunity to obtain necessary foods such as fluid milk at prices which do not prohibit purchase of the amounts needed to maintain a high state of health and vigor. Likewise, the welfare of milk producers is enhanced by being able to dispose of sustained or increasing quantities of milk at acceptable prices.

For almost eight years fluid-milk producers in many markets have been demanding and obtaining state or federal aid to assist in maintaining satisfactory prices. While this price maintenance has had a stabilizing and mollifying influence of producer conditions, it has by no means provided a lasting cure.

What will the next step be? To this no one can give a final answer. It may be suggestive to note the trend of thought of some lawmaking bodies. For example, in 1935 a bill was presented in the Wisconsin legislature to permit cities to distribute fluid milk to the exclusion of private capital with the hope of reducing the "spread" of distributing milk. The bill passed the assembly and lost in the senate by only five votes. Two years later a similar but more detailed bill was presented, recommended for passage by the committee on agriculture, but was lost in sine die adjournment. Out of the general public interest which then existed, together with that which arose out of these legislative discussions and deliberations, grew requests that the College of Agriculture of the University of Wisconsin make a study to determine the advantage and limitations of milk distribution under public utility control.

The findings show that, if the functions of processing and of distributing fluid milk were operated as an efficient unified system publicly controlled, the possible economies and resultant savings would be considerable. But while these purely economic questions can be answered rather positively, many other considerations must be taken into account. Among the most important are two which would seem paramount, namely, (1) "Will the general public accept the different approach to the milk-distribution problem and lend the new undertaking continuous and unqualified support?" and (2) "Will those in public office have the desire and capacity to operate the enterprise efficiently and in the public interest, or will they give greater consideration to their own personal and political interests?" Neither the economist, the social psychologist, nor the political scientist can answer these questions with finality. Indeed, experience alone will provide the information with which to give the answers.

This volume has been improved distinctly through the suggestions of several of my colleagues to whom I make grateful acknowledgments. Professors B. H. Hibbard and Asher Hobson have offered general guidance and encouragement. They have read the manuscript and suggested additions and changes. Charles Bunn, professor of law in the University of Wisconsin, has made fundamental suggestions on the legal section. Professors Edwin E. Witte and Martin L. Glaeser of the Economics Department have likewise read the entire manuscript and recommended changes. W. A. Sumner, professor of agricultural journalism, read some chapters, contributing much to style and form.

On many occasions the project has been discussed with members of the staff of the Agricultural Economics Department, especially Professors H. H. Erdmann, P. E. McNall, D. R. Mitchell, Don S. Anderson, R. K. Froker, and Carl F. Wehrwein. Five graduate students have helped compile, tabulate, and interpret material: Ray Strauss, graduate student in marketing; Lawrence Witt, Donald Keyes, Carl Heisig, and Gale Johnson, all graduate students in agricultural economics.

It goes without saying, of course, that the author assumes full responsibility for all statements made and for omissions and errors.

W. P. MORTENSON

MADISON, WISCONSIN
   February 1940

TABLE OF CONTENTS

LIST OF TABLES

LIST OF TABLES

APPENDIX TABLES

PART I
HISTORICAL AND INTRODUCTORY BACKGROUND

CHAPTER I

HISTORY AND BACKGROUND OF FLUID-MILK REGULATION

HISTORICAL SKETCH

FOR a long stretch of years the functions of processing and distributing fluid milk in urban centers were performed in an atmosphere of almost complete laissez faire. Indeed, this freedom of economic activity was enjoyed by virtually all American enterprises. Coupled with the "let-alone" philosophy was apparently the belief that unlimited freedom of competition as it then functioned in business and industry would create efficiency of operation, eliminate wasteful business practices, and best serve the public welfare.

The turn of the tide from unhampered freedom of action in American economic activity came in 1876, when the United States Supreme Court handed down a number of decisions in what became known as the "Granger cases." These cases centered their attention primarily on questions of (1) the power of the state to fix maximum freight rates and railroad fares and (2) the charges permitted to be made by public warehouses for the storage of farm products. For the first time it became evident that the public and the courts began to doubt the desirability of untrammeled freedom of private enterprise in the operation of agencies in which arbitrary charges were coming to predominate. Another telling blow was aimed at laissez faire in 1890 with the passage of the Sherman Anti-trust Act, which made it illegal for a business to monopolize trade or attempt to do so by combining into trusts or similar organizations in restraint of trade. While the general import of this act was similar to that which grew out of the Granger cases—namely, to break down complete freedom of action on the part of entrepreneurs—the method of accomplishing this purpose was different. The Granger cases involved the question of direct fixing of rates and charges by the state. The

Sherman Anti-trust Act was designed to force competition for the public benefit.

The Clayton Act, passed in 1914, contained among others certain provisions to supplement existing laws on monopolies and restraint of trade. Again, seven years later, the Packers and Stockyards Act re-emphasized some of the provisions of earlier regulatory acts and specifically prohibited (1) unfair trade practices; (2) the giving of special advantages to individuals, firms, or localities or subjecting them to disadvantages; and (3) the apportionment of territory in carrying on business.[1] The Clayton Act and the Packers and Stockyards Act, like the Sherman Anti-trust Act, were premised upon the desirability of maintaining—indeed, of forcing—free competition. Philosophically, America, rural and urban, has been anti-monopolistic. Briefly, "collective action in control of individual action"[2] developed gradually but rather continuously for a period of fifty years. Even with this increase in regulation, American business, industry, and agriculture, with the notable exception of rail transportation, coasted along with relatively few obstructions until the time of the world-wide crash which began with real force in the early 1930's.

EVENTS LEADING TO PRICE CONTROL IN THE FLUID-MILK INDUSTRY

As the severity of the depression increased, large numbers of individuals as well as business and industrial concerns began to clamor for public control. Farmers demanded higher prices for their products; industrial workers wanted economic security and protection against declining wage rates; business and industry insisted on aid and regulation designed to promote economic stability. Price-fixing at higher price levels struck a popular keynote with industry and agriculture alike. The urge that the government "do something" became more and more general and was pressed with increasing intensity. Many acts were discussed by Congress and state legislatures, and numerous laws were passed by the federal government and by several states in answer to these insistent demands.

[1] *United States Code, Annotated*, Title 7: *Agriculture* (St. Paul, 1927), p. 77, esp. chap. ix.

[2] See John R. Commons, *Institutional Economics* (New York, 1934), pp. 69–93, esp. chap. ii.

In the fluid-milk business regulation involving health and sanitation had been common for at least two or three decades, but it was not until the 1930's that price regulation also made its impression upon the industry. The pressure for this type of control came mainly from milk producers but also somewhat from milk distributors. Legislation by several states and by the federal government brought forth a new type of control in the field of milk production and distribution.

The general economic conditions at the time, especially as they affected agriculture, were more instrumental than were conditions peculiar to the fluid-milk business in bringing about control of fluid-milk prices. Prices paid producers for milk going to urban centers dropped to discouragingly low levels in 1932 and 1933, but this decline had been preceded by an even more precipitous fall in other farm prices, especially manufactured dairy products—butter, cheese, and evaporated milk. In fact, this latter condition was largely responsible for the conditions in the fluid-milk market.

One of the reasons why farm prices of milk for fluid uses remained relatively more stable than the prices of other farm products was due to the organization of producers in fluid-milk markets. In the early 1920's producers selling fluid milk to cities had organized and maintained measurably effective producers' associations whose primary function was to bargain with city milk distributors for the farm price to be paid for milk sold for fluid consumption. As a general rule, these prices were noticeably above those paid for milk used for manufacturing purposes. Even two or three years after the great depression began these producers' associations were able to retard the decrease in prices paid their members for milk directed to fluid use. In areas where milk production was well controlled by the associations, it had been the practice to discourage new producers from entering the market. This was done partly by limiting the amount of milk which incoming producers were permitted to sell at the relatively favorable "Class I," or fluid-milk, price. In many cases these incoming producers were obliged to accept the less favorable, "manufactured" milk prices for as much as half of the milk delivered by them during the first year. Various other methods were practiced to discourage the entrance of new producers.

However, in 1931 and 1932, when prices of manufactured dairy products reached the lowest point within a quarter-century,[3] the situation became more difficult to control. The dairy farmer who had been selling his product to creameries, cheese factories, or condenseries for manufacturing purposes was forced to exercise every possible effort to save his farm from bankruptcy. One way to increase his income was to obtain higher prices for milk either by distributing it directly to consumers in fluid form or by selling it through a milk distributor.

In the cities and villages unfavorable conditions in industry and trade had forced many people out of their businesses. The starting of a small milk-distributing company appealed to some of these as offering a way of making a livelihood, and many found their way into this business. A quick and relatively easy method of building up the volume of sales was by selling to the wholesale and retail trade at prices below those prevailing in the market. This method was common if not almost universal among both the dealer-distributors and the producer-distributors who were attempting to get a foothold.[4] Many consumers whose incomes had been reduced responded to price reductions with the result that "price-cutting" had a demoralizing effect upon the whole market.

These new dealer-distributors, the so-called "price-cutters," commonly obtained milk from producers who had previously sold their milk for manufactured uses at prices below those enjoyed by farmers producing city fluid milk. Through this source these new distributors were able to obtain milk at a price somewhat and often appreciably below that paid by the established dealers for milk going to fluid resale. The buying advantage of the new distributors, often amounting to as much as a cent a quart or more, made it relatively easy to undersell their competitors who were paying prices determined through bargaining between producers and distributors. In the

---

[3] W. P. Mortenson, H. H. Erdmann, and J. H. Draxler, *Wisconsin Farm Prices, 1841–1933* (University of Wisconsin Research Bull. 119 [Madison, 1933]).

[4] A dealer-distributor is one who purchases his entire milk supply from farmers, processing and delivering it to the wholesale (stores, hotels, restaurants, etc.) and retail trade. A producer-distributor is one who produces all, or a considerable portion, of his milk supply, purchasing the balance from near-by producers.

attempt to hold their trade, the old distributors answered by meeting the price cuts and by passing all or part of the reduction back to the producers. Disturbances followed which in some cases led to farmer strikes and a method of picketing which could not be characterized as "peaceful."

STATE PRICE-CONTROL MEASURES

By 1932 the situation in many markets had reached a point where public welfare, health, and safety were being jeopardized. The "unfair and destructive trade practices" and generally unsettled conditions resulted in reducing prices below those which seemed justified by demand, supply, and general economic conditions. While the price-cutting practices were usually focused at the point of re-sale, the low resale prices often reflected themselves back to the producers in the form of lower farm prices for Class I milk—the milk sold for fluid use to customers.

Legislatures in at least fifteen states passed legislation setting up state milk control boards to regulate distribution.[5] These control boards in most cases were composed, or were under the direction, of some of the personnel of the State Department of Agriculture and Markets designated as a "commission" for the purpose of control. While the control measures differed in detail, certain fundamental features were common to all of them.

Broadly speaking, the legislation was designed to "stabilize and protect the dairy industry." Actually, however, it affected primarily the fluid-milk industry and mainly the producer of this milk. The

[5] Acts relating to the regulation of the distribution of milk for fifteen states are as follows: *California Laws, 1937*, c. 413; *Connecticut Acts, 1933*, c. 22634; Florida Joint Com. Substitute for Senate Bill No. 786, 1933; *Georgia Acts, 1937*, pp. 247 and 725; *Indiana Acts, 1935*, p. 1365; *Maryland Acts, 1935*, c. 310 (held invalid by Court of Appeals); *Massachusetts Acts, 1934*, c. 376 and *ibid., 1938*, c. 334, 428; *New Hampshire Laws of 1937*, c. 107; *New Jersey Laws, 1935*, c. 175; *New York Laws, 1933*, c. 226; Ohio House Bill No. 671, 1933; Oregon State Bill No. 44, 1933; *Pennsylvania Acts, 1937*, No. 105; Vermont House Bill No. 2, 1933; *Wisconsin Acts*, No. 235, 1933. Similar acts have been introduced in several other states but failed of passage. Again, some states are carrying out regulation under laws not particularly designed to regulate the milk business. These acts were all designed primarily to meet the emergency arising out of the depression and were intended to continue until the following session of legislature. Some of them were not re-enacted at the date of expiration.

production, processing, distribution, and sale of milk was declared to be "affected with a public interest." Thus, in a broad sense, milk was declared to fall within the sphere of a public utility. More specifically, the legislative measures granted power to

1. Supervise and regulate matters pertaining to the production, manufacture, distribution, and sale of milk and its products
2. Provide a commission to act as mediator and arbitrator in controversies arising between dealers and producers or among either dealers or producers
3. Investigate the books and accounts of dealers to determine the disposal of milk made for various uses, the cost of distribution, profits or losses, etc.
4. Fix prices, when necessary, to be paid producers and to be received by dealers from wholesale and retail trade

Stripped of accessories and details, the fundamental purpose of milk control in most states was to stabilize and to maintain—or raise—the farm price of fluid milk within the established city milk-sheds. This was to be accomplished by (1) preventing the effects of price wars among distributors from being passed back to the source of supply and (2) preventing distributors from reaching out beyond the established milkshed in an attempt to obtain milk at prices below those established within the shed.

Usually the legislation has covered a two-year period. The legislators who passed the acts expected that the "emergency" which was declared to exist would be over at the end of the period. Most of the control acts were first passed in 1933, the majority being re-enacted in 1935 and again in 1937, but each time on the two-year basis.

The price fixed by the control boards to be paid producers was legally a minimum price, but in practice this minimum became the actual price. It was always established at a point high enough to attract all the milk utilized for fluid use in the market. In fact, it was generally set so high, relative to the price of manufactured milk, that it attracted noticeably more milk than was consumed as fluid milk and cream, thus tending to build up a surplus supply of fluid milk which had to be turned into manufacturing channels. As a result, certain distributors violated the regulation by purchasing milk at prices below the established minimum.

Likewise, the retail prices for fluid milk and cream established by the control boards were legally merely minimum prices. However, as long as competition for the sale of milk was maintained, it was impossible for any seller to obtain more than the minimum price established. In any attempt to sell at prices below the established minimum, and thereby to increase their volume of sales, distributors violated the regulations on the resale price.

PROGRESS OF STATE CONTROL

State control boards[6] had a decided public value in bringing order out of the chaotic condition existing in 1933 and 1934 and since then have exercised a real influence in stabilizing sadly disrupted markets. Complete regulation of the fluid-milk business is not a simple and easy matter, and most of the control boards wisely followed the policy of not enlarging the scope of their functions beyond those which to them seemed essential to meet the existing emergency and to carry out the provisions of the acts under which they were operating. Control boards were and still are feeling their way. Most of their attention has been centered—and perhaps rightly so—upon the question of establishing and enforcing a price structure which would appear equitable under the existing conditions. Many of the major issues of the industry have scarcely been touched, to say nothing of having been solved, by the control boards. Little attention has been given by these boards to studies concerning marketing efficiency, methods of reducing costs, and ways of narrowing margins of milk distribution.

The regulation has not adjusted itself entirely to the industry, nor has the industry adjusted itself to regulation. This is not surprising since so many conflicting interests pervade the milk business— a business which has long followed established trade practices under freely competitive conditions and which, in consequence, does not readily lend itself to rigid regulation.

While state control boards have set up no highly standardized method of arriving at the prices to be established, the Wisconsin

[6] In addition to state control, the Dairy Section of the Agricultural Adjustment Administration had and still has milk-marketing agreements with various markets in the United States. The number reached its peak in 1934 of about fifty markets or market areas.

system, which is fairly typical, has been somewhat as follows. On the basis of findings, the accountants decide which distributor in a market is operating with the lowest degree of efficiency, or its counterpart, the highest cost, that should be permitted to continue. Such a company may be designated as the "marginal included dealer." The prices to be paid farmers and those to be charged at resale are then established at points which will permit this distributor to remain in business and to realize a slight profit. Companies less efficient than this one, or for any other reason in a weaker position, will find it necessary to withdraw from business unless they can improve their status, while companies in a stronger position than the "marginal included dealer" will be able to continue in business. Factual data upon which to base decisions in methods of approach and policy have been, and in most areas still are, noticeably lacking. Add to these difficulties the handicap of operating under temporary legislation, and one sees the obstructions acting as stumbling blocks to constant and rapid progress.

It should be remembered that regulation of the fluid-milk industry had until recently received little review by the courts. Hence the control boards were not certain of their legal rights and powers, and few of them pressed vigorously for court action. First, they were too busy with administrative procedure and, second, they preferred to wait until they could prosecute a particular case in which the facts were such that the power of regulation would be likely to receive favorable consideration by the courts.

Until 1937 the control boards had felt that little would be gained by gathering detailed information concerning the industry. About that year, however, it became apparent that more information was essential if satisfactory regulation was to be established. Some of the control boards are to this end striving to build up a body of factual data. With such facts available, the rate of progress should be more rapid.

In the meantime violations of orders have been numerous—and in some cases so extensive that people have lost respect for the law under which the control operated. Legal procedure for enforcement has been slow and costly, and the progress made in enforcement came only after constant hindrance and obstruction. Recently, however, lines have been more clearly drawn, and policies are gradually being formed. Hence, despite the many unhappy experiences, this form of regulation has had and is having a stabilizing influence in the fluid-milk industry. Even so, if this type of regulation is to improve milk-marketing conditions permanently, new regulatory features will need to be added as the situation demands. Effective fact-finding and educational programs will have to be established for the purpose of renewing the possibilities of increased efficiencies in milk distribution. The "educational" approach may need to be supplemented with a carefully planned and executed system of persuasion and enforcement of commission orders necessary to bring about the changes essential for increased effectiveness of regulation.

PROBABLE TRENDS IN FUTURE CONTROL

Future regulation can be expected to take a more permanent form and to work toward fundamental goals. It is generally agreed that if real progress is to be made in milk control, as it affects the functions of milk processing and distribution, more attention must be given to increase the efficiency of these functions. If efficiency can be increased and costs lowered accordingly, then the margin or spread between prices paid for milk by city consumers and those received by farmers for that same milk can likewise be narrowed.

Efficiency in distribution as it now functions could be increased by (1) reducing the duplication of delivery service through a voluntary or obligatory exchange of customers between distributors (this might eventually lead to districting the market between distributors); (2) inaugurating a system to reduce the amount of special-delivery service, bad debts, bottle losses, and cost of collecting accounts; (3) reducing, where necessary, capital valuations to a point more nearly in line with actual present values; (4) reducing salaries, dividends, profits, and bonuses, to amounts just necessary to attract the needed capital, qualified management, and labor to the industry; and (5) gradually eliminating the less efficient and highest-cost distributors who are unable to continue operation under gradually narrowing margins of distribution established by the price-fixing board or commission. Adjustments such as these may call for more regulatory power than the present types of boards are willing to muster and perhaps greater powers than the present control acts permit.

Fluid-milk producers will likely continue to demand some types of regulation in the milk business unless conditions on dairy farms improve greatly. Assuming that regulation continues, there is every reason to believe that increased attention will be centered on the fundamental problem of narrowing the margin between producer and consumer prices.

CHAPTER II

CHARACTERISTICS OF PUBLIC UTILITIES AND COMPARISONS WITH THE FLUID-MILK BUSINESS

DEFINITION OF A PUBLIC UTILITY AS IT OPERATES IN OUR MODERN ECONOMY

MODERN economic activities vary between two extreme categories. On the one extreme are those activities, commonly referred to as *public services*, which are owned and operated for the common benefit by federal, state, or municipal governments as a government monopoly. On the other extreme are those businesses the operations of which are left almost entirely to the volition and direction of individuals. These enterprises are referred to as *private business*. They have relatively little if any public regulation involving economic considerations imposed directly upon them.

Between these two categories is another group of activities which are operated by private enterprise but subject to relatively complete public regulation. Enterprises in this group include what are ordinarily referred to as *public utilities*—private enterprises in which there is a high degree of public interest. The classification is such that the lines of division between the three categories are wavering and blurred. One category shades into the other, leaving a doubt as to exactly where one ends and another begins. This doubt exists not only in the minds of the general public but also in the minds of legislators as well as in those of economists and of the judiciary.

The meaning of the term "public utility" varies, depending upon the point of view from which it is defined. There are at least three common definitions.

1. The "average citizen" usually thinks of a public utility in terms of the local gas, electric, city bus, or telephone company—a definition based upon the way the enterprise functions or the type of

enterprise. These so-called "average citizens" who comprise the bulk of voters, and in the final analysis the lawmakers, are inclined to think in terms of tangible things such as buildings, equipment, and type of service.

2. Usually state legislatures specifically designate the enterprises which are to be classed as public utilities. These embrace among others the common carriers such as streetcar and city bus systems and water, gas, electricity, telephone, and telegraph corporations. The lawyer and the judge will thus point out that a public utility is any business which has been declared by legislation to be such and in which the public has a closer interest than is true of the ordinary private business. On the basis of this definition, any enterprise which is "clothed with a public interest" is or can be made a public utility. Such a definition is based upon state and federal constitutional sanction, emphasizing a purely legalistic interpretation of the rights and powers of the state. The lawyer thinks in terms of constitutional rights, legal development as manifested by court decisions, and, perhaps to a much lesser extent, of public purposes— economic or social. Recent United States Supreme Court decisions have recognized that to some extent all businesses are "clothed with a public interest." This increases the difficulty of rigidly defining the term "public utility" from a legal point of view.

3. For our purpose we shall assume a public utility to be a business having certain economic characteristics, and one in which only those may engage who have been granted a franchise by the government (federal, state, or a department of the state). This is the generally accepted definition of economists.[1] Thus, in the milk business the right of monopoly or quasi-monopoly would be conferred upon a single milk distributor or upon a very small number in a market or market area. Milk distributors under this system would be peculiarly subject to intensive regulation, on the one hand, with regard to the prices paid farmers and, on the other hand, with regard to those required of customers (wholesale to stores, restaurants, and hotels, and retail to family trade); likewise, the type and quality of service rendered to the consuming public would be prescribed.

Such an arrangement may be referred to as a *unified system* of

[1] Martin G. Glaeser, *Outlines of Public Utility Economics* (New York, 1927), chap. i.

milk distribution since it would operate as *one unit* throughout the market, or as an integrated system in case two or three distributors were engaged in the business, each assigned to a specific area of the city. Obviously this is in sharp contrast with the existing system of milk distribution in which a large number of competing distributors operate substantially independently of one another.

From the standpoint of legal sanction as well as organizational and administrative arrangement, ownership and operation by a government unit, such as a city or municipality, is not the same as the privately owned, publicly controlled utility. However, from the standpoint of operation of the enterprise, the two systems would be similar. Both would operate on a unified basis and thus permit economic savings in the distribution of fluid milk and cream to city consumers.[2]

TESTS OF DESIRABILITY OF PUBLIC UTILITY CONTROL[3]

From an economic point of view there is one overmastering test as to whether an enterprise should be operated as a competitive business or as a controlled monopoly—namely, Which system will best serve the public interest? More specifically: (1) Are the characteristics of the business such that it may expand operations with measurably increasing physical efficiency until the whole of the market area is covered? (2) Will this increasing physical efficiency result in a corresponding, though not necessarily proportional, decrease in operating cost per unit of output? (3) Will the savings of the system, under proper control, redound to either consumers or producers of the product in question? Applying this test to the fluid-milk business, it would seem that, if it can be shown that the spread between what the consumer pays and what the producer properly receives for milk will be narrower under a unified system

[2] The advantages and disadvantages of public ownership compared with private ownership under public control will be discussed in chap. vii.

[3] We shall presume that public utility operation will begin when the milk reaches the city. No control would be carried into the sources of production. The farmer-producers would not be affected by any of the control operations except as they may indirectly influence the prices producers receive.

than under a competitive system, then the change to unification will be to the public advantage.[4]

The fact is reasonably well established that, in a given-sized city, the larger milk-distributing companies generally operate at a lower unit cost, or its counterpart, a higher profit, than do the smaller companies.[5] The difference is fundamentally the result of increased physical efficiency due to size.[6]

The question is often asked, "If the business of processing and distributing milk tends toward what has been termed a 'natural monopoly,'[7] permitting increased efficiency with size of distributor, why have not the larger and presumably the more efficient distributors driven the smaller and weaker competitors from the field?" There are at least three reasons for this.

1. Even though physical efficiency in distribution may be increased until the whole of the market is covered, this efficiency likely increases at a decreasing rate after a substantial portion of the city is covered. The increased physical efficiency, after a certain

[4] This would, of course, assume reasonable comparability of service between the two systems.

[5] See chap. v, pp. 98–100.

[6] Since it is impossible to obtain information from markets where milk is distributed through a unified system with monopolistic control, it will be necessary to base our analysis upon information obtained from markets where distribution is carried on through a competitive system. While the analysis resulting from this approach leaves something to be desired, it will, nevertheless, throw much light upon the question concerning the economic advantage of a publicly controlled unified milk-distributing system. So far as is known to the writer, there has been no experience in the United States in which a milk-distributing company has supplied an entire market of considerable size. Hence, it is impossible to obtain statistical facts to show the advantages caused by increased physical efficiency resulting from such monopoly.

In Tarboro, North Carolina, whose population is 6,400, milk processing and distribution is operated as a public enterprise, but a study of the market gives little or no information on economic advantages or disadvantages of that system compared with a competitive one (A. J. Nixon and O. M. Reed, *Municipal Milk Distribution in Tarboro, North Carolina* ["U.S.D.A. and A.A.A. Market Information Series," DM–5 (Washington, December, 1938)], p. 2).

Wellington, New Zealand, a city of about 150,000 population, has operated a municipal milk plant since 1918, although not as a complete monopoly (*Municipal Milk Plant of Wellington, New Zealand* ["Bulletin of the International Association of Milk Dealers," No. 12 (May 23, 1939)]).

[7] See Richard T. Ely, *Monopolies and Trusts* (New York, 1912), chap. i.

size is attained, may account for only a small decrease in cost per unit of product handled; that is, small in relation to the total distribution cost. Even under a unified system, the scattered, outlying sections of a city can probably not be served at as low a unit cost as can the more concentrated areas. In those sections there may actually be slight increasing costs.

2. As long as opportunities are open for additional distributors to enter the market, some will do so even though their efficiency of operation is lower than is that of a larger, established company. Their operating costs (to be contrasted with physical efficiency) may be kept down by adopting practices not open to the larger company. For example, a family of grown and capable boys may enter the milk business, realizing that they may not necessarily be able to obtain a large income but that it may be greater than other alternatives open to them. Their guess may be correct, and they may meet with fair success, if defined according to their own standards. Even though they have overestimated their possible income, they can still stay in business for a considerable period of time, if not indefinitely. They may be able to purchase milk at prices below those paid by their competitors, unless the producers are strongly organized or the market rigidly regulated. Even in a market organized by producers selling on the basis of a "two-price" plan, small distributors may be able to obtain "unorganized" milk, buying on a "flat-price" plan. They may pay lower wage rates and lower salaries than do their competitors, and, if need be, they may actually reduce their own income until it is just sufficient to provide an acceptable standard of living for themselves and their families.

Once the original, large distributor begins to lose business to the newcomer, his cost per unit of product will tend to climb because of decreased efficiency due to unused capacity of plant, equipment, operating capital, and of personnel working less than full time or working at lower efficiency than before. The greatest inefficiency arises from the fact that milk deliverymen find it necessary to travel a greater distance per unit of milk delivered than before the new competitor came into the market. Thus, even though an enterprise may fall into the category of a "natural monopoly," it does not follow that one company will be able to absorb and hold the entire

In actual Practice you get 3 large and a number of small distributors

market under conditions where all are free to enter and free to determine or influence the wage rates, salaries, working conditions, and prices of raw products.

3. Even though the larger distributor might be able to freeze others out by a reduction of the margin of distribution—the difference between what he pays producers for milk and what he receives for it from consumers—it usually does not pay him to do so. The president of one of the most efficient and successful milk-distributing companies in the Middle West once stated: "If one competitor is squeezed out, two more will come in. The newcomers do not know ahead of time that success is impossible. Once they start business, they hang on—unless they are able to sell their business—until they have lost their last dollar and all the credit they can get." Continuing, he said: "It pays us better to let in a few competitors because they demonstrate to prospective competitors that there is little opportunity for profit in the business."

During periods of relatively economic stability there has been in many cities a gradual concentration of the fluid-milk business into the hands of a relatively few large and efficient distributors. They were able to keep down their costs and to operate at a sufficiently low margin so that the smaller companies were unable to compete. When a period of economic depression sets in, new distributors find their way into the market because it offers what appears to them the best, or only, opportunity to earn a livelihood, and, even though they have difficulty in meeting competition, they are able to hang on at least for a time.

If a single, regulated milk distributor operated under an exclusive franchise, the market would be closed to the newcomers. Only under such a unified system will the advantages of increasing physical efficiency have an unhindered opportunity to manifest itself.

It is significant that even those enterprises which have become our more typical public utilities and clearly "natural" monopolies, as commonly defined—such as the street railway and city gas, electric, and water systems—were competitive until public policy changed, authorizing—indeed, compelling—them to operate as publicly owned or as controlled monopolies. Seldom did one company drive all others out of existence. Through time, those in the weakest position failed, but in many cities several, or more correctly a few, enterprises continued to operate. They operated at relatively low efficiency and at correspondingly high costs, which were passed on to the consuming public in the form of higher prices than would have been necessary under a unified system.

A second test as to whether an enterprise should be operated under competitive conditions or as a controlled monopoly is the extent to which the service rendered is essential to the public. For example, it is said that water for drinking purposes is indispensable for life itself and necessary for personal and household uses as well as for extinguishing fires, sprinkling lawns and streets, etc. Electricity is necessary for modern lighting and power purposes; gas for heating; and streetcar or bus systems are essential to provide effective transportation in our cities.

That fluid milk is also an important or necessary product hardly needs supporting evidence. It is commonly accepted that fluid milk is a desirable food for all and a necessity for infants and growing children. Indeed, it is a common necessity. If it can be made available through an improved method of distribution at less cost to consumers without a corresponding reduction in price to producers, then, from the points of view of these two groups, efforts in this direction are amply justified.[8]

[8] A third test commonly applied as to whether an enterprise falls into the category of a public utility is that of public convenience. Several series of overhead telephone lines to blot out the natural and man-made beauty, two or more streetcar or bus systems to obstruct street traffic, or a number of water or gas mains buried under the streets to be disinterred at irregular intervals for examination, repair, or replacement would obviously become an inconvenience and even a public nuisance. With the present crowded condition of most city streets it is desirable to reduce all traffic obstructions and remove unessential obstacles. A unified milk-distributing system would reduce the number of milk wagons or trucks traveling and parking on the streets, hence would likewise reduce the inconvenience or nuisance of traffic congestion—an inconvenience of no minor importance.

PART II

COSTS AND PROFITS OF DISTRIBUTING MILK AND SAVINGS THROUGH UNIFICATION

CHAPTER III

GENERAL SURVEY OF COSTS OF MILK DISTRIBUTION

GENERAL CONSIDERATIONS

TO BOTH producers and consumers the retail price of fluid milk has seemed high in relation to the receipts of farmers for the milk furnished for city consumption. This wide margin of distribution is one of the phases of the milk business which has prompted much public discussion. Producers of city milk, largely through producer co-operative associations, have probably been more instrumental than any other individuals or groups in focusing public attention on the industry, especially on prices paid to their members.

From the standpoint of consumers, however, there are at least four characteristics of milk and of the milk business which have contributed to the ease of keeping public attention directed to questions of city milk prices, processing, and distribution. First, milk is an essential food for infants and growing children around whom center much family concern. Second, it receives separate attention because it is delivered to the family doorstep as an isolated article, not with a larger bill of goods as is the case with groceries. Third, the milk bill is paid as a separate account, thus again tending to focus attention on it. Fourth, while it does not account for an extremely large proportion of the weekly or monthly family food expenditure, it is, nevertheless, a sizeable consideration for families with low or even medium incomes. These conditions all tend to focus attention on the price paid for milk; on the more general questions involving methods of distribution; and especially on profits in the industry and salaries paid to those who own and operate the business. Recently, the public attention has apparently shifted somewhat away from the items of profits and salaries of distributors to the items of wages paid in the industry and, to a lesser extent, to the inefficiencies of distribution.

In many localities there has arisen a desire on the part of producers and, to a lesser extent, on the part of consumers to determine what, if any, changes can be made in the present system of milk distribution to reduce the amount of price "spread" or margin between the farmer who produces milk and the consumer who uses it. If this margin cannot be reduced under the present system, can a new and different system be established which will perform the operations of processing and delivering fluid milk at lower costs and at a correspondingly lower margin?

In an attempt to present a general picture of the industry, including the efficiencies, costs, and profits involved, a somewhat detailed analysis of costs of processing and distribution will be presented.

SURVEY OF THE DIVISION OF THE SALES DOLLAR

Numerous sources of information were drawn on in the presentation of the facts involved: (1) detailed records of thirteen Wisconsin milk-distributing companies covering an eleven-year period (cf. Fig. 1);[1] (2) information on milk delivery obtained through a survey of some 275 milk routes in 82 markets, together with a detailed study of 8 routes; (3) records of about a dozen additional companies located in Wisconsin, including Milwaukee companies, for which no complete breakdown could be made because of the lack of detailed information in the company records; (4) records from the Federal Trade Commission reports; (5) studies made by various research workers in California, Connecticut, Illinois, Maine, Massachusetts, New York, and West Virginia; and (6) study made of the Milwaukee market by the Agricultural Adjustment Administration.

It must be emphasized at the outset that it is not presumed that this study permits of a broad generalization beyond the period of time covered, or for milk markets throughout the country. The research worker, limited by funds and personnel, has no choice but to limit the research problem to keep within the budget available. Rather than make overbold generalizations from limited data, this

---

[1] Records of all the thirteen companies could not be carried back for the entire eleven-year period (see Table A, Appen. A, for the exact years for which information was available by companies). These companies were all located in Wisconsin cities of 70,000 population or less.

analysis is intended to support only those conclusions which the facts appear clearly to dictate. The data available are presented in rather complete form so that the reader may have an opportunity to study them in some detail.

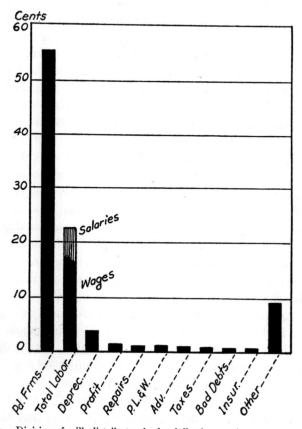

Fig. 1.—Division of milk distributors' sales dollar into various cost items. Average of thirteen Wisconsin companies for the eleven-year period 1927–37, inclusive. Pd. Frms. = amount paid farmers for milk; Deprec. = total amount of depreciation; P.L. & W. = power, light, and water.

In order to obtain an over-all picture of the actual operation of the milk distributors covered in this study, it seemed desirable to make available first a summary diagram setting forth a general picture of costs. Accordingly, in Figure 1 the entire milk distributors' sales dollar—whether it was obtained through the sale of fluid milk and cream or from manufactured products—is divided into various cost items, including (1) costs of raw products (or amount paid farmers), (2) the several items involving all manufacturing and delivery costs, and (3) profits.

Let it be said that this chart showing a "thumbnail" sketch of the division of the sales dollar of the milk-processing and milk-distributing companies will give the reader only a general picture of the main items. Detailed data are necessary for the purpose of critical analysis. The reader is cautioned not to draw final conclusions from this chart but rather to examine the more complete and detailed tables which follow. It may, however, be of interest and value to call attention to at least the more important items in the chart. For instance, the proportion of the total sales dollar going to farmers—about 56 cents—is higher than is commonly believed.

The usual popular comparison made is that between the average price received for milk by the producer with that paid by the city housewife for milk delivered at her doorstep. Such a method of calculation is incorrect because virtually all distributors dispose of some of the milk at wholesale to stores, hotels, and restaurants at a price below that sold at retail. In Wisconsin, until stopped recently by the milk-regulating commission, the Wisconsin Department of Agriculture and Markets, quantity discounts were given to the retail trade. Families consuming over a certain amount of milk per month—usually 90–110 quarts—received a certain discount, generally a cent a quart. Also, most distributors sell some milk in the form of manufactured dairy products which bring even lower prices than milk or cream at wholesale. Generally, however, milk not sold for liquid use is purchased at a price lower than that paid for milk sold in fluid form.

For purposes of this analysis it did not seem desirable to attempt a separation of the fluid-milk business as such from the incidental business of manufacturing butter, ice cream, and other products. Instead, every operation of the distributing company, manufacture of dairy products as well as fluid-milk distribution, was considered as a part and parcel of the milk business. An analysis on the basis of only the milk sold at retail in fluid form, or even of all the fluid milk and cream sold at retail and wholesale, leaving out of account the manufactured dairy products, would have shown only a part of the total operations of the companies. In order to avoid placing overemphasis on the manufacturing processes carried on in connection with the fluid-milk-distributing business, only companies were included which received at least 60 per cent of their income from the sale of fluid milk.[2] Hence, in the entire analysis of the Wisconsin companies, the "amount paid farmers,"[3] for example, is the total amount paid farmers taken as a percentage of the total amount received from the finished products sold by the distributor, including manufactured dairy products as well as fluid milk and cream. This method of calculation will show that producers get a larger percentage of the dealers' sales dollar than if retail milk prices only had been compared with average prices paid farmers. Farmers receive a much larger proportion of the retail price of butter—into which much of the manufactured or "surplus" milk is diverted—than they do of fluid milk. This is largely because the processing and distributing costs of butter are relatively low compared to those of milk.

Next to the amount paid farmers (Fig. 1), the item of wages accounts for the largest amount. In fact, it was over three times as large as the next highest item, the combined salaries of operators, managers, and foremen. Depreciation of plant and equipment was the fourth largest cost, being over twice that of the one which

[2] This does not hold, of course, for the supporting information. The data there were taken from secondary sources, hence there was no certain way of determining the relative importance of the dairy-manufacturing operations.

[3] The term "amount paid for raw products" would be more strictly correct than the term "amount paid farmers." When butter, cheese, or ice cream are manufactured, some "raw products" in addition to the milk bought from the farmer must be purchased. In the case of the dealer who makes butter, the salt added—the only other important item of cost—amounts to about one-half of 1 per cent of the cost of the milk so used. In the case of cheese, the costs of rennet and one or two other minor items amount to a fraction of a cent per dollar cost of milk. For ice cream the cost of flavors, sugar, gelatin, fruits, etc., amounts to almost 30 per cent of the "raw products." Even so, the amount shown above, within probably one or two cents per sales dollar, goes to the farmer-producer for milk. The exact amount varies among dealers depending upon what percentage of the milk purchased is sold at retail, wholesale, or is manufactured into butter, cheese, or ice cream.

TABLE 1

DIVISION OF SALES DOLLAR INTO MAJOR ITEMS BY INDIVIDUAL COMPANIES, ARRANGED IN DESCENDING ORDER OF SIZE, BY YEARS, 1927-37, INCLUSIVE

(Expressed as a Percentage of Total Sales)

	1927	1928	1929	1930	1931	1932	1933	1934	1935	1936	1937
Company A:											
Amount paid farmers*	68.7	65.5	64.9	61.7	60.3	51.8	50.2	53.9	55.1	56.8	57.7
Total operating cost	31.7	31.5	32.7	34.8	38.9	45.6	48.4	45.3	43.3	42.0	39.8
Net operating profit	− 0.4	3.0	2.4	3.5	0.8	2.6	1.4	0.8	1.6	1.2	2.5
Total sales value	100.0	100.0	100.0	100.0	100.0	100.0	100.0	100.0	100.0	100.0	100.0
Company B:											
Amount paid farmers*	......	......	......	......	......	58.1	56.6	60.5	63.9	64.2	62.7
Total operating cost	......	......	......	......	......	42.2	43.3	39.5	37.4	36.1	35.6
Net operating profit	......	......	......	......	......	− 0.3	0.1	0.0	− 1.3	− 0.3	1.7
Total sales value	......	......	......	......	......	100.0	100.0	100.0	100.0	100.0	100.0
Company C:											
Amount paid farmers*	50.4	51.4	50.4	46.6	41.9	38.8	37.9	39.0	40.5	42.8	44.1
Total operating cost	43.5	46.0	45.8	46.8	52.4	60.8	63.2	60.2	57.3	55.7	52.1
Net operating profit	6.1	2.6	3.8	6.6	5.7	0.4	− 1.1	0.8	2.2	1.5	3.8
Total sales value	100.0	100.0	100.0	100.0	100.0	100.0	100.0	100.0	100.0	100.0	100.0
Company D:											
Amount paid farmers*	......	......	77.9	74.3	69.2	65.8	60.2	58.2	59.4	62.6	61.4
Total operating cost	......	......	18.4	24.0	28.8	37.0	40.4	41.8	40.4	36.9	38.1
Net operating profit	......	......	3.7	1.7	2.0	− 2.8	− 0.6	0.0	0.2	0.5	0.5
Total sales value	......	......	100.0	100.0	100.0	100.0	100.0	100.0	100.0	100.0	100.0

* Cost of goods sold.

TABLE 1—Continued

	1927	1928	1929	1930	1931	1932	1933	1934	1935	1936	1937
Company E:											
Amount paid farmers*	53.6	52.6	50.4	47.2	41.4	37.0	49.2	51.2	54.4	49.2	49.0
Total operating cost	36.1	35.7	34.8	42.2	49.4	59.9	50.6	43.4	45.5	49.4	49.6
Net operating profit	10.3	11.7	14.8	10.6	9.2	3.1	0.2	5.4	0.1	1.4	1.4
Total sales value	100.0	100.0	100.0	100.0	100.0	100.0	100.0	100.0	100.0	100.0	100.0
Company F:											
Amount paid farmers*	.....	.....	.....	.....	.....	46.5	53.9	52.4	53.9	56.8	55.0
Total operating cost						57.5	48.6	45.2	41.7	37.2	41.6
Net operating profit						—4.0	—2.5	2.4	4.4	6.0	3.4
Total sales value	.....	.....	.....	.....	.....	100.0	100.0	100.0	100.0	100.0	100.0
Company G:											
Amount paid farmers*	60.5	57.8	53.7	49.9	43.5	41.7	45.9	47.4	50.6	52.6	52.4
Total operating cost	33.5	35.9	36.5	36.7	45.2	56.5	51.7	50.0	45.2	42.9	43.4
Net operating profit	6.0	6.3	9.8	13.4	11.3	1.8	2.4	2.6	4.2	4.5	4.2
Total sales value	100.0	100.0	100.0	100.0	100.0	100.0	100.0	100.0	100.0	100.0	100.0
Company H:											
Amount paid farmers*	67.3	61.2	58.7	54.1	49.3	45.0	47.3	50.5	52.3	54.0	54.9
Total operating cost	33.2	36.2	35.9	37.2	44.4	61.9	65.6	57.3	50.4	47.8	47.9
Net operating profit	—0.5	2.6	5.4	8.7	6.3	—6.9	—12.9	—7.8	—2.7	—1.8	—2.8
Total sales value	100.0	100.0	100.0	100.0	100.0	100.0	100.0	100.0	100.0	100.0	100.0
Company I:											
Amount paid farmers*	.....	.....	61.1	50.6	45.1	46.9	52.2	53.2	53.0	59.0	55.6
Total operating cost			33.9	46.3	54.7	53.3	47.7	46.4	47.0	40.3	43.5
Net operating profit			5.0	3.1	0.2	—0.2	0.1	0.4	0.2	0.7	0.9
Total sales value	.....	.....	100.0	100.0	100.0	100.0	100.0	100.0	100.0	100.0	100.0

TABLE 1—Continued

	1927	1928	1929	1930	1931	1932	1933	1934	1935	1936	1937
Company J:											
Amount paid farmers*	65.3	56.2	54.1	47.2	45.0	46.4	43.3	45.6	49.5	52.9	56.0
Total operating cost	34.8	53.2	52.4	47.9	51.2	55.6	57.7	54.4	48.9	47.5	45.2
Net operating profit	−0.1	−9.4	−6.5	4.9	3.8	−2.0	−1.0	0.0	1.6	−0.4	−1.2
Total sales value	100.0	100.0	100.0	100.0	100.0	100.0	100.0	100.0	100.0	100.0	100.0
Company K:											
Amount paid farmers*	83.2	82.8	79.4	70.1	64.9	59.5	61.2	63.5	63.8	64.8	61.7
Total operating cost	15.4†	15.2†	17.9†	29.5†	35.4	40.1	43.0	39.4	36.1	34.9	37.0
Net operating profit	1.4	2.0	2.7	0.4	−0.3	0.4	−4.2	−2.9	0.1	0.3	1.3
Total sales value	100.0	100.0	100.0	100.0	100.0	100.0	100.0	100.0	100.0	100.0	100.0
Company L:											
Amount paid farmers*	63.2	59.9	59.3	54.5	47.7	43.6	46.4	49.0	51.8	53.7	53.3
Total operating cost	42.0	40.2	37.6	42.7	49.5	57.1	53.4	50.9	47.0	45.9	47.0
Net operating profit	−5.2	−0.1	3.1	2.8	2.8	−0.7	0.2	0.1	1.2	0.4	−0.3
Total sales value	100.0	100.0	100.0	100.0	100.0	100.0	100.0	100.0	100.0	100.0	100.0
Company M:											
Amount paid farmers*	......	......	60.2	60.9	61.6	61.4	58.4	60.1	61.7	59.2	61.0
Total operating cost	......	......	32.5	31.9	35.8	38.1	39.3	35.4	38.4	34.9	37.0
Net operating profit	......	......	7.3	7.2	2.6	0.5	2.3	4.5	0.1	5.9	2.0
Total sales value	......	......	100.0	100.0	100.0	100.0	100.0	100.0	100.0	100.0	100.0
Average amount paid farmers	64.0†‡	60.9†‡	60.9†‡	56.1†‡	51.8	49.4	51.0	52.6	54.6	56.0	55.8

† Company K sold a considerable portion of milk as fluid cream at wholesale during the years 1927–30. The processing and distribution costs of this phase of the milk business was relatively low, and accordingly the proportion of the sales dollar paid farmers was high. If the figures of this company for these four years had been eliminated from the study, the amount of the sales dollar paid farmers for milk as shown in the summary chart (Fig. 1) would have been reduced by about 0.8 cent, and the combined items included in operating costs would have been increased by a similar amount. Profits would have shown no change in the first decimal place.

‡ "The average amount paid farmers" when Company K is excluded are 61.3 for 1927, 57.8 for 1928, 59.1 for 1929, and 54.7 for 1930.

followed it, namely, operating profit of the business. Repairs, advertising, taxes, bad debts, and insurance aggregated less than six cents of the sales dollar. These five items combined were less than one-third as much as wages alone.

Table 1 sets forth for each of thirteen Wisconsin companies a division of the sales dollar into three major items: (1) amount paid farmers for milk (cost of goods sold), (2) operating costs, and (3) profits. Only the first of these items will be discussed at this point.

AMOUNT PAID FARMERS

The item "amount paid farmers" in Table 1 has been averaged, and the averages are shown at the end of the table. These averages should, however, be considered with reference to the figures of the individual companies because the deviations from the averages are considerable.

The averages show an interesting, though not pronounced, trend. The percentage of the sales dollar going to farmers was considerably smaller during the early thirties than before or since. As early as 1933 the percentage had begun to increase, and it has continued to do so since that time except for 1937. It is, however, still slightly lower than it was in the predepression period.

CHAPTER IV

ANALYSIS OF OPERATING COSTS AND THE POS-
SIBLE SAVINGS THROUGH UNIFICATION

IF ACTUAL examples of milk distribution under a unified system were available so that one could make direct comparisons
between that system and a competitive system, the problem
of showing the advantages and disadvantages of unification would
be relatively simple. It might then be possible to make a detailed
analysis of each of the cost items which would provide facts for
making comparisons item by item between the two systems. Such
a study would permit of straightforward and relatively simple
methods of approach. However, even though we have no actual experiences of milk distribution under a unified system, it is possible
from an analysis of the competitive system to throw considerable
light upon the probable economic savings which might result from
unification because there would be many parallels in the functions
of the two systems, and it is not difficult to recognize where these
parallels would diverge and to determine within reasonable limits
the extent of this divergence.

Fundamentally, the functions connected with the processing and
distribution of milk would be similar whether they were performed
under one system or the other. Pasteurization, bottling, refrigeration, delivery of the milk, and similar functions would naturally
have to be performed under either system. An analysis of the detailed costs in the competitive system will show which cost items
are large and which are small. With this information one will be
able to determine how important a reduction in each of these cost
items would be under the unified system in performing the services
of processing and distribution. Naturally, a given percentage reduction of a large cost item would be more significant in reducing the
cost of distributing a quart of milk than would an equal percentage
reduction in a smaller cost item.

For a breakdown of these costs we shall rely in the main upon detailed information from 13 Wisconsin milk-distributing companies the data of each of which cover a span of eleven years.[1] Data for the cost of delivering milk are based on a survey of some 275 delivery routes from 82 Wisconsin distributing companies and on a detailed study of 8 selected milk-delivery routes.[2]

No attempt has been made to separate those operations involving the processing and sale of fluid milk and cream from the remainder of the business of the milk distributor. Most distributors, except those whose business is relatively small, manufacture some dairy products in addition to their major business of selling fluid milk and cream. The costs of operating the fluid-milk and cream business as such cannot be separated from the costs incurred in manufacturing dairy products except on a somewhat arbitrary basis. In some operations the costs are purely joint costs for which there is virtually no logical basis of separation. In other operations, costs, while not truly joint, are sufficiently involved so that a separation into milk-processing and milk-delivering costs, on the one hand, and costs of manufacturing butter or other dairy products, on the other hand, is without real meaning. In order to reduce the difficulties associated with the segregation of costs of the fluid-milk business from those of manufactured dairy products, only companies which received at least 60 per cent of their income from the fluid-milk business were included in the sample.

The detailed data of the thirteen companies are supplemented by reliable, though less detailed, information from other primary sources. In addition, a large amount of information was assembled from other studies giving costs and profits of milk distribution.

[1] See Table A, Appen. A, for detailed figures.

[2] It was originally intended to include a relatively large number of companies for study. One hundred companies in Wisconsin cities ranging in size from 10,000 to 70,000 population were selected. Of this number, only about fifty had records sufficiently detailed to provide the information desired, and only twenty-five of these fifty had continuous records for more than two years. By analyzing further, it was found that some of these twenty-five had to be eliminated because in one or more of the years covered by the analysis as much as half of their sales came from sources other than fluid milk, sales from manufactured products such as ice cream and butter being the most common.

Highly important is the fact that this supplementary information clearly supports the conclusions reached through the analysis of the primary data, hence it furnishes quite convincing evidence that a larger sample would not have changed the results significantly.

Although records of a larger number of companies would have been desirable for an analysis, it can be easily demonstrated that complete records from a smaller number of companies for several consecutive years will permit of a more fruitful analysis and will culminate in more dependable conclusions than will data from a larger number of companies with less complete information and for a shorter period of years. Accounting systems are seldom as complete and detailed as may be desirable to permit of an economic analysis upon which one can place unlimited confidence. Certain cost items of necessity must be fixed arbitrarily even with an elaborate accounting system.

The longer the period of the record, the more accurate will be both cost and the evaluation figures. This is true because accounting "errors" are constantly being corrected as assets are sold, worn out, discarded, or otherwise disposed of. It follows, of course, that the more accurate the cost and valuation figures, the more accurate will also be the figures showing profit. Suppose, for example, that the accounts were set up on the basis of a milk delivery truck having a life of five years, at the end of which time it would have only a "turn-in" value. If later events proved that the truck had to be replaced at the end of four years, the annual depreciation rate as carried on the books was obviously too low. This "error" might not have been corrected until the beginning or even the end of the fourth year, when the truck was replaced. The amount of the underestimated depreciation would thus be charged entirely to the fourth year of the truck's operation. The depreciation would have been understated for three years and overstated for one—the fourth year. Clearly the record of any one, two, or even three years would have been less accurate than a record covering the entire five-year period.

Cost of repairs may also vary considerably from year to year, depending, among other things, upon the changes necessary to meet city and state health requirements and upon the desire on the part of the directors in office to keep or not to keep the plant and equipment well repaired. Here again the accounts covering a longer period of years will present a more accurate picture of the business than will be the case if figures are available for, say, two or three years

TABLE 2

DIVISION OF MILK DISTRIBUTORS' OPERATING COSTS, 1927–37, INCLUSIVE, FOR CERTAIN WISCONSIN MILK-DISTRIBUTING COMPANIES*

(In Percentage of Total Operating Cost)†

Cost Item	1927 (8)‡	1928 (8)	1929 (11)	1930 (11)	1931 (11)	1932 (13)	1933 (13)	1934 (13)	1935 (13)	1936 (13)	1937 (13)
Salaries.............	12.1§	13.7	13.1	14.0	14.6	11.9	12.8	12.7	11.9	12.0	11.1
Wages..............	42.7	38.9	40.7	41.5	42.1	39.8	43.1	42.0	43.0	41.8	43.6
Total labor......	54.8	52.6	53.8	55.5	56.7	51.7	55.9	54.7	54.9	53.8	54.7
Depreciation........	7.4	8.0	8.9	8.4	8.8	9.2	9.8	8.6	7.8	7.4	6.7
Bad debts...........	1.0	1.4	1.4	1.7	1.3	4.3	2.6	3.0	1.8	1.5	2.1
Taxes..............	2.5	3.0	2.5	2.8	3.0	2.8	2.8	2.1	2.2	2.1	2.5
Insurance..........	1.6	1.7	1.7	1.5	1.3	2.2	2.4	2.4	2.8	2.3	2.3
Advertising.........	3.1	3.4	3.3	3.3	3.0	3.4	2.5	2.6	3.2	3.3	3.7
Repairs.............	2.8	3.1	4.8	4.0	4.3	3.4	3.1	2.9	3.9	4.8	4.5
Light, power, and water............	3.3	2.7	3.3	3.3	3.1	3.4	3.6	3.4	3.3	3.2	3.0
All other............	26.8	26.4	22.8	21.5	20.5	20.3	19.3	22.5	21.7	22.8	20.8

* These items are simple averages of the number of milk-distributing companies shown in each column. The companies included are identical for the entire period of years listed in the table. For example, the eight companies beginning in 1927 were carried throughout the entire eleven-year period. In 1929 three more companies were added and two years later another two companies. Once a company was included, it was carried for the entire period of years. Three or four company records (depending upon the year) did not permit of a complete breakdown of every minor item. For example, (a) repairs and (b) the combined items of light, water, and power were not obtainable for a few distributors (see Table A, Appen. A, for a complete breakdown of costs by individual distributing company).

† Percentage figures of operating costs of the various cost items do not total to exactly 100 per cent for every year. There are two reasons for this. First, data were not available for all these items for every company every year. For example, the books of Company C did not segregate repair costs until 1937. Before 1937 these were included with the general cost item referred to as "all other." Only those companies which had data for an item were included in the average of that item. To illustrate, in those years when twelve of the thirteen companies segregated the item of repairs, the average figure was obtained by adding the percentage figures of the twelve companies and then dividing by 12, not 13. This method of calculation results in a larger average (and a figure more representative of the individual companies) than would be obtained if the divisor consisted of a larger number, that is, if all the companies had been included in the divisor, some of which showed zero for the item in question. Second, when a company's books showed no breakdown for a specific cost item, the amount which would have been involved therein was included in the "all other" item, thereby accentuating it.

‡ Numbers in parentheses refer to the number of companies included.

§ See Table B, Appen. A, for the standard error of the means of these cost items.

only. This same situation applies to all items carried in the books such as machines, equipment, furniture, and buildings.

In the thirteen Wisconsin companies whose records were analyzed, one characteristic stands out above the rest, namely, although there was considerable variation from company to company, all showed the same general proportion going to each of the various cost items. This is shown in Table 2 and in Table A of Appendix A. Out of every dollar expended for operation, an average of around 40–44 cents went for wages; 12 cents for salaries of officers, managers, and foremen; 8 cents for depreciation of buildings, equipment, and minor items; 3 cents for each of advertising and repairs; 2–2½ cents for

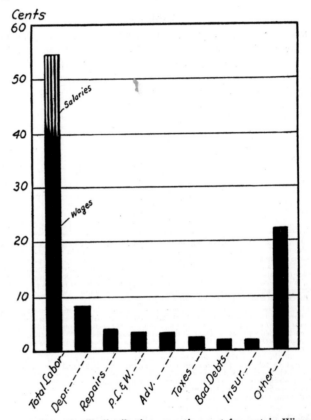

Fig. 2.—Division of milk-distribution operating cost for certain Wisconsin milk-distributing companies (average eleven-year period 1927–37, inclusive). Depr.= total amount of depreciation; P.L. & W.=power, light, and water.

each of the items of taxes, insurance, and bad debts; 3–3½ cents for the combined items of light, water, and power; and the remainder of about 22–25 cents for "all other" items (Fig. 2). While the degree of variation in the operating-cost items from company to company is relatively wide, it is largely negligible in the broader cost problem.

A detailed breakdown of the figures expressed in terms of percentages of total operating cost is shown in Table A of Appendix A. Considerable between-company variations in the cost items would be expected to, and do, occur not only in the milk-distribution business but in all businesses except those which have attained virtually complete standardization of operating methods and technique. Because these between-company variations existed, we have not relied upon averages in determining the possible savings which might result from unification of the milk-distribution system. Instead, we have used figures showing a range within which savings might be expected to occur.[3]

Variations in costs of these items may also be expected to occur between all the milk-distributing companies of one city and those of another city of a similar size. Accordingly, a city in which the existing milk-distribution system is operating with a combination of relatively low distribution costs and relatively low profits could not expect to save as much through unification as could a market where the opposite of these conditions prevails.

Salaries, expressed as a proportion of total operating cost, varied noticeably from company to company. Wages showed a less pronounced variation, and, if the two items are combined as "total labor," the variation between companies is still smaller. One would expect a relatively wide between-company variation of the items of salary and wages as a percentage of total operating cost for several reasons, two of which are especially important: (1) the actual amount paid as salaries and wages will vary for similar-sized companies and (2) there is no fixed standard by which all companies carry these items in their accounting systems. The first of these reasons is largely self-explanatory. The second is less so. One milk-distributing company may carry only one person's name, say that of the president of the company, on the books as receiving a salary. Two or three others may be listed as receiving wages even though they are officers or managers of certain operating departments of the company. In such a case the item of wages will be swelled by the amount of the inclusions of what would be more strictly classed as salary. On the contrary, the accounts of another company may carry individuals as receiving salary when in reality these persons

[3] See Table 10, p. 82.

perform functions for which payment in form of wages would be more accurate. Again, in the case of some companies, especially the smaller ones, some of the actual functions ordinarily classed as labor are performed by the owners or managers.

Thus, if one were to secure strict comparability as between wages or salaries for two or more companies, it would be necessary that, in the accounting records, wages and salary be allocated on the basis of the relative amount of effort actually devoted to labor, for which wages would be paid and to management for which salary would be paid. No attempt was made in this study to segregate arbitrarily the company payments into the items of wages or salaries on the basis of functions performed—labor or management. The records of those companies used for the study were accepted as showing a reasonable division of these items. Even when salary and wages are combined into one item, labor costs, the between-company variations are considerable. This does not necessarily mean that the company with the relatively low labor cost is operating with a high degree of efficiency and vice versa. This low cost may be entirely or in part the result of paying low wage and salary rates to employees and managers. On the basis of such cost figures, we are not justified in assuming that the methods of operation followed by the "low-cost" company are such that they would result in a similar low cost if adopted by a unified system. If a company can be shown to have relatively low total labor costs per unit of product handled because of high physical efficiency of operation, then something could be learned by a study of its operating methods; but if that low cost is due to low wage and salary rates, or in part to these and in part to high efficiency, then the analysis would yield little usable information since it would not be expected that the same low wage and salary rates could be continued until the whole of the market was served as would be the case under a unified milk-distribution system.

Turning again our attention to the central problem of costs, the following summary facts are highly significant.

1. If wages and salaries are combined into one item, total labor, then for the eight-year period during which data were available for all thirteen companies (except for two companies for 1930 and 1931),

the cost of this total labor amounted to more than half of the total operating cost. For the other three companies the percentage figures were in the high forties. An average for the period was 55 per cent with a standard error of the mean of 6.3 per cent (Table B, Appen. A).

2. On the basis of the annual figures of these companies for the same eight years, data showed that, in over two cases out of three, depreciation ranged within 6 per cent and 10 per cent, inclusive, of the total operating cost. The average was 8.2 per cent with a standard error of the mean of 2.6 per cent.

3. The combined items of (a) bad debts, (b) taxes, (c) insurance, (d) advertising, (e) repairs, and (f) power, light, and water—averages of thirteen companies by years—varied from 15.6 per cent in 1934 to 18.9 per cent in 1932 of total operating cost. The balance of the cost comprised a large number of smaller items listed under the heading "all other." This points out rather vividly that, despite the variation which exists between companies in the different cost items, it is still obvious that the big cost is for total labor (wages and salaries) and that the cost of no one or even the entire six items above is of any great significance. The company-to-company variations of any specific cost item is but a ripple on the larger wave—the variation between one (a large) cost item, such as total labor, and another (a small) item, such as repairs or insurance.

Obviously, if costs of processing and distributing fluid milk are to be reduced materially, the major reduction must come from the large cost item—total labor—and to a lesser extent from the next highest cost item—depreciation. Even though the other six items were reduced by a large proportional amount, the actual reduction per quart of milk handled would be of a distinctly minor consequence.

In an attempt to determine the extent to which savings may be made under a unified system of milk distribution, we shall discuss the items set forth in Table 2 in the order in which they are listed.

WAGES

As pointed out earlier, the division between the item of wages and that of salaries is of necessity made on a somewhat arbitrary basis. Especially in the smaller companies, the officers and managers very frequently work at operations which might be more correctly classed as the type of work for which wages rather than salaries should be paid. The most common method of division between salary and wages is to class officers and managers as receiving salaries regardless of what functions they actually perform. In general, wages amount to from three to four times as much of the total operating cost as the next largest individual item—salaries. The importance of this fact must not be overlooked.

Or increased volume

A reduction in wage costs means either less people employed or lower wage rates or both. Lower wage rates will not be acceptable to the wage-earners without protest. In fact, their strength, through labor organizations, has become so great that a reduction would very probably be virtually impossible at the present time even if it were desirable from the standpoint of the distributors and the milk consumers and producers. This would suggest that virtually the only way the wage bill can be reduced is by reducing the number of laborers employed and making such adjustments as will increase the output of the remaining workers. Some increase in wage rates to employees in milk-distributing companies has been common everywhere during the past few years. As one would expect, the greatest wage increases have been those obtained through the organized effort of employees. The present policy of labor leaders and, to a lesser extent, of employees in general is to maintain or increase wage rates even though such a policy may mean a maintenance or an increase in wholesale and retail fluid-milk prices.

While at first glance it may seem that labor costs take an unduly high percentage of total costs of milk distribution, it must, of course, be recognized that marketing fluid milk to the family trade under the present competitive system involves a greater proportional element of personal service than does the marketing of most other products. Each delivery is relatively small, amounting to one, two, or three quarts of milk per day for most families. Indeed, many more families take one quart per day than any other quantity. Two-quart customers are next in importance, and those who purchase more than two quarts daily are uncommon and considered sufficiently valuable accounts to be sought after by all alert distributors. The amount delivered per customer in Milwaukee averaged from 1.3 to 1.5 "points."[4] The one-quart account involves only about ten to twelve cents per sale, depending upon the price of milk in the market. For this consideration, not only must daily delivery be made but, except for a relatively few cash customers, a record must be kept of each sale and a bill rendered once a month or oftener. In many cases the costly practice of making personal collections is necessary. Constant checking to minimize bottle losses and past-due accounts also requires time and attention. Under a competitive system of distribution, this item of personal service is important; consequently, it should be expected that the item of wages will be higher and that the margin of distribution will be wider than at first appearance would seem necessary.

A comparison of the delivery costs of small and of large companies should throw light upon the question as to whether noticeable savings could be made in this item if the milk business were operated as a publicly controlled unified system. Even a cursory search shows that such a comparison does not yield so clear results as are at first anticipated. Two important factors, not easily separated without detailed information, are involved in making such a comparison: (1) the comparative physical efficiency between the small and the large companies with respect to the use of labor and (2) the relative wage rates paid employees as well as the number of hours worked per day. Generally speaking, the larger the company, the greater the opportunity for efficiency in the use of labor. This is especially true on the milk-delivery routes. Within any market a large distributor delivers milk to a greater proportion of the city consumers and usually has more concentrated routes than does the smaller company. Hence, the larger company is able to make delivery at less distance traveled per unit delivered and to spend less time for each unit delivered, with a correspondingly high efficiency. On the other hand, the larger companies often pay higher wage rates than do the smaller ones, mainly because their employees are generally more effectively organized, and, while proof would be difficult, it is often said that they are better qualified for their occupation. The

---

[4] Agricultural Adjustment Administration, *A Survey of Milk Marketing in Milwaukee* ("U.S. Department of Agriculture, Market Information Series," DM-1 [Washington, May, 1937]), Table 51. A "point" is a quart of milk, whether regular, chocolate, or vitamin D milk, etc.; or a half-pint of cream, etc.

two influences—relative efficiency and relative wage rates—tend to counteract each other with the result that there appears to be no highly significant relationship between size of company and wage cost calculated as a percentage of total operating cost. For the entire eleven-year period total wages for the companies classified as "small" were 43.7 per cent of the total operating costs as compared with 39.8 per cent for those companies classified as "large."

Expenses of delivery directly to the family retail trade accounts for roughly two-thirds of the total cost of retail milk distribution. This cost can be reduced by a reduction of the duplication of retail delivery routes, thus permitting more efficient use of the milk deliverymen, or by a system of distributing fluid milk through the local grocery store or any other type of dispensary easily accessible to consumers. The second method suggested would make milk available at a lower cost than is possible if it is delivered to the family doorstep. Such a system would, however, fall short of providing the type of service desired by many city consumers. Though acknowledged to be worthy of consideration, it would not solve the problems of milk distribution. Inasmuch as it is not a fundamental part of the question of milk distribution under public utility control, we shall not include it as a part of this book.

Assuming no change in the rate of wages, what savings would be possible in the wage bill if milk were processed and distributed under a unified system? In order to make detailed analysis of these costs and possible savings, we shall need to make a division of the labor employed (a) in the milk plant, (b) in milk delivery, and (c) in the office.

a) *Plant labor.*—For the most part, the amount of plant labor is in direct proportion to the volume of milk handled. However, the use of larger units and more automatic features in processing machinery such as pasteurizers, bottle-washers, filling and capping machines, and conveyors will make possible some reduction of the labor cost per unit of plant output. A fuller use of these machines will also tend to increase labor efficiency. For example, the time spent in cleaning the plant, machines, and equipment after the daily run is about the same whether the plant has been in operation for three hours or for six hours.

On the basis of observation in a number of plants over the state and the opinions of a number of milk-plant operators, it is estimated that under a unified system of milk processing and distribution, if the plants were efficiently operated, plant labor per unit of output could be reduced somewhere between 15 and 25 per cent. The savings would be brought about through (1) a longer daily utilization of machines and consequently less time spent in cleaning them per unit of output, (2) the use of larger and more automatic features on the machines, and (3) more automatic conveyors. These savings would result in no change in the type of service rendered consumers.

Another plant saving, perhaps even larger proportionately, could be brought about by handling fewer or none of the special brands of milk and other dairy products. Under the present system it is not uncommon for distributors to handle from three to six special brands of milk featuring varying butterfat content, special bottles or bottle caps, etc. Most of these are properly classed by milk deliverymen as "novelties." In addition, there is "soft curd" milk, homogenized milk, raw milk, and certified milk. Some of these special brands and special products are said to have their primary value in meeting competition from other dealers rather than in meeting a demand originating from consumers. Only a relatively small number of consumers take these specialty products, but milk distributors believe it necessary to carry them in order to meet competition. While it would be difficult to obtain the facts needed upon which to allocate total costs of handling these special products if such allocations could be made, they would likely show that the prices charged are generally not high enough to cover their handling costs. From the standpoint of fairness to all milk consumers in a market, should these products not be so priced as to at least pay their own way?

Even though the total output of all specialty packages is but a small proportion of the total plant output, they add materially to the unit cost of the entire plant output because they cannot be handled as a part of the continuing plant operations. Either additional smaller machines must be provided for their processing, or, if the regular machines are used, they will be operated at a slower rate of output than is the case when processing the standard product. Moreover, these products must be placed in the cooler so as to be easily accessible, hence requiring extra labor as well as cooler space. In the daily routine of plant operation these products may not appear to involve a noticeably increased amount of labor time, but the plant labor per unit of output is vastly greater for the special products than for the standard product handled. This cost is spread over the entire output. When it can be reasonably shown that changes or new processes make for an actual improvement in the nutritive or health-giving quality of milk, or in any other way is to the public advantage, then such improvements should be encouraged and introduced. But a practice of providing specialty products or attempting to differentiate a product even though it is not significantly different from that regularly provided and which serves only as a means of inducing customers to shift to a different milkman has nothing to recommend it from a public point of view. Such practices add to the unit cost of handling and may actually tend to confuse consumers. Can they be justified except as competitive weapons? The writer appreciates, of course, that practices of this nature are not peculiar to the fluid-milk business only, but does that serve as a justification?

On the basis of calculation in this study, the labor cost (plant, office, and delivery), not including management, amounts to 40–45 per cent of the total operating cost.[5] While no comprehensive determinations were made to establish the proportion of the labor which was assigned to plant operations, a study indicated that plant labor accounted for approximately 18–25 per cent of total labor.[6]

[5] See Table 2, p. 35, and Table A, Appen. A.

[6] A study made by the Wisconsin Department of Agriculture and Markets in 1938 covering three selected months—two in 1937 and one in 1938—gives the distribution of total labor costs into three items—plant, delivery, and office—for each of nine Wisconsin companies. The table below gives the distribution of labor costs into these three items by company. It should be noted that, though there is some variation between companies, the deviation from the mean is reasonably small. This is especially true of the two largest items—plant and delivery labor.

PERCENTAGE DIVISION OF TOTAL LABOR COSTS INTO THREE CATEGORIES—PLANT, DELIVERY, AND OFFICE

Labor Cost Category	Company									Average
	A	B	C	D	E	F	G	H	I	
Plant	26.7	19.5	18.0	19.4	16.5	20.8	20.9	22.0	17.6	20.2
Delivery	69.9	76.8	76.8	75.0	76.8	70.0	69.2	71.5	75.4	73.5
Office	3.4	3.7	5.2	5.6	6.7	9.2	9.9	6.5	7.0	6.4
Total labor cost	100.0	100.0	100.0	100.0	100.0	100.0	100.0	100.0	100.0	100.0

On the basis of total operating costs of 5 cents per quart of milk, the total labor would thus amount to 2–2.25 cents per quart.[7]

As mentioned earlier, rather than to set forth information in terms of averages, we shall set up what may be termed the probable range within which savings in plant labor might be expected if the distribution of milk were operated as a unified system under public utility control. Taking first the smaller probability or likelihood, we might calculate on a basis as follows:

Total cost of all labor equals 2 cents per quart of milk; plant labor equal to 18 per cent of total labor and a saving of 15 per cent on this plant labor. Eighteen per cent of 2 cents equals 0.36 cent. Fifteen per cent of 0.36 cent equals 0.054 cent, the probable saving per quart.

Using the figure representing the larger probability, we shall calculate on the basis of plant labor being equal to 25 per cent of the total labor and a possible savings of 25 per cent on this plant labor. On the same basis as before, of 2 cents per quart for total labor cost, plant labor would be 25 per cent of 2 cents or 0.5 of a cent per quart. Twenty-five per cent of this 0.5 cent would be 0.125 of a cent. That is, the probability of savings in plant labor should be within a range of 0.054 of a cent and 0.125 of a cent per quart of milk handled.[8]

b) Delivery labor.—In the main, unit cost of milk delivery is determined by the size of load carried and by the daily, weekly, or monthly wage rate of the deliverymen. The variation between the lowest unit cost route of the lowest cost company and that of the highest unit cost route of the highest cost company of the same city may be expected to be extremely wide. Even within one company the unit cost varies from route to route, depending upon the relative efficiency of the deliverymen, the concentration of customers on the delivery route, the type of vehicle used, the ease of collecting from customers, and a few other less important considerations.

Where delivery is made before breakfast, the length of time to cover the route is more limited than where delivery is made during

[7] Five cents per quart is assumed to be an approximation of the milk distributors' margin in a city of the size included in this study. At the end of the chapter calculations are also made on the basis of a 6-cent margin (see Tables 10 and 11).

[8] See Table 10, p. 82.

the day, but under any condition time is a fundamental factor. If increased volume of milk is to be delivered per route and per hour of work by the deliverymen, the dwellings served must be concentrated so that delivery can be made more easily and rapidly. A unified system would permit of a greater concentration of dwellings served by a deliveryman than does a competitive system. Under unification it should be possible to maintain as low a unit cost on the majority of its routes as is achieved in similar areas by the lower, or the lowest, cost routes under the existing system. The present competitive system—regulated or unregulated—offers little opportunity for a high degree of concentration of delivered routes with the resulting dispatch and economy of delivery.

In some markets of the country the milk deliverymen, largely through organized efforts, have laid down regulations placing a maximum on the amount of milk which is to be delivered daily per deliveryman. If this should become the common practice and if the trend should be for still smaller loads, then any effort on the part of either the private milk companies or a unified system to increase the concentration of routes by reorganizing them would result largely in a gain to deliverymen by reducing their hours of work rather than in reducing the cost of delivery. Indeed, if the labor organizations should decide that the size load to be delivered per deliveryman is to stay at or below the present level, and they should become sufficiently powerful to carry out such a policy, then a unified milk-distributing system would not be in a position to pass the savings resulting from delivery efficiencies on to consumers. Instead, the gain would be enjoyed by those who delivered the milk.

One of the most important considerations, often overlooked in discussions of efficiency of retail delivery under the present competitive system, is the time spent in the collection of accounts and the solicitation of "new" customers. Both are important cost items. These two activities are essentially problems which arise under a competitive system and could be largely or entirely eliminated under a unified system. Especially wasteful is the practice of soliciting new customers by the route salesmen or by solicitors hired for that particular purpose. Solicitation, in practically all cases, is an economic waste of time and money from the standpoint of the market as a whole, although to any individual company such activity may be profitable. Indeed, if the practice is common in a market, an individual company which does not fall in line with this practice may find it impossible to increase or even maintain its business. Soliciting is largely a process of Company A taking a customer away from Company B and the latter retaliating by immediately attempting to get two customers from A or C.

Even though it be granted that there is an economic justification for a type of sales promotion which increases the total sales of fluid milk, it does not follow that the kind of soliciting now being carried on is socially desirable since it results almost entirely in the promotion of one company's sales at the expense of another with no net social gain; instead it may be in the nature of an imposition upon the time and patience of the prospective convert—the housewife. To the extent that housewives become annoyed by solicitation of milk salesmen, which is probably true in many cases, such solicitation does not serve to promote milk consumption—quite the contrary. Nor would it seem logical that personal calls to collect the milk accounts would serve to promote milk sales.

That a unified system would permit of a savings of delivery expense by eliminating the time of soliciting is hardly open to question. It is somewhat less obvious that a like saving could be made in eliminating or in reducing the time in collecting accounts. However, there are some aspects of this latter question about which there is no doubt. Under the present system the responsibility of collection falls to the deliveryman. Competition for business is so intense that he cannot insist upon prompt payment for fear that the consumer will become offended, discontinue her patronage, and transfer to another company. Because of this condition, a deliveryman may be forced to call upon not a few housewives as often as five to ten times each during a month for the collection of the milk bill. Under a unified system the route men would not be required to face this problem; it would instead become the consumers' responsibility to see that the milk bills were paid. A definite date could be set when the route man would call on his customers for payment, or it could be sent directly to the main office or paid in the form of checks left in the empty milk bottles. If payment were not made at that time or within a limited time thereafter, service could be discontinued until the bill was paid. Since the consumer would not be able to obtain service from a competing dairy, payments would likely be both prompt and regular.

Some might object to such a "business-like" or perhaps even harsh manner of collection on the grounds that those out of employment, or for other reasons unable to pay, may find themselves without milk for the family. However, one might argue with equal force that those unable to make payment for gas and electricity should be provided these essential services free of cost. Such problems should perhaps be handled by the relief authorities. It is to be observed that city water, electricity, and gas have been dispensed through public utilities for decades, yet it has apparently worked no particular hardship upon those in economic distress any more than have the methods used in supplying the products and services handled through private competitive enterprise. It would seem logical that those who pay their milk bills regularly and promptly should not be required to pay higher prices because others are lax in payment or neglect payment entirely.

Data obtained by the writer from some eighty milk distributors located in Wisconsin cities varying in population from 10,000 to 70,000 show that collecting accounts and soliciting new customers required over two-fifths as much time as was absorbed by the actual delivery and almost one-third of the deliverymen's working time.[9] Table 3 presents the essential facts for 274 retail or mixed routes of the eighty-two milk-distributing companies.

The weighted average time spent per load in actual delivery was 5.6 hours; collecting, 1.7; and soliciting, 0.6 hour, totaling 8 hours. If only the larger companies are considered (over four loads per day), 6.1 hours are spent in delivery and 2.8 hours in soliciting and collecting, a total of 8.9 hours daily.

In a detailed study made by C. W. Pierce of 42 retail and mixed routes in New York City, it was found that, on an average, collect-

9 The following operations are included in "actual delivery": loading and unloading at the plant; driving to and from the routes; placing the milk at the doorstep and picking up the empty bottles; entering customer accounts in the customer's book; and checking in at the plant. "Total delivery" included the above operations and in addition the time spent in collecting accounts and soliciting new customers.

ing and soliciting required about 2–2¼ hours out of a total of 9¼ hours spent daily by the deliveryman.[10] This meant that roughly one-fourth of the total time of the deliverymen was spent in collecting milk bills and soliciting new business.

Charles Blanford found that for 745 New York City routes, on the average, 5.4 hours were spent in actual delivery and 2.4 hours

TABLE 3

AVERAGE TIME SPENT BY MILK DELIVERYMEN PER LOAD ON EACH OF THREE
FUNCTIONS—ACTUAL DELIVERY, COLLECTING ACCOUNTS, AND SOLIC-
ITING NEW CUSTOMERS—82 WISCONSIN DISTRIBUTORS

(Time in Hours)

NUMBER OF LOADS PER DAY	NUM-BER OF COM-PANIES	NUM-BER OF ROUTES	TIME OF AC-TUAL DELIV-ERY	TIME COL-LECT-ING	TIME SO-LICIT-ING	TOTAL TIME ON ROUTE	TIME COL-LECT-ING AND SO-LICIT-ING	COLLECTING AND SOLICIT-ING AS PER-CENTAGE OF	
								Actual Deliv-ery Time	Total Time
Over 4...........	15	171	6.1	2.0	0.8	8.9	2.8	46	31
4...............	4	16	6.4	1.9	.8	9.1	2.7	44	30
3...............	9	27	5.1	1.7	.6	7.4	2.3	45	31
2...............	6	12	5.0	0.7	.5	6.2	1.2	24	20
1...............	48	48	3.9	0.7	0.3	4.9	1.0	26	20
Total or weight-ed average...	82	274	5.60	1.70	0.64	8.0	2.4	43	30

in collecting, a daily total of 7.8 hours.[11] That is, slightly more than 30 per cent of the total time was devoted to collecting. The amount of time spent in soliciting by deliverymen was not ascertained.

[10] "Survey of Milk Routes in New York City," *Farm Economics*, February, 1935, p. 2131. A small part of the time designated for collections and solicitations was actually used in picking up milk bottles from stores and returning to some of the larger retail customers to determine if additional milk was required. Since these routes averaged only seven wholesale customers, the time required for picking up bottles would be small and the return trip to customers could be considered as part of solicitation, as this was no doubt one of the means used to keep their patronage.

[11] *An Economic Study of the Costs of Selling and Delivering Milk in the New York Markets* (Cornell University Agricultural Experiment Station Bull. 686 [Ithaca, 1938]), p. 24.

However, it was shown that, of the total of 4.87 cents spent in selling and delivering a quart of milk, 0.18 cent was expended for salaries of special salesmen and collectors or 4 per cent of the total in addition to the above 30 per cent.

In the study of the Milwaukee market made by the Agricultural Adjustment Administration, no data were given concerning the time spent on collections and solicitations, but some idea of the evident importance of these factors is revealed by the fact that deliverymen spent less than five hours daily in actual delivery.[12] Even if the deliverymen worked only a seven-hour day, the time spent in collecting and soliciting would amount to almost 30 per cent of the total.

Thus, briefly, the available evidence indicates that, as a rather general practice, 30 per cent or more of the total daily time of deliverymen is spent soliciting and collecting.

If, under a unified system, soliciting were dispensed with and the time required for collections were reduced to a minimum—say, to not more than 3–5 per cent of the total time now spent for delivery—then, as a conservative estimate, roughly one-fourth of the work now done in a day by the deliverymen would be saved. Put in another way, if no efficiencies other than savings in collecting and soliciting were possible, milk could be delivered under a unified system by about three-fourths of the present number of deliverymen. This means that the cost of delivery-truck operation and total wages of drivers could be reduced by approximately the same proportion.

No small amount of public criticism has been leveled at the common practice of permitting as many as eight, ten, or more wagons to deliver milk in the same block. In some cities the number of miles traveled by milk delivery trucks aggregates several times the total street mileage.

For the purpose of obtaining detailed data concerning the amount of time consumed by unnecessary driving on milk routes under the system now in effect, an observer who collaborated in this project under the general direction of the writer accompanied deliverymen on eight representative routes of four companies in a midwestern

---

[12] *Op. cit.*, p. 74.

city of some 70,000 population.[13] The various operations performed by the route men were timed with a stop watch and the time recorded on a tally sheet designed for that purpose. The following activities were timed: (1) loading and arranging load; (2) driving to place of first delivery; (3) walking from truck, depositing milk at each home, and returning to truck; (4) driving from one stop to the next; (5) working in the truck, arranging load and filling bottle-carrier; (6) tabulating customers' accounts; (7) soliciting customers; (8) collecting; (9) driving from the last stop to plant; (10) unloading; and (11) checking in at plant. These various figures were ascertained for 1,600 customers or approximately 10 per cent of all the milk customers in the city. The routes on which data were obtained were primarily retail. The number of wholesale delivery stops per route varied from two to six. Excluding the time spent in soliciting and collecting, the drivers averaged about 5.5 hours of work for the tasks enumerated above to serve retail customers, and an additional 20 minutes were required to serve the wholesale trade, making a total of approximately 6 hours daily for what may be termed actual delivery time. However, since the survey was made under conditions of daylight delivery, it was difficult to segregate the amount of time spent in collecting and soliciting, and, as a result, some time devoted to soliciting and collecting was included in the above total.

The information revealed by the summary of the observations permit of some interesting conclusions. First, there appears to be some economy worthy of consideration when a deliveryman serves more than one dwelling before returning to the truck. When only one dwelling was served before returning to the truck, it required an average of 41 seconds of the deliveryman's time to make the delivery (the time spent carrying the milk to the house and returning with the empty bottles). When two houses were served, the average time was 36 seconds, and, if three or more houses, the average was 33 seconds per house.[14] The possible economy under a unified sys-

---

[13] In order to permit of continuity of discussion and ease of reading, a portion of the material on milk delivery has been set forth in Appen. B.

[14] In each case only one customer was served in each residence. If the observer obtained any evidence that a collection had been made on the same trip or the driver spent time for purposes other than making the delivery, the figure was edited out.

tem would no doubt be greater than that exhibited by the averages given. In probably half of the cases where the deliverymen served two or more dwellings before returning to the truck, those dwellings were not adjacent to each other. Under a unified system, all the dwellings served would be adjacent since every dwelling in an area would be served by the same deliveryman.

Second, three of the drivers ran rather than walked much of the distance in order to increase speed of delivery. According to labor-union regulations, drivers were not permitted to start delivery before a stated hour. Some customers preferred obtaining milk from the wagon making the earliest delivery which urged drivers to complete their deliveries ahead of their competitors. As a result, they made a better showing, on an average, than did drivers who walked. The three drivers who ran had an average of 38 seconds for going from the truck to the house and return, compared to 52 seconds for the five who walked. The saving that would result from delivering to more than one dwelling at a time would be about offset by the fact that the men would no doubt find it necessary to walk in order to conserve their energy if the size of their load were increased materially. As would be expected, the older and more experienced men seldom, if ever, ran. It is significant that apparently only about one-fourth of the time spent away from the truck was saved by running instead of walking.

Third, special brands of milk and other products required noticeably more time per unit delivered than did "standard" milk. If the number of different types of products delivered were reduced to one, two, or at the most three kinds of milk and, say, two grades of cream (coffee and whipping), the time required for work in the truck, filling the trays in which the bottles are carried, and finding the proper products or containers, etc., could be reduced greatly. Under the existing system, it is not at all uncommon for a route man to carry twenty or more different kinds, sizes, and types of containers.[15]

[15] As an example, on one of the wagons carrying a typical load, the following items were included: regular milk in two styles of quart bottles and one in pints; Guernsey milk in quarts and pints; certified raw milk in quarts; Grade A in quarts; vitamin D milk in quarts; acidophilous milk in quarts; buttermilk in quarts; light and heavy

Although the exact amount of time required for the driver to locate the special brand of milk (or other special products) was not tabulated, it was a noticeable proportion of the total time required in filling the tray. In addition to the time required in locating the special products, the driver usually had to return to the truck from the house to get a special item which was ordered only at irregular intervals. The time consumed in returning to the truck from the dwelling to serve customers with a special product aggregated over 3 seconds per customer for the whole route or a total of from 30 to 40 seconds for each customer so served. Likewise, the time devoted to checking-in at the plant and recording customers' orders in the account book would be reduced if the milk wagons carried fewer products.

It should be mentioned that the savings indicated under a unified system would result partly by reducing some of the services now offered consumers. However, consumers would still receive adequate service though perhaps not the amount of special products or personal attention now made available to or urged upon them. It is argued by some that this personal attention advertises milk, thus tending to increase the consumption of it. Others point out that the additional attention given it serves to call price to the attention of consumers thus increasing their price consciousness of the product and thereby inducing them to lessen consumption rather than increase it.

Fourth, generally speaking, each route which had a high percentage of stops in the same block had a low average driving time per dwelling and vice versa. This fact is pointed out in Table 4. For

---

cream in quarts, pints, and half-pints; sour cream in quarts and pints; cottage cheese in glasses, jars, and paper cartons; butter in two different types of packages; chocolate milk in quarts and pints; and an orange drink in quarts and pints. Another truck carried eggs, American cheese, and a grape drink, though not quite all of the above combination of items.

In a summary statement the Federal Trade Commission points out that "as many as nineteen different classes and grades of milk, cream, butter, buttermilk, cheese, eggs and other commodities are carried on and delivered from the same milk vehicle in as many as 63 sizes and shapes of packages" (*Distribution and Sale of Milk and Milk Products* [*Boston, Baltimore, Cincinnati, and St. Louis*] [House Document No. 501 (74th Cong.; 2d sess.)], p. 10). This is apparently not an unusual situation which exists only in scattered markets.

Route A, the most highly concentrated route, with 76 per cent of the stops within blocks, the average driving time per dwelling was only 9 seconds compared with about 20 seconds for the somewhat less concentrated routes (D, H, G, B, and C). The two most scattered routes, F and E, where only a third or less of the stops were made within the same block, required from four to six times as many seconds driving as did those with the greatest concentration.

TABLE 4

RELATIONSHIP BETWEEN PERCENTAGE OF TOTAL STOPS MADE WITHIN THE SAME BLOCK AND THE AVERAGE DRIVING TIME PER DWELLING SERVED*

(Time in Seconds)

Route	Total Number of Houses Served (1)	Number of Times Two or More Stops Were Made in Same Block (2)	Percentage of Total Stops Which Were Made within the Same Block (3)	Average Driving Time per Dwelling (4)
A..........	185	141	76	9
D..........	188	121	64	21
H..........	201	122	61	20
G..........	155	86	56	20
B..........	164	92	56	24
C..........	187	99	53	28
F..........	145	50	34	64
E..........	155	43	28	40

* When two or more stops (deliveries) were made within the same block before crossing the street to the next block, they are referred to as "stops within the same block" or "within blocks," in contrast to stops between blocks. In the between-block stops one or more blocks were sometimes skipped entirely because no milk deliveries were made in them.

In general terms, Route A made about three out of every four stops within the same block as compared with only one out of four for Route E (col. 3). The driving time per dwelling for Route A was about one-fourth of that for Route E (col. 4).

In Table 5 comparison is made between the average time for driving between stops in the same block and the average time between successive stops in different blocks. For six out of the eight routes, the average driving time between stops in different blocks was at least four times as great as that between stops in the same block. In the other two cases (Routes E and G) the necessary time required for consecutive stops in different blocks was more than twice that for stops within the same block. This shows that economy of driving time between stops in the same block in relation to stops in different blocks is of major consequence.[16]

The average time for driving between stops in the same block for the most concentrated route (Route A) would probably approach the time required if a truck served every house in the block in a similar residential district. On Route A the average driving time

TABLE 5

COMPARISON BETWEEN DRIVING TIME WHEN
STOPS ARE MADE IN SAME BLOCK
AND IN DIFFERENT BLOCKS

(Time in Seconds)

Route	Average Time between Stops in Same Block	Average Time between Stops in Different Blocks	Difference between the Two
A.........	4	22	18
B.........	9	44	35
C.........	9	50	41
D.........	9	43	34
E.........	19	54	35
F.........	14	91	77
G.........	13	29	16
H.........	9	36	27

between stops in the same block was only 4 seconds. This was the time the truck was actually in motion while traveling between dwellings. Although Deliveryman A made deliveries in thirty blocks, in only five of these blocks did he serve more than half of the dwellings. Since the district in which this route was operated was one of not more than average concentration of dwellings, it would seem that 4–6 seconds per dwelling would be a conservative estimate for the driving time needed in a residential area under a unified system.

Table 6 indicates the savings which would be made possible if the

[16] This increase in time consumed in delivering in different blocks over that of delivering within a block is greater than most individuals would expect because the difference in distance traveled was considerable. It was a common occurrence for deliverymen to skip two or three blocks between deliveries.

driving time of all routes could be reduced to between 4 and 6 seconds per dwelling—a goal easily within the range of possibility. In this table it was assumed that economy of time would be possible in only two of the six functions: a reduction of the driving time while making the actual delivery and a (smaller) reduction made in driving from the plant to the first stop and again from the last delivery back to the plant. The first would result from a saving of driving distance per customer served because of increased concentra-

TABLE 6

DIVISION OF TIME REQUIRED TO SERVE A CUSTOMER UNDER COMPETITIVE AND UNIFIED SYSTEMS COMPARED*

(Time in Seconds)

Function	Competitive System	Unified System
Going from truck to dwelling and return.	45	45
Work in truck.	18	18
Truck in motion on route.	23	5
Drive to and from route.	6	4
Load and unload at plant.	4	4
Check in at plant.	13	13
Total.	109	89

* Based upon driving time of 5 seconds per customer. Since there was an average of slightly more than 1 customer per dwelling, there is some difference between the average time required to serve a house and a customer. The routes studied had, on an average, about 200 customers who lived in 175 dwellings. Thus, there would be 1⅐ customers per house. Table 6 is based upon time required to serve a customer rather than in terms of serving a dwelling.

tion of customers on the routes. The second would arise because a smaller number of trucks would travel to and from the routes in serving the same total number of customers. The full saving of time of 20 seconds per customer amounts to a reduction of 18 per cent. The time requirement in the other four functions of actual delivery was assumed to remain unchanged.

Under a unified system of delivery there is every reason to believe that some time could also be saved in going from truck to dwelling and return and also in the time spent in work in truck because of fewer products carried. Thus, the estimate made here is distinctly conservative.

To summarize the findings of this survey, it seems clear that under a unified system there are three important phases of delivery wherein an appreciable amount of time could be saved: (1) collecting accounts and soliciting business, (2) in the driving time consumed in covering the route, and (3) in supplying special products.

The first two of these savings could be achieved without any reduction in the kind or quality of fundamental services offered or in the variety of products made available at the consumer's doorstep. The only change from the present system would be that involved in a possible inconvenience to the consumer through the adoption of a more businesslike or aggressive method of collecting accounts. If special milk and other products now carried on the wagons were eliminated, the service resulting might be looked upon as somewhat restricted. As mentioned earlier, there is real doubt as to whether these special products are carried as a result of a demand arising from the consumer or whether distributors have created a demand for them in order to push their sales at the expense of competitors. They may add no fundamental utility to the consumer.

The amount of the savings which could be brought about through the adoption of these three changes can be estimated roughly. Eliminating the solicitation and reducing collecting to a minimum would mean a savings of about 25 per cent of the total working time of the deliverymen. Of the remaining 75 per cent (this 75 per cent of the total time constitutes the time spent in actual delivery), increased concentration of customers would account for an economy of about 18 per cent of actual delivery time or 13 per cent of the total time now spent by deliverymen (18 per cent of 75 per cent = 0.135 or 13.5 per cent). The elimination of special products now handled would result in a further economy of approximately 4 per cent (0.75 × 0.05 = 0.0375 or 3.75 per cent) of the total time. Thus, under a unified system, it would seem altogether within the realm of possibility that the total delivery time saved would amount to about 42 per cent (25 + 13 + 4 = 42). Accordingly, the savings in delivery labor and hence the amount of the delivery wage could be reduced by a like amount.[17] Delivery labor constitutes from 65 to 75 per cent of the total labor cost in most markets.[18]

[17] This estimate is based upon the assumption that time required in collection would amount to 5 per cent of the total time required to serve the customers. This would allow for the equivalent of a full day and a half a month for collections. However, if the collections were made in the manner similar to that commonly used by most public utilities, this collection time could be eliminated entirely.

[18] Cf. n. 6, p. 44.

Following the procedure used in the discussion of plant labor, we shall set up a probable range within which savings in delivery labor per quart of milk handled may be expected if the distribution of milk were operated as a unified system. Allowing for about 10 per cent range on either side of the calculated savings of 42 per cent, the upper and lower limits of the possible savings can be calculated.

Taking the lower likelihood, 38 per cent (10 per cent of 42 = 4.2; 42 − 4.2 = 37.8), one may calculate as follows: total cost of all labor, 2 cents per quart; delivery labor equal to 65 per cent of total labor and a saving of 38 per cent on this delivery labor. Sixty-five per cent of 2 cents equals 1.35 cents—38 per cent of 1.35 cents equals 0.51 cent per quart of milk.

Using the upper probability, we shall calculate on the basis of delivery labor being equal to 75 per cent of total labor and a possible saving of 46 per cent on this labor. On the same basis as before of 2 cents a quart for total labor cost, delivery labor would be 75 per cent of 2 cents or 1.5 cents per quart. Forty-six per cent of this 1.5 cents would be 0.69 cent, or roughly 0.7 cent per quart of milk.

If 42 per cent fewer deliverymen and trucks were employed, each route would have an average of approximately 330 customers as compared with the 200 customers for the routes studied in this survey, which appear to be rather typical in volume of routes of other cities. Serving 330 customers would necessitate carrying approximately a 500-point load of milk and milk products. The existing type of delivery equipment would permit hauling this size load. The observer on the milk routes was of the opinion that from 12 to 16 additional cases of milk of 12 bottles each could be carried in any of the trucks without interfering with the driver. In fact, two of the route men had previously hauled over 500 points.

In the Milwaukee market the average capacity of retail trucks was 506 points at the time of the Agricultural Adjustment Administration study. The average per capita fluid-milk consumption was slightly less in Milwaukee than in the market covered in this study. Thus the number of points carried per customer (or for the load) would be lower than indicated above. It was also found in the Milwaukee study that retail and mixed-route trucks were utilized at only 54 per cent of possible capacity.[19] In apartment-house areas larger trucks than are now common on retail routes could be used and appreciably more than 330 customers could be served in an eight-hour day.

However, if the unified system adopted the ordinary public utility method of collecting accounts, namely, by requiring all accounts to be paid at the main office, an additional saving of about 5 per cent could be realized. This means that the lower limit of possible reduction in cost of delivery labor would be 0.56 cent and the upper limit of probable saving would be increased to 0.75 cent per quart of milk handled with no particular strain on the delivery equipment or burden on the deliverymen. If we assume, as in Table 6, that a customer could be served in, say, 90 seconds, a conservative estimate, then 330 customers could be served each day in 8.25 hours. This estimate of 90 seconds per customer assumes that the wagons would carry the same number of special brands of milk and other products as is carried by delivery wagons at present. The time required to serve 330 customers if special products were eliminated would probably not be more than 7.9 hours a day.

Naturally this would vary materially from area to area. In apartment-house districts it should be possible to make deliveries to 330 customers in much less than this amount of time.

It is evident that more customers are served in one section of a city than in another, or in one city than in another. Despite these relatively minor variations—except in apartment districts—studies made in other markets indicate that the routes analyzed in detail in our study were by and large rather typical of retail routes in other cities with respect to size of load carried. For example, in Milwaukee in 1934 the average number of customers per route (for more than 700 routes) was 204, compared with our 200. The average points delivered was 273 as compared with about 300 for our study.[20] For the 274 routes from various Wisconsin cities, referred to earlier, the average number of customers per route was a little smaller, averaging 187. However, if the producer-distributor routes —comprising virtually all the one- and two-route distributors—had been excluded from the sample, the average would have been about

[19] *Op. cit.*, pp. 79–80.　　　[20] *Ibid.*, p. 74.

210 customers and 325 points delivered per route. From 745 routes in New York City there was an average of 196 customers per route and 313 points per load.[21]

Table 7 gives the average size load in points for eleven companies in six Wisconsin markets for various years since 1929. This table shows that the size load varies from a low of 219 points for Company W (for 1933) and a high of 469 for Company U (in 1932). These companies are not the same ones as referred to in Tables 1 or 2.

Because of the variation from company to company and market to market used in the "point" system,[22] an arithmetic average was not calculated, but it is interesting to note that 13 of the 45 averages fall below 280 points, 20 between 280 and 320 points, and only 12 over 320. This indicates clearly that the size load carried on the routes studied in detail in our survey compares quite closely with the modal size for the 45 loads of eleven companies shown in Table 7.

Some years ago two studies involving experimental milk deliveries were made to determine the extent of possible savings if milk were delivered under a unified system. One was made by B. H. Hibbard and H. E. Erdman in Chicago,[23] and the other by John R. Williams in Rochester, New York.[24] The findings of both of these studies

---

[21] Blanford, *op. cit.*, p. 26.

[22] It should be mentioned that the difference in points per load obtained by using different systems of determining points is slight, and it might be that, if enough loads were considered, the average would be substantially the same regardless of which of the two most common point systems were used. To illustrate this, a small number of route loads were picked at random from a large number that were available to the writer and the number of points were calculated, first, on the basis of counting each unit of product handled as a point and, second, by counting a quart of milk or a half-pint of cream as a point and other sized units on the basis of their proportional size to these units with each unit of special product being counted as one point. For the eight routes on which such calculations were made, the following results were obtained: (1) 303 and 299, (2) 364 and 358, (3) 352 and 348, (4) 323 and 329, (5) 268 and 268, (6) 376 and 387, (7) 281 and 278, and (8) 275 and 276. The results obtained by these two point systems appear substantially identical for practical purposes.

[23] *Marketing Wisconsin Milk* (University of Wisconsin Bull. 285 [Madison, December, 1917]), pp. 66–70.

[24] "The Economic Problems of Milk Distribution in Their Relation to Public Health," in *Transactions of the Fifteenth International Congress on Hygiene and Demography,* V (Washington, 1913), 128–40.

have been criticized somewhat because it was believed by some that it is impossible to duplicate actual conditions in a trial delivery where all the actual processes were not carried out. Such criticisms as the following were directed against the studies. The deliverymen were not required to return to the truck if the housewife wanted more than the usual quantity of milk or cream, and the deliverymen did not have to spend any time talking with the housewife.

TABLE 7

POINTS CARRIED ON RETAIL AND MIXED ROUTES FOR VARIOUS WISCONSIN COMPANIES*

YEAR	ANNUAL AVERAGES					MONTHLY AVERAGE (APRIL)					
	M	N	O	P	Q	R	S	T	U	V	W
1929	259										
1930	263					330	290		296		
1931	276					320	288		349		
1932	251				279	347	308		469		
1933	263	255	305	325	314	307	288	288	428		219
1934	292	276	303	328	344	278	244	240	354	318	224
1935	315	296	314	330	365						
1936	300	302									
1937	316	333									
1938		303†									

* The approximate number of routes for each company are as follows: M, 10; N, 25; O, 7; P, 24; Q, 17; R, 280; S, 200; T, 27; U, 18; V, 63, W, 16. Routes shown for Companies R to W inclusive are for retail routes only.

† Three months only.

From this study it was found in one section of Chicago that the milk deliverymen actually delivered milk at the rate of a bottle a minute, while the men on trial delivery were able to deliver 1.87 bottles per minute, almost twice the amount disposed of by those who actually delivered milk under the then existing system. In the other section of the city, 120 bottles were delivered in 76 minutes in contrast to the 139 minutes required by the actual deliverymen. This showed substantially the same degree of efficiency as was obtained in the other section of the city.

The conservative nature of the Hibbard and Erdman estimates should be emphasized. As they pointed out, the actual drivers obviously made much better time in the blocks in which the study was made than for the route as a whole, since drivers lost much time in driving past blocks in which no deliveries were made.

Williams found in Rochester that the total miles traveled by distributors could be reduced from 2,509 to about 300 miles and the estimated cost of delivery reduced from $2,000 daily to $600, a reduction of over two-thirds from that existing at the time. It should be pointed out that, while these surveys were made several years ago, the conditions of the trial delivery would be just as applicable to present-day conditions as they were at that time.

By using a three-man crew, it was found that it would be possible to serve customers in the more densely populated districts at the rate of 35 seconds per customer, and in the well-to-do, less densely populated sections the average time required was 45 seconds. If the average of two sections was typical of the city, one man could serve over 500 customers in 6 hours of actual delivery excluding the loading and unloading time, driving to and from the route, and checking in. It is probably true that this experimental delivery was carried on under very satisfactory conditions, but it could have been in error by 20 or even 30 per cent without invalidating the general conclusions drawn from the experiment.

During the recent survey of milk marketing in Milwaukee by the Agricultural Adjustment Administration, a number of trial deliveries were evidently made in which it was found that a customer could be served in 40 seconds. Though it was not made clear how much of the total service was included in this 40 seconds, it is probably safe to assume that loading and unloading and checking-in at the plant were not included. If the time required for these activities is added, the total time would be about 60 seconds per customer, a third less than the average found in our study. On the basis of 60 seconds per customer, a deliveryman could serve 420 customers in a seven-hour day.[25]

[25] There is relatively little information available on the amount of duplication of delivery service with the resulting efficiency of delivery in apartment houses. Blanford, in his study of delivery routes in New York City, found that over 63 per cent of the apartment houses were served by two or more dealers and over 23 per cent by three or more distributors. This indicates that the duplication in service is quite prevalent, though it does not give any indication of the additional cost incurred because of the practice.

Judging from the results of other studies which suggest possible economies ranging from 54 to 60 per cent in delivery through a unified milk-distribution system, it would seem that an estimated saving of 38–46 per cent, assumed in our calculations, are extremely conservative.[26]

c) Office labor.—Roughly 6 per cent of the total labor cost of the milk-distributing business is classified as office labor.[27] Under a unified system this cost item would perhaps not be decreased even though all the accounting procedure involved in the milk business of a city were brought into one general office. While some economy might arise because the books and accounts of only one distributor would be kept instead of many, as under the existing system, it is generally assumed that, as the size of any business enterprise increases, the accounting procedure becomes more comprehensive and complex, thus increasing rather than decreasing the cost of office labor per unit of product handled.

In this analysis we shall assume that unification of the milk business would not alter the expense for office labor. If this expense were increased or decreased, such a change would have little influence upon the total labor cost of the business because the total of the office-labor expense is comparatively low. For example, a reduction or increase of 10 per cent in this item would bring about a change of only 0.6 per cent in the total labor cost of the business.

SALARIES

Out of every dollar of total operating cost, an average of approximately 12 cents went for the salaries of officers, managers, and foremen. There was decided variation from company to company in the sizes of salaries paid officers who were usually also managers or foremen (Table A, Appen. A). The bulk of the salaries ranged from $2,200 to $3,000 or $3,500 per year. In some cases they were as high as $5,000, and a few were $7,000 or over per year. There were, in fact, a few instances where the salaries paid seemed out of line with the responsibility involved.

From the standpoint of the milk-distributing business, dispropor-

[26] The reader is referred to Appen. B for other information on delivery cost and for a discussion on the number of daily deliveries made by urban mail-carriers.

[27] See n. 6, p. 35.

tionately high salaries are unfortunate, not so much because of the amount by which they directly increase the cost of distribution per quart of milk handled, because such increases would for the most part be negligible as we shall see later, but more because the general public sentiment is against the idea of high salaries. To be sure, the public is in sharp disagreement with the idea of any private or public industry paying what appears to them as high salaries to entrepreneurs or managers, but in most businesses other than milk distribution the salaries paid seldom become public knowledge, hence the public has given little attention to the question. Not so in the fluid-milk business. The great amount of public attention recently centered on it has brought to the fore not only questions of salaries, profits, and "monopoly" practices but also a host of other questions including regulation of prices, type and extent of public control, etc. In short, the public has become milk conscious, or, perhaps stated more correctly, it has become "milk-price conscious."

In some cities general sentiment has been so strong against the ideas of high salaries that no small number of consumers are said to have reduced their milk consumption in protest of such practices; others have changed their patronage to a different distributor in the belief or hope that its salaries were lower. Indeed, new distributing companies have gained entrance to the market largely because of adverse publicity which existed concerning those operating in the market at the time. As new distributing companies enter a market, the increased duplication of efforts brings about greater inefficiencies and higher costs of distribution. This tendency on the part of the public to become emotionally stirred up over what seems to it to be unduly high salaries (or profits) brings about unfortunate results because it often means the public attention becomes sidetracked on those issues rather than becoming centered upon the larger and more central problem—the efficiency of milk distribution. Inefficiencies in the operation of milk distribution increase the cost of milk to consumers. Yet, even though such inefficiencies bulk a large proportion of the total costs of distribution because they are not easily noticed, the public seldom concerns itself about them.

Serious question might well be raised as to whether or not it is either desirable or justifiable from the public point of view to pay salaries beyond those necessary to make it worth while for capable men to come into and stay in this industry. From a purely business point of view, however, the important consideration for either producer or consumer is not the exact amounts of the individual salaries paid but rather what percentage of the total or unit cost of operation consists of salaries, and how much the cost would be lowered if salaries were reduced to a lower level.

Suppose, for example, that all salaries were reduced to a point equal to that of wages of deliverymen. How much would that reduce distribution costs? Taking the companies covered in this study over a period of eleven years, it was found that if salaries had not exceeded an average paid to the deliverymen, the savings would have amounted to from 2 to 2.5 cents of the sales dollar. This means that there would have been a saving of about 0.2 cent per quart of milk sold by the milk distributors.

There is, indeed, another important consideration. Suppose salaries were reduced to this level, let us say, by order of a state control board; some managers and officers would doubtless leave the milk business to obtain positions with other types of businesses. Lower salaries would mean less capable men being attracted, and, as a result, there would be lower efficiency of operation and probably as high—or even a higher—unit cost of distributing milk as before the salary reduction. The item of salary as a percentage of the total operating cost, while important, is not so large as many people have believed. This is because only one, two, or at the most three men in a company of the size discussed here receive what is termed "salary." The balance receive wages. Thus, the total amount of business done is relatively large for each salaried employee. This suggests strongly that under the competitive system the costs of milk distribution cannot be reduced much by a reduction in salaries.

However, these costs can be appreciably reduced if a unified milk-distribution system is adopted and the number of salaried workers is thus reduced. Consider, for example, the situation in a Wisconsin market of about 60,000 population. Suppose that in addition to a few small distributors there are a half-dozen medium-sized or large distributing companies each employing two or three salaried people. This would aggregate a dozen to fifteen salaried persons in the market. Under a unified system of milk distribution whereby one distributing organization handled all the fluid milk in this market, the number of salaried employees might be reduced by one-half, or even a little more than half in some cases. Of the total cost of distribution, an average of about 10–14 per cent goes for salaries with a wider variation than this in some cases.[28] Using 5 cents per quart as the distributors' total operation cost, we find that the amount per quart of milk going for the item of salary would vary from 0.5 cent to 0.7 cent per quart. Suppose that under a unified system one-half of the total bill for salaries could be saved, then the saving per quart of milk handled would be 0.25–0.35 cent per quart.

DEPRECIATION

The depreciation in reality includes three kinds: (1) that brought about through wear and tear on the entire physical structure (including buildings, machinery, equipment, milk delivery wagons, delivery trucks, furniture, furnishings, etc.) which is due to use and not currently replaced or repaired; (2) that caused by the general action of natural elements such as heat, frost, moisture, etc.; and (3) that resulting from new inventions creating more efficient types of (or for other reasons improved) machines, equipment, or buildings than those in use—obsolescence.

In the case of machinery, obsolescence represents the greatest depreciation cost, but for delivery equipment the relative importance of the three forms is somewhat different. Here the largest amount of depreciation is due to wear and tear. The amount of depreciation caused by obsolescence is more difficult to forecast than are the other two forms. A new invention may suddenly make a machine or a costly piece of equipment obsolete because of the economic saving resulting from the invention or because of the ability to process a better quality of milk than could be processed without it. Because of such improvements or inventions, coolers, pasteurizers, bottle-washers and bottle-cappers, or systems for conveying the milk or the bottles may need to be replaced long before the old equipment is actually worn out.

Considering the changes which have taken place during recent

[28] See Table A, Appen. A.

years in the machinery, equipment, trucks, etc., used to process and distribute fluid milk, the rapidity with which obsolescence has taken place may be appreciated. Because of these changes, coupled with the fact that the fixed capital required in the milk business is relatively large, it is not surprising that the item of depreciation has amounted to from 7 to 10 per cent of the total cost of milk distribution. The average figure for companies listed in Table 2 during the eleven-year period was 8.3 per cent of the total operating cost. The depreciation items aggregate about two-thirds as much as the cost of salaries for the same companies covering the same period of years.[29]

Changing and increasing sanitary regulations have been important factors necessitating relatively rapid changes in machinery and equipment, thus forcing a correspondingly rapid rate of obsolescence. Sanitary requirements have also increased wear and tear of equipment and of some machines because, in an attempt to secure a highly sanitary plant, more and more caustic cleaners have been used and more drastic cleaning methods have been adopted.

Delivery trucks and wagons are comparatively short lived and must be replaced before there is danger of breakdown causing delay in service and complaint from or even loss of customers. Delivery equipment must, therefore, be replaced often even though it is kept in a reasonably high state of repair.[30]

Would a unified system of distributing fluid milk permit of a reduction in the cost of depreciation? If so, what would be the amount

---

[29] It may be of interest to compare the rates of depreciation of these milk companies with depreciation rates in other fields. For example, "the records of five companies among each of four utilities covering the eight years from 1917 to 1924 showed that . . . . the average percentage of depreciation charge to total operating expenses had the following range: telephone companies, 21.2 to 27.7; electric light and power companies, 6.7 to 13.7; gas companies, 3.9 to 7.8; and water companies, 8.9 to 11.9" (Eliot Jones and Truman Bigham, *Principles of Public Utilities* [New York, 1931], p. 466).

[30] The following schedule of depreciation rates per year is in common practice among milk-distributing companies and has been approved by the accountants of the Wisconsin Department of Agriculture and Markets as being a reasonably close approximation of the actual depreciation over a period of years:

	Per Cent		Per Cent
Buildings	3–5	Office fixtures	10
Milk machinery	12½	Automobiles and trucks	25
Power and refrigeration	10	Milk cases and cans	33

of the savings? The rate of depreciation probably would not differ greatly between a unified and a competitive system. Wear and tear of machinery, equipment, delivery trucks, furniture, and furnishings will still continue. The natural elements—heat, cold, wind, sun, and moisture—will also continue to take their toll. New inventions, if science advances, will still make it necessary or desirable to replace the machines in use before they are entirely worn out. Buildings, pasteurizers, coolers, and trucks, assuming comparable use and care, will last no longer under one system of distribution than under another. Therefore, if savings in the item of depreciation are to be made by operating the milk business under a unified system, they must be the result of handling a larger volume of milk per unit of fixed and movable capital employed under such a system.

No study known to the writer can be accepted as having set up conclusive measures or indexes of milk-plant capacity or efficiency. Neither have acceptable standards or norms been established for comparative purposes—nor is it a simple matter to establish them. It is recognized, of course, that the volume handled per unit of capital employed depends upon how completely both the fixed and the movable capital is utilized and upon how efficiently it is employed.

Information obtained in this study indicates that only a very small percentage of the milk-distributing companies are operating at more than 80 per cent of plant capacity. Many are operating at from 60 to 80 per cent, with the majority of these nearer the 60 than the 80 per cent mark. Operations at 50 per cent capacity or below are not uncommon, and many plants are running as low as 30–40 per cent of their optimum output.[31] If the aggregate of all distributors in a market were considered, the operation now common

31 A survey of fourteen companies located in various sections of the state indicates that the pasteurizers and washing, filling, and capping machines were being operated at much below optimum capacity. In only two of these companies were these machines active more than 5½ hours per day. The lowest was 1 hour daily (one company), but the machinery of six of the fourteen was in active operation 3½ hours or less daily. Eight of the fourteen were operating their machines at 4½ hours or less per day. The time for the others varied from 3½ to 5½ hours daily. General observation and information from many other companies seemed to indicate that this situation was probably not dissimilar from conditions elsewhere in the state or in this general geographic region.

in the markets of the size studied is probably in the neighborhood of 50–70 per cent of the optimum.

It is recognized, of course, that a general statement of capacity has but limited meaning. For instance, the building space may be utilized to 75 per cent capacity, pasteurizers to 40 per cent, and bottle-filling machines to 80 per cent. Moreover, the entire machinery may be operating at only 50 per cent, but the delivery wagons or trucks at 80 per cent of capacity. The relative percentage use of capacity of various machines would depend upon whether the company was gaining or losing business, upon the age, condition, and capacity of the machines in use, and upon other less important considerations. Another reason why it is difficult to determine the extent of the full capacity utilized is that plant managers and engineers often differ concerning the most practicable number of hours each machine should be operated per day. While it might be physically possible to operate a pasteurizer, a bottle-filling, or a bottle-washing machine 18 out of 24 hours, it would not be economically practical to do so.

Manufacturers of milk-plant machinery commonly consider the daily capacity to be the amount handled in 8 hours, but plant operators usually consider 5–7 hours daily use as practically full utilization. In a study of the Milwaukee milk market, it was estimated that, on the basis of 5.5 hours daily as the optimum use, the machines mentioned above were operating at 45–55 per cent capacity as an average (April, 1934). On this basis of calculation, using 5.5 hours as 100 per cent utilization, the range between the companies varied from 4.9 to 117.9 per cent of practically full capacity. The larger distributors consistently had a higher percentage utilization than did the smaller ones.[32] Tinley estimated that as a rather typical situation of twelve distributing plants, the four operating under the lowest cost had sufficient capacity to supply an entire market.[33] This suggests that for an entire market only about one-third of the practical capacity was being utilized.

We will not be far afield if we assume that in the aggregate the

[32] Agricultural Adjustment Administration, *op. cit.*, Table 49.

[33] J. M. Tinley, *Public Regulation of Milk Marketing in California* (Berkeley: University of California Press, 1938), Table 4, pp. 125–26.

existing milk-distributing companies in a representative Wisconsin market are operating at from 50 to 70 per cent of optimum capacity. On that basis and with no change in the distributing system but with all existing plants adjusted to operate at optimum capacity (an average of 85–90 per cent of full capacity), it would be possible to reduce the total fixed and movable capital employed at least 20–30 per cent. With no change in the rate of depreciation or quality of construction, this reduction in capital would mean a corresponding decrease in the total amount of depreciation for the market as a whole.[34]

If a unified system were established, the size of plant and machines in each market could be adjusted so as to operate at or near optimum practical capacity. Clearly, the job of adjusting a unified system to fit the whole market would be much less difficult than it would be for the individual competitive companies to arrange a system capable of operating at full or near full capacity under competitive conditions. Whenever a new distributing company enters a market, it builds up its business largely at the expense of the established companies. Thus, the added plant brings about additional capacity for the distributive system as a whole, and consequently the probability of adjusting the aggregate capacity of all plants to fit the market is quite remote.[35]

In the preceding general discussion on depreciation an attempt has been made to point out the savings of fixed and movable capital—as distinct from current or working capital—which might be made through full utilization of plant capacity with no change in the type of distribution system. In comparing the cost of depreciation of a unified system with that of a competitive one, a more detailed and thorough analysis will be necessary. Such an analysis will require separate consideration of each of the three major items

[34] It is possible that, with the fuller use of plant and equipment, the rate of depreciation would be slightly higher due to the additional wear and tear, but the added amount would be hardly noticeable.

[35] Unfortunately, it does not follow that investments in land, buildings, and equipment under a unified system will always be prudently made. To the extent that they are not, the result may be to create an investment in fixed capital which is out of line with market requirements. Thus, the opportunities for savings may be dissipated.

of fixed and movable capital: (*a*) buildings, (*b*) machines, and (*c*) delivery equipment.

a) Of buildings.—In a small city with a population of 50,000 or less operating under a unified milk-distribution system, a central plant would likely be established where all processing would be done and from which all milk delivery wagons would start. In larger cities it would be necessary to provide branch plants to store bottled milk for delivery. The goal toward which the designers of such a system should strive would be to obtain maximum efficiency of delivery routes rather than minimum capital invested in buildings. Accordingly, investment in buildings may not be decreased much if any under a unified system. True, more complete utilization of buildings, hence reduced building space per unit of output, would bring about a saving in the item of building depreciation. These savings would, of course, vary from market to market depending upon the efficiency in the operation of the existing competitive system and also upon the efficiency in utilizing buildings under a newly established unified system. The exact extent of such probable savings could be arrived at only after a thorough study of the market in question.

According to estimates made in the Milwaukee study, the building cost under a unified system would be about 18 per cent greater than the reproductive value and about 47 per cent greater than the "sound" value of the total investment of the companies then operating.[36] The significance of such comparisons may easily be overstressed. If the establishment of a unified system would necessitate constructing practically all new buildings rather than using some of the more efficient ones then in use, the new ones could not be compared directly with those being replaced. The new and improved buildings would naturally represent a greater capital investment than the old. On the other hand, the rate of depreciation would likely be reduced noticeably, especially if the new buildings were of a steel and concrete construction. The longer serviceable life of the

[36] Agricultural Adjustment Administration, *op. cit.* Percentage figures were obtained from a calculation of amounts given in Tables 28 and 58. The capital of these twenty-three companies represented substantially the entire investment in the market at the time, only two peddlers, operating one route each, being omitted. All costs and values were calculated as of April, 1934.

new buildings would bring about a corresponding decrease in depreciation rate.

While it might be possible to reduce the cost of depreciation of buildings under a unified as compared with a competitive system, the reduction per quart of milk delivered would be negligible. The lower the building utilization under the existing system, the greater would be the opportunity for reducing depreciation costs through unification. If the total depreciation of buildings could be reduced as much as 20 per cent, the savings would only be about 0.01 of a cent per quart of milk handled (Table 9).

b) Of machines.—The rate of depreciation of machines (pasteurizers, washing and filling machines, conveyors, etc.) could be reduced very little, if at all, through a change in the system. Some savings might be possible by replacing the machines in use with different types and larger sizes, but the important saving would be made by increasing the utilization of the machines.

In order to estimate the savings in capital—hence a saving in depreciation—resulting from larger-sized machines, a comparison of the cost of operating each machine at various capacities would be required. Suppose a unified system would use machines three or four times larger than those used in a competitive system; would the total investment in the necessary machinery be reduced? Larger machines usually result in lower unit labor costs but not necessarily in lower unit capital costs. A large machine may require no more personal supervision than a small one turning out half or a third the volume. On the other hand, the larger machines are usually as expensive or even more so in relation to output than are the smaller ones. More automatic features and more sturdy construction ordinarily characterize the larger units. The small number manufactured also means little opportunity for economies resulting from mass production of them. Hence, the cost of such machines is relatively high.

For example, a bottle-washing machine of a certain type with a capacity of 180 bottles per minute is quoted at $32,000–$36,000; one of 100-bottle capacity will cost $18,000–$22,000, while a 24-bottle capacity machine can be purchased for $1,800–$2,200. In this case, the larger the machine, the greater is the cost per unit of capacity.

A bottle-filler and bottle-capper of 120 quarts per minute capacity will cost $4,200–$4,500. One of the 35-quart capacity sells for about $1,400–$1,600. Here the cost per unit capacity is about the same for either size machine. Additional quotations could be cited, but these will serve to show that the investment, and therefore the depreciation per unit on machines of larger capacity, will probably be equal to or above those of smaller output.[37] As one would expect, a wide price variation exists between different makes of machines with identical capacities. These variations depend to a certain extent upon the materials used in their construction and upon the special and automatic features of the machines.

Even though we assume that depreciation would not be noticeably reduced by replacing smaller machines with larger ones, a unified system would still reduce machine depreciation per unit of output because of greater utilization of the machine capacity. This increased utilization would reduce depreciation even if the existing size and type of machines were still used under the new system. We have already pointed out that as a general practice machinery in milk-distributing companies was probably being operated at from 50 to 70 per cent of optimum capacity. With operation at optimum capacity the machine utilization could thus be increased as much as 30–50 per cent. If the utilization of existing machines—or others of larger size—could be increased 40 per cent, then both the capital invested in the necessary machines and the depreciation cost would be decreased accordingly. The importance of this reduction is shown in Tables 8 and 9.

c) Of delivery equipment.—The possible reduction of capital invested in delivery trucks would depend largely upon the increase in size of loads delivered under a unified system compared with those delivered under a competitive one. We shall assume that the number of trucks could be reduced by 42 per cent—the same proportion as delivery labor.[38] With no change in the type of trucks used, the capital invested in trucks, hence the amount of depreciation, could

[37] The writer expresses appreciation to Professor L. C. Thomsen, Department of Dairy Industry, College of Agriculture, for his counsel in the preparation of the discussion involving milk-processing machines.

[38] See discussion on delivery labor earlier in this chapter, pp. 45–63.

be reduced by substantially the same amount. In this study the discussion of assets and rate of depreciation is made on the basis of the use of motor trucks rather than horses and wagons.

We are now able to bring the different parts of this discussion into juxtaposition. The information is condensed in Tables 8 and 9. Column 7 of Table 8 shows the depreciation cost per quart of

TABLE 8

THE DIVISION OF ASSETS ON THE BASIS OF TOTAL ASSETS AND CERTAIN DEPRECIATING ASSETS, THE RATES OF DEPRECIATION, AND THE PROPORTION OF THE TOTAL DEPRECIATION DUE TO EACH*

Asset	Certain Depreciating Assets as Percentage of Total Assets	Percentage of Depreciating Assets†	Rate of Depreciation as Percentage per Annum	Annual Rate × Proportion of Depreciating Assets	Percentage Each Item Is of Total Depreciation‡	Percentage Each Item Is of Total Operating Costs§	Depreciation Cost in Cents for Each Form Borne by Each Quart of Milk
	(1)	(2)	(3)	(4)	(5)	(6)	(7)
Buildings........	21	37	4	1.5	13	1.1	0.05
Machines.......	23	41	12½	5.1	42	3.5	.18
Delivery equipment.........	12	22	25	5.5	45	3.7	0.19
Total.......	56¶	100	....	12.1	100	8.3	0.42

* The depreciation of each of these three classes of assets is shown in relation to the total depreciation cost of 0.42 cent per quart (col. 7).

† Figures in col. 2 represent the proportion each item in col. 1 is of the total of col. 1.

‡ Figures represent percentage each item in col. 4 is of the total of col. 4.

§ Figures in this column were obtained by multiplying the percentage figures in col. 5 by 8.3 per cent, the proportion which depreciation is of the total operating cost.

¶ Working capital and miscellaneous assets account for the other 44 per cent of the total assets. For this purpose these are classified as nondepreciating assets.

milk for each form of depreciating asset—buildings, machines, and delivery equipment. The method of arriving at the results shown in column 7 requires brief explanation. In column 1 the investment in each of the three classes of depreciating assets is expressed as a percentage of total assets. In the next column the total of depreciating assets is used as a basis for the distribution between the three classes. The rates of depreciation are given in column 3, while the next column shows the product of the respective figures of the preceding two columns. Figures in column 5 were obtained directly from those in column 4. The last column indicates the actual cost of depreciation per quart of milk handled assignable to each class of depreciating assets.

It is interesting to note that delivery equipment constitutes the largest depreciation cost per quart (0.19 cent compared with 0.18 cent for machinery and 0.05 cent for buildings), although the proportionate amount of capital invested in delivery equipment is only about one-half that of either buildings or machines. This is quite

TABLE 9

AMOUNT OF DEPRECIATION PER QUART OF MILK
HANDLED; PERCENTAGE AND AMOUNT SAVED
PER QUART THROUGH UNIFICATION

Asset	Cost of Depreciation per Quart of Milk (1)	Percentage Saved by Unified System (2)	Amount Saved per Quart through Unification (3)
Buildings......	0.05	20	0.01
Machines.....	.18	40	.07
Delivery equipment.......	0.19	42	0.08
Total.....	0.42	....	0.16

obviously the result of the relatively high depreciation rate on delivery equipment—25 per cent per year.

Table 9 presents the summary facts regarding the possible savings in the item of depreciation which may be made through unification. Column 3 of this table shows the possible savings in depreciation per quart of milk, assuming that the amount of depreciation cost for buildings, machinery, and delivery equipment could be reduced by 20, 40, and 42 per cent, respectively (col. 2). The savings would amount to approximately the same for each, machines and delivery equipment, but would be much smaller for buildings. On the basis of these figures, the total savings would be 0.16 cent per quart of milk. If a 15 per cent deviation on each side of this 0.16 cent is allowed, the range within which savings could be expected would vary between 0.14 and 0.18 cent per quart of milk handled.

REPAIRS

In the milk business service must be made available without delay. Moreover, customers often associate poorly kept milk plants and especially delivery equipment, which is before the public notice, with poor quality products. For these reasons, a high state of repair must be maintained, thus bringing about relatively high repair bills. Total repairs amount to from 3 to 4 per cent of the operating cost.[39] Since about 1934, the cost of repairs has increased in relation to other costs. This was caused in part by deferred maintenance of plant and equipment during the depression period of the early thirties. In those years replacements of machines, plant equipment, and perhaps to a lesser extent delivery wagons and trucks were not adequate to keep them in a superior condition. Naturally, a poorer condition of plant and equipment when continued means higher repair bills later. Generally, however, distributors have made a serious effort to maintain a state of repair sufficiently high to process and distribute milk of a superior quality.

No attempt will be made in this analysis to show a breakdown of repairs between buildings, machines, and delivery equipment. It will be assumed that under unification the repairs would be reduced proportionately the same as the reduction of fixed capital, namely, 30–40 per cent. This assumption may not be wholly correct because under unification the entire distributing system would operate at more nearly full capacity than does the existing competitive system. The increased use would also increase the amount of necessary repair. For buildings this would be almost negligible, but for machines which would be operated more hours per day the repairs would be somewhat higher than under the present distributing system in proportion to machine investment. For delivery equipment, on the contrary, the repair bill would probably be reduced proportionately more than the capital investment. Although heavier loads would be carried under unification, the daily distance traveled by trucks would be reduced, consequently the wear and tear per truck and hence the repair would be reduced. The tendency for the repair bills of delivery equipment to decrease proportionately greater than the investments in it would likely more than offset the opposite situa-

[39] Table 2, p. 35.

tion with respect to buildings and machines. On the basis of repair costs amounting to 3 per cent of a total of 5 cents per quart operating cost, the repair item would amount to 0.15 cent per quart. Forty per cent of this amount is 0.06 cent. If the saving in the repair bill were 30 per cent, the amount would be 0.045 cent per quart.

ADVERTISING

Under a competitive system of operation, advertising may have any of three aims: (1) to induce a general increase in the demand for the product advertised, (2) to sustain the present demand for the product, or (3) to increase consumer purchases from one company at the expense of another. To the extent that funds are spent for competitive advertising by the fluid-milk distributors, they probably have little direct effect upon bringing about an increased total milk consumption in the city. It is true, of course, that the advertising appeal to purchase milk from Dealer A rather than from Dealer B or C may indirectly influence consumers to actually increase the amount of their purchases. However, it should be observed that funds spent for competitive advertising are less effective in increasing the general demand for milk than would a like amount spent with the direct view of increasing milk consumption in general.

At 5 cents per quart as a distribution cost, the advertising cost of about 3 per cent would be 0.15 cent per quart. While the control made possible through a unified system of distribution would permit the complete elimination of advertising, thus saving the 0.15 cent per quart, such a policy would probably not be adopted. Perhaps the greatest or only saving which would be made in this item would be that resulting from a change in the type of advertising to focus its emphasis upon milk as such rather than the particular milk supplied by a specific distributor. Such advertising (or shall we say "educational work") may tend to influence the total milk consumption in the market. This might be especially true if it were coupled with lowered resale milk prices.

TAXES

Under unification the costs of machinery and delivery equipment could be reduced materially more, proportionately, than could building cost—which might not be reduced at all and might even be increased. If the total amount of fixed capital necessary to operate the milk-distributing system of a city could be reduced by 20–30 per cent, as we have suggested might be possible,[40] and the tax rate per dollar of property valuation remained unchanged, then the amount paid as property taxes would be reduced by the same proportion as the reduction of fixed capital. Taxes amounted to roughly 2.5 per cent of the total cost of milk distribution. On the basis of a cost of 5 cents per quart of milk distributed, the total amount of the tax per quart handled is 0.125 cent. If as much as 30 per cent of the tax bill could be saved by operating the milk business through a unified milk-distributing system, the savings per quart would be 0.0375 cent. The fact must be recognized, of course, that the reduction of income to the city treasury because of the decrease of taxes from this source of income would need to be compensated from other tax sources. Thus, actually the amount gained by the milk consumers of a city through a reduction of taxes on the milk business will in reality not be a net gain to the residents as a body. When considered on this basis, the savings in taxes would be nothing. Indeed, the amount of taxes assessed against the enterprise as a public utility might be greater than the total amount assessed against the existing milk-distribution system. From the point of view of the milk business only the savings would not be expected to exceed 0.038 cent per quart. We shall, therefore, place the range from 0.0 to 0.038 cent per quart.

BAD DEBTS

Over the eleven-year period covered, 2 per cent as an average of the total operating costs went for bad debts.[41] The possibility of saving any part of this item under a system of public control or public ownership would depend almost entirely upon the policy adopted by those who directed the enterprise. If a so-called liberal policy were adopted whereby no special effort were made to collect the accounts, it is easily conceivable that the item of bad debts would be as great or even greater than under a privately operated com-

40 See discussion under "Depreciation," pp. 66–75.

41 See Table A, Appen. A, for detailed figures.

petitive system. If the other extreme were adopted whereby consumers were required to make a deposit to insure payment, and service were discontinued if and when bills were not paid—the policy followed by many or most public utility services—then the losses from bad debts would be nil. At 5 cents per quart as the total cost of operation, bad debts have amounted to 0.1 cent per quart, substantially all of which could be saved under unification.

INSURANCE

The amount of the insurance item is almost identical to that of bad debts or of taxes—around 2 per cent of the total operating cost. If we assume that the total amount of fixed capital can be reduced by 20–30 per cent, then the item of insurance can be decreased by a similar percentage without changing the insurance protection. The amount will vary depending upon the reduction in the number of delivery trucks which often carry a rather high insurance rate. Using 5 cents per quart as the cost figure and under the assumption that 30 per cent of the insurance bill could be saved, the savings would amount to 0.03 cent per quart of milk handled. A conservative estimate would place the amount between 0.02 and 0.03 cent per quart.

LIGHT, POWER, AND WATER

Power includes electric motors and steam or gasoline engines for running machinery.

Cost of light, which is primarily electricity, is dependent mainly upon type of building and building space (cubical contents of buildings) and the number of hours the building space is actually utilized. If a unified system decreased the building space, the change would permit of a saving of light; but, if this decreased space were utilized more hours, especially during those of natural darkness, the light consumption might actually be increased.

The amount of water used is doubtless a more direct function of the amount of fluid milk and manufactured dairy commodities sold than of the amount of capital invested or the size of plant or percentage of capacity utilized. However, power consumption varies inversely with the efficiency of the machines. Hence up-to-date and efficient machines will consume less power per unit of product handled than will small machines or those which are beginning to become obsolete.

There is no way of foretelling whether a unified publicly owned or controlled milk-distributing system would employ more up-to-date machines than would a private competitive system, but it is clear that such a one would permit of larger and hence more efficient plants and machines than a competitive system, thus making possible certain savings in the cost of power.

While a unified system efficiently operated would likely reduce the cost of these three combined items, the amount of the savings would probably be of minor consideration and will not be tabulated in this analysis.

ALL OTHER EXPENSES

Bottles, bottle caps, and cases, fuel, gasoline, and oil used in trucks, feed and horseshoeing, supplies for the accounting department, and many other items too small to be grouped under a particular heading are included in "all other" costs. Among the largest of these items is the expense for milk bottles. The cost of bottles usually amounted to from 2 to 3 per cent of total operating costs. It was about as large as taxes or insurance or advertising and almost as large as the total expense of power, light, and water combined. Where no charge is made to consumers if bottles are lost, this cost naturally runs higher. Under some conditions a bottle may make as few as ten trips, while under others the number may be as high as thirty. Naturally the bottle losses are greater for store trade than for family trade. Ordinarily the family makes the empty bottles available at the doorstep for the deliveryman, whereas many who purchase from stores do not take the trouble to return the empties unless a charge is made, and even then losses are more common than for family trade.

No records were obtainable from which to determine whether the bottle losses were due to accidental breakage and other causes which would also exist under a unified system, and we are making no determination of possible saving in this item.

Gasoline and oil for delivery trucks amounted to 3–5 per cent of the total cost of operation. For those companies which delivered milk mostly or entirely with horses and wagons instead of trucks, the cost of feed and horseshoeing amounted to over 2 per cent of the total cost. Under unification it should be entirely possible to save, say, 40 per cent of this gas and oil bill. This saving would amount to from 0.06 cent to 0.1 cent per quart of milk distributed.

Certain other cost items in this group of "all other" would clearly lend themselves to savings under a unified system; others would be changed very little, and one or two would actually be increased. The net, however, would likely be a reduction. Supplies for the accounting department would go up, but, since they are but a small proportional cost, the increase would be small and canceled by other items not considered here where savings would be made. The cost of items such as bottle caps and cases would change very little.

Having pointed out the major items which would permit of savings under unification of the milk-processing and milk-distributing business, we shall now attempt to bring into a summary form the list of possible savings in these items. Table 10 sets forth this summary.

In the main portion of Table 10 calculations are made on the basis of distribution cost of 5 cents per quart. Normally this will be a representative figure for the markets of 10,000–50,000 or even 100,000 population in which there is relatively high efficiency of milk distribution. The estimated minimum savings of 1.25 cents is perhaps overconservative and the maximum 1.92 greater than one should expect would be saved in markets where the existing system is operating at a relatively high degree of efficiency, or its counterpart relatively narrow distributors' margins. In markets where the existing margin of distribution is wider, larger savings should be possible. Here the range between 1.50 and 2.29 cents would be closer to expectation. On the basis of this study and the supporting evidence cited, it would be conservative to estimate that unification of milk distribution would make possible a saving of 1.5–2 cents per quart of milk handled. The extent of possible savings would naturally vary from market to market. Such variations would be determined in part by the variations prevailing in the distributors' margins under the competitive system. The extent of this margin and the relative variation between markets is shown in Table 11.

This table shows the average margin or spread between the family retail price and dealers' buying price for 19 markets (17 or 18 for some years). The markets represented have populations varying from about 20,000 to 100,000 located in ten states in the East North

TABLE 10

ESTIMATED SAVING THROUGH UNIFICATION
OF MILK DISTRIBUTION

(Based on 5-Cent Distribution Cost per Quart of Milk)

OPERATING COST	ESTIMATED SAVINGS (CENTS PER QUART)	
	Minimum	Maximum
Plant labor......................	0.054	0.125
Delivery labor..................	.56*	.75
Office labor......................	....	....
Salaries.........................	.25	.35
Depreciation....................	.14	.18
Repairs.........................	.045	.06
Advertising.....................	.0	.15(?)
Taxes..........................	.0	.038
Bad debts......................	.10	.10
Insurance......................	.02	.03
Light, power, and water........	(?)	(?)
"All other"		
Gasoline and oil..............	.06	.10
Bottle losses................	(?)	(?)
Profit (see chap. vi)...........	0.02	0.04
Total estimated savings on basis of 5¢ distribution cost.	1.25†	1.923
Total estimated savings on basis of 6¢ distribution cost‡	1.50	2.29

* If cost of collecting accounts were not eliminated, the savings would be 0.51 and 0.70 cent, respectively.

† Actually 1.249.

‡ The estimate on the basis of a 6-cent cost was obtained by raising the 5-cent cost figure 20 per cent.

Central and West North Central states. Dealers' buying prices for different cities are not strictly comparable because in some markets they represent the price paid for all milk bought by dealers while in others they represent only the "basic" quantities—the quantities sold by dealers for fluid use. During the 1920's most of these 19 markets operated on a "flat-price" plan wherein the buying prices represented that paid for all milk purchased. During the 1930's many of these cities changed to a "base-surplus" plan of purchasing, hence the buying prices represent the prices paid only for that milk used for fluid purposes.

TABLE 11

AVERAGE MARGIN BETWEEN DEALERS' SELLING PRICE IN CENTS PER QUART FAMILY TRADE AND DEALERS' BUYING PRICE, 19 CITIES IN CENTRAL UNITED STATES, 1922–38

Year	Number of Cities	Average Margin (Family Retail Price *less* Dealers' Buying Price) (1)	Standard Deviation (2)	Coefficient of Variation (Per Cent) (3)
1922.........	17	5.7	±1.0	17
1923.........	19	5.9	0.7	12
1924.........	19	6.3	0.8	13
1925.........	19	6.0	0.8	13
1926.........	18	6.1	0.9	15
1927.........	16	6.0	1.0	17
1928.........	18	6.2	1.0	16
1929.........	18	6.3	0.9	14
1930.........	18	6.4	0.8	13
1931.........	19	5.8	0.6	10
1932.........	17	5.6	0.7	13
1933.........	17	5.3	0.7	13
1934.........	19	5.6	0.6	11
1935.........	18	5.9	0.7	12
1936.........	19	6.0	0.8	13
1937.........	19	6.3	0.8	13
1938.........	18	6.3	±0.9	14
Annual average...	....	6.0	....	....

The average margin for this list of cities was 6 cents per quart for the seventeen-year period from 1922 to 1938, inclusive. The lowest was 5.3 cents in 1933 and the highest 6.4 cents in 1930. Column 2 shows the standard deviation, and column 3 the coefficient of variation between markets by years for the same period. The difference between markets as shown by these deviations, while not large, does show noticeable market-to-market variation. One has reason to expect that, where the margin of distribution is relatively wide under the existing system, the opportunities for savings would be relatively large, and vice versa. It will be remembered, of course, that this margin represents the difference in dealer buying and selling prices for only the milk sold at retail to family trade. It does not include the milk sold at wholesale by dealers to hotels, restaurants, and stores, either in bulk or in quart bottles, which is sold at lower prices than is that going to family trade. This means that the margin on all wholesale and retail milk handled by dealers would be perhaps $\frac{1}{4}$ to $\frac{1}{2}$ cent less than this amount. The margin includes all cost of handling and the profit of the dealers, if any. While these figures representing dealer margins cannot be translated into figures representing distribution costs, they do suggest that the cost of distribution, taken as a general average figure, is below 6 cents for the size city covered in the study. During the years of relatively low margin—and, in general, relatively low cost—1931–34, inclusive, the cost of distribution would be closer to 5 than to 6 cents. On the other hand, since 1936, and especially in 1937 and in 1938, this cost would likely be closer to 6 than 5 cents.

In conclusion, it may be of interest to see what the possible savings in Table 10 would amount to for an average family, assuming the entire amount went to them in the form of lower fluid-milk prices. To a family which averaged only one quart of milk per day, the saving on the basis of 1.25 cents per quart would amount to $4.56 per year. Suppose, however, the savings were, say, 1.5 cents per quart, then a family using two quarts per day would save annually $12.77 on the milk bill. At 2 cents per quart saving, a family using three quarts daily would save $21.90 annually. The latter two amounts can hardly be dismissed as being insignificant for a family of small or moderate income. It is recognized, of course, that in some markets of the country consumers can purchase milk over the store counter and save amounts equal to those indicated above. It is interesting to note that, where store prices are noticeably below delivery-wagon prices, store sales have increased at the expense of wagon sales.

TABLE 12

DIVISION OF MILK DISTRIBUTORS' OPERATING COSTS

OPERATING COST	1930*				1932*				1933*				1936*			1937*			
	Wisconsin Large Companies†	Wisconsin Small Companies‡	New York Upstate§	New York City¶	Wisconsin Large Companies	Wisconsin Small Companies	New York Upstate§	New York City¶	Wisconsin Large Companies	Wisconsin Small Companies	Milwaukee‖	West Virginia**	Wisconsin Large Companies	Wisconsin Small Companies	New York City††	Wisconsin Large Companies	Wisconsin Small Companies	New York City††	California‡‡
Total labor	52.3	58.3	54.7	56.4	52.0	51.4	54.1	54.4	55.8	56.0	61.2	41.0	53.0	56.0	55.1	52.5	57.2	54.7	55.7
Depreciation	10.0	7.0	7.0	6.1	8.4	10.2	7.0	6.5	9.3	10.4	5.9	10.7	7.8	7.7	4.7	6.7	6.6	4.9	4.2
Bad debts	1.0	2.3	1.1	0.4	4.6	4.0	1.2	0.9	2.7	2.5		3.4	2.0	2.0		1.7	2.5		2.5
Taxes	4.5	1.4	1.8	1.4	3.7	2.0	2.4	1.3	3.4	2.2		1.5	3.6	1.7	2.5¶¶	2.6	2.4	3.5¶¶	
Insurance	1.3	1.7	2.3	0.8	1.9	2.2	2.4	1.0	2.8	2.6	1.3	1.9	1.8	2.2		2.0	2.6		7.0§§
Advertising	3.8	2.7	1.4	1.8	4.0	2.8	2.4	1.8	3.2	2.2	2.0	1.1	3.6	2.6	2.3	4.6	2.6	2.6	1.2
Repairs	4.4	3.6	3.7	3.8	3.2	3.8	3.6	4.2		3.0	4.2		3.7	3.6	3.8	4.1	5.0	3.2	7.4
Light, power, and water	3.2	3.3			3.5	3.2			3.9	3.5		≡	3.4	3.1		3.0	3.0		
Total repairs and depreciation	14.4	10.6	10.7	9.9	11.6	14.0	10.6	10.7	12.5	13.4	10.1		11.5	11.3	8.5	10.8	11.6	8.1	11.6

* Years selected on basis of availability of data from various sources. To supplement Table 2, p. 35.

† Data on companies classified as large in this study include 5 companies in 1930 and 7 thereafter.

‡ Data on companies classified as small in this study include 6 companies.

§ *Report of the Joint Legislative Committee To Investigate the Milk Industry* (New York Legislative Document No. 114 [Albany, 1933]), pp. 231, 233–34. Data are for the month of April for both years except that salaries are for the year 1931 in both cases.

¶ *Ibid.*, pp. 196, 207, 215, 216, 217, 222. In order to make the New York City data comparable to the rest of the data used here, transportation costs from country receiving stations were not included as a part of the costs of distribution. This analysis was presumably based upon 24 upstate and 29 New York City companies.

‖ A.A.A., *A Survey of Milk Marketing in Milwaukee* ("U.S.D.A. Marketing Information Ser.," DM-1 [Washington, May, 1937]), p. 60. Averages are for 6 companies.

** R. O. Stelzer and L. M. Thurston, *Milk Distribution Costs in West Virginia* (West Virginia Agricultural Experiment Station Bull. 266 [1935]), p. 20.

†† Audit by Ernst and Ernst reported in the *American Produce Review*, February 23, 1938, pp. 498–99. Averages are for 14 companies.

‡‡ J. M. Tinley, *Public Regulation of Milk Marketing in California* (Berkeley: University of California Press, 1938), p. 130. Although the study involved an analysis of 39 distributors, detailed cost data were presented for only one company. Data are for retail sales only. For the wholesale sales the figures were as follows: wages and salaries, 47.2 per cent of total cost; depreciation, 3.7 per cent; bad debts, 3.4 per cent; taxes, insurance, and license, 6.7 per cent; repairs, 7.2 per cent; light, water, and power, 0.9 per cent.

§§ License, insurance, and taxes.

¶¶ Rent and insurance costs were totaled as one figure in the original data, the total being 3 per cent for 1936 and 2.6 per cent for 1937. In 1930 for the companies covered by the study referred to in n. § above, rent was less than 1 per cent of the total and fell to half that in 1932. In 1933 Spencer found that rent amounted to less than 0.5 per cent of the total. If the same situation held through time, insurance costs would have amounted to about 2.5 per cent and 2.1 per cent in 1936 and 1937.

‖‖ The figure given in this case was 6.3 per cent, which included fuel. If fuel were added to the light, power, and water of the large Wisconsin companies for which the data are available, the total would be 5.9 per cent, showing relatively close comparability.

The supplementary material involving some ninety to a hundred companies will be presented largely in the form of summary tables

TABLE 13

COMPARISON OF THE COMBINED ITEMS OF SALARIES AND WAGES OF
VARIOUS GROUPS OF COMPANIES FOR CERTAIN YEARS

(Percentage of Total Operating Costs)

	No. of Companies	1931	1932	1933	1934	1935	1936	1937
Connecticut large companies*	3	53.4	54.4	52.4				
Connecticut small companies*	6	50.6	48.5	48.2				
Philadelphia large companies*	2	59.0	59.9	58.9				
Philadelphia small companies*	3	56.7	55.0	54.4				
New York upstate†	21			55.7				
New York City‡	14			56.0				
Connecticut§	47						53.6	
Maine¶	266						50.8	
Milwaukee‖	5							63.4
Racine and Kenosha‖	2							62.0
Madison‖	2							55.8
Wisconsin large companies**	7	53.4	53.0	55.8	54.0	54.6	53.0	52.5
Wisconsin small companies**	6	59.5	51.4	56.0	55.5	55.3	56.0	57.2

* Federal Trade Commission, *Distribution and Sale of Milk and Milk Products: Philadelphia and Connecticut Milksheds* (House Document No. 387 [74th Cong.; 2d sess.] [Washington, 1936]), p. 120.

† Leland Spencer, "Costs and Profits of Milk Dealers in Up-state Cities, August, 1933" (Report to the New York State Milk Control Board, March 24, 1934), p. 9 (mimeographed). Data are for the month of August, 1933, only.

‡ Leland Spencer, "Costs and Profits of Milk Dealers in New York City, August, 1933" (Report to Division of Milk Control, New York State Department of Agriculture and Markets, April 16, 1934), p. 12 (mimeographed). Data are for the month of August only.

§ S. McLean Buckingham (Connecticut Milk Administrator), "Dealers' Spread in Connecticut" (January, 1938) (mimeographed).

¶ George L. Dow, "Ways of Reducing Cost of Distributing Milk in Maine" (1938), p. 12 (mimeographed). The vast majority of these dealers were producer-distributors; only 17 of them had average annual sales in excess of $17,500. Data are for 1935 and 1936.

‖ Unpublished data compiled by the Wisconsin Department of Agriculture and Markets. Figures for July and October, 1937, and July, 1938.

** Data are similar to those in Table 2 (p. 35) except that the companies have been classified as "large" and "small" to facilitate comparison.

and discussed only briefly. Table 12 makes available a comparison between the Wisconsin companies studied and other milk-distributing companies for which data have been made available through other studies. One is impressed with the general similarity in the relationships between the various cost items of the companies represented. While there is some variation from market to market, the general relationships are substantially the same in all of them, sufficiently so that the analysis presented of the selected Wisconsin markets will hold, in the main, for the other markets here shown. For example, in the item of total labor comprising over half of the entire operating cost, in only one case was there a variation of more than 5.2 between the average percentage figures of the Wisconsin companies studied and those companies of the other studies. Relatively, the variations in depreciation were somewhat wider than those of total labor as were those of most other items, but all these items are sufficiently small so that the conclusions arrived at in this chapter are not invalidated by the variations.

While information from a larger number of milk-distributing companies might have altered the conclusions in minor respects, the main features of the entire picture would remain unchanged.

The sources listed for Table 12 were the only data available to the author from which could be obtained as complete a breakdown as is set forth there. There are, however, other studies giving less detailed data, some of which will be utilized for comparative purposes. For example, the combined items of salaries and wages as shown in other studies are compared in Table 13 with the data from the Wisconsin companies.

TYPE OF SERVICE DESIRED BY CONSUMERS AND THE EFFECT UPON COST OF DISTRIBUTION

Determination of the advantages and disadvantages of public utility operation as compared with operation under the present competitive system cannot be reached unless there is agreement as to the type of service to be provided by the city milk-processing and milk-distributing system. In general, should the goal be to perform a service just adequate to satisfy the ordinary requirement at the lowest possible cost? Or, on the contrary, should emphasis be centered on a very superior type of service including such items as (a) the supplying of special brands of milk for the few who prefer them, milk varying in butterfat content, and specialty products other than milk; (*b*) the catering to the convenience and personal pride of consumers in providing for special deliveries of milk upon short notice or in rendering one or more statements and making personal calls to remind consumers courteously of accounts due or overdue; and (*c*) the maintaining of the labor load and wage rates in order not to reduce the income to labor. These are only a few of the items which determine the expense of milk distribution. It goes without saying that it is possible to provide a type of service varying from that which may be looked upon as scarcely adequate to a type which is better than that commonly demanded, hence is more expensive than is necessary for practical purposes.

Many consumers will prefer the competitive system, even though they know it to be more expensive than operation under a public utility system offering substantially equivalent service, because it affords them the psychic satisfaction of discontinuing the patronage of one company and engaging another for purely emotional rather than logical or economic reasons. Lack of sufficient courtesy of deliverymen, lack of extreme promptness of special-delivery service, the pressing of a customer for an overdue account, the result of arguments between deliverymen and consumer concerning noise on the street or in entering the house in the process of making delivery, personal acquaintance with another milk salesman, and many other equally trivial reasons have been causes for changing milkmen. Under a unified system of distribution through a public utility the choice of milkmen would, for the most part, be beyond the prerogative of the consumer. To the extent that the majority of consumers prefer lower prices together with adequate standardized service to higher prices and superior service the following standard would seem to recommend itself.

1. Milk delivery once daily only—no special delivery except at an extra charge. Under this arrangement consumers would have to depend upon the local stores for extra milk desired before the next regular milk delivery.

2. Attention centered largely or entirely upon one or two classes and quality of milk and cream rather than upon products relatively similar but each differentiated from the other and specialty products priced so as to cover the cost of handling them.

3. Deposits required from consumers to assure full payment of the product, and a policy of discontinuing service in the event of non-payment, and of charging for all bottles not returned to distributor.

The above standard of service would have its critics. As an example, suppose milk were withheld from a family because of an unpaid milk bill, what might be the outcome? Would it not afford an ideal opportunity for the opponents of the system to muster public support against it? Imagine the effectiveness of the following headline in the local press: "Babies Starve! Local Monopoly Withholds Milk from Distressed Families." If milk were discontinued from customers for nonpayment of bills, then the relief or other agencies would perhaps need to be in a position to act with more dispatch than is now generally the case in order to provide distressed families with milk when necessary because of discontinuance of delivery by the utility.

The opposite extreme would be one which might be termed more "liberal" and doubtless more popular but would also be distinctly more costly. Under this plan of operation, specific desires of customers would be catered to by (1) making available various brands of milk and cream each presumed to possess a distinct quality or characteristic, (2) special-delivery service to customers, and (3) continuing to serve customers after bills were overdue, thus permitting bad debts to be incurred.

This is more comparable to the practice now being followed in most markets and the one which many individuals would favor unless an educational policy were instituted to show the possible savings through the adoption of the first policy.

It is to be remembered, of course, that some of these economies of service mentioned above could be instituted under the present competitive system if the competing milk distributors would agree on such policy and then all carry it out. The difficulty arises from the fact that, where several firms are competing for business, it is almost certain that some will fail to adhere to an agreed policy. Consequently, if savings are to be made through standardization of service and product, it will undoubtedly have to be accomplished through unification of the milk-distribution system.

CHAPTER V

PROFITS

HISTORICAL CONSIDERATIONS

DURING the period of the 1920's, especially the last five years of it, and to a lesser extent during 1930 and 1931, consolidations and mergers of milk-distribution companies were taking place at a rapid rate. As an example, the number of companies in Milwaukee was reduced from thirty-two in 1920 to eleven in 1930.[1] When two or more companies operating within the same city merged, it was not uncommon for the least well-equipped or favorably situated plant to be partly or entirely abandoned or to be sold, for what it would bring, for uses other than distributing milk. The more efficient equipment which could be used advantageously was continued in use or disposed of to the best advantage. Commonly some equipment was replaced by types more modern and efficient.

Consolidation of this nature tended to reduce processing and distributing costs in at least three ways: (1) plants and equipment were operated at more nearly full capacity after the merger than before; (2) the use of modern and, in some cases, larger units of equipment resulted in economies, especially in the use of labor; and (3) to a considerable extent delivery routes were combined, hence duplication in delivery was reduced with a corresponding reduction in costs. To the extent that distributors' margins remained the same after as before the merger, the merged companies enjoyed the result of these economies, and the savings tended to swell the profits of the new and larger company. Indeed these margins changed very little during the decade of the 1920's (Table 11). Thus in many cases the efficient distributors enjoyed handsome profits during this period, as will be pointed out later in this chapter.

When the depression came on in real force in 1930 and 1931, new

[1] W. P. Mortenson, *An Economic Study of the Milwaukee Milk Market* (University of Wisconsin Research Bull. 113 [Madison, January, 1932]), p. 5.

milk dealers of many types entered the markets. With them came intensely increased competition, entirely new problems, and a different situation with respect to profits of milk distributors. This new competition took the following forms:

1. Some people whose livelihood had been taken away by the depression entered the market not with any great hope of making large profits but more particularly to make a living.
2. Producer co-operatives, consumer co-operatives, and combinations of these two set out to deliver milk directly to the family and to the wholesale trade (stores, hotels, and restaurants).
3. In the smaller or even middle-sized markets, farmer-producers who were pressed to meet certain fixed obligations entered the market in order to swell their farm income by carrying their product direct to the consumer.

During this time the per capita city milk consumption was barely holding its own or was even being reduced, in some cases substantially (Appen. C). This meant that the new distributors were taking customers from distributors formerly established. When the established dealers suffered losses in volume of sales, they were not able to reduce their expenses in the same proportion. Indeed many of their expenses remained constant. The items of taxes, insurance, and repairs were reduced very little, if at all. The amount of bad debts actually increased during the depression. The number of employees could be reduced very little, if any, until volume of sales had been reduced decidedly. In fact, public sentiment was so strongly set against discharging employees that many of the established companies chose to suffer financial loss rather than have public sentiment turned against them. Employees resisted the reduction of the rate of pay even though their output had been decreased materially because of the reduced volume of business. Few, if any, of the expenses of the established distributors decreased in proportion to the decrease in sales receipts.

After such dynamic changes had been made, the industry faced, and still faces, the problem of reducing expenses of distribution with many of the plants operating at much less than full capacity. The industry is now operating with a much larger capital equipment than is necessary (chap. iv). The larger number of dealers in the market has resulted in competition becoming extremely intensive and in many cases expensive or even wasteful. As one would expect, under such conditions, profits have shrunk appreciably as compared with the earlier period.

MEANING OF TERM

We have used the term "net operating profit" to mean the remainder or residual from gross earnings after making deductions of operating costs but not of interest on either owned or borrowed capital. That is, the interest has been included with the net operating profit, not with the operating cost. This classification makes for clearer comparability between companies than if the interest obligation had been left as a cost. It is recognized, of course, that if capital is to continue to flow into the milk business to maintain the industry, some return upon the investment will be necessary. Some of the companies were financed almost entirely from within through investments of one owner or at most a very small number such as three or four owners, who were also officers of the corporation. These members of the firm put funds into the enterprise in anticipation of earning at least the going rate of return on the money invested. Other companies obtained an appreciable amount of funds from the outside through the issue of bonds or preferred stock which act as direct claims against the assets of the company.

To illustrate this difference between companies, let us suppose that Company A and Company B were operating similar-sized milk businesses, each doing an annual business of $250,000, with an investment of $100,000, but that the two were differently financed. Assume that Company A borrowed no funds but that B borrowed $25,000. Suppose, further, that, after meeting all operating costs (not including interest), each had a remainder or residual of $5,000. For Company A, who borrowed no funds, the net operating profit shown in form of percentages would be as follows:

Profit as a per cent of sales 5,000 ÷ 250,000 = 0.02 or 2 per cent
Profit as a per cent of capital invested 5,000 ÷ 100,000 = 0.05 or 5 per cent

Company B, doing the same amount of business, with the same amount of total investment and finishing the year with the same amount of residual as Company A, would be shown to have made the same rate of return on investment and on sales as did Company

A if interest on borrowed capital was included with the net operating profit. If, on the other hand, the interest due had been included as an operating cost, the accounting would be as follows:

Interest on $25,000 borrowed at 5 per cent = $1,250
Residual of $5,000 − $1,250 = $3,750

Thus, if interest on borrowed capital had been included as a cost, this $3,750 would have been left as the net operating profit for the year—not $5,000 as in the case of Company A. On the basis of $3,750, the profit as a per cent of sales would be 1.5 as compared with 2 per cent for Company A. Again for Company B, profit as a per cent of capital invested would be 3.7 as compared with 5 per cent for Company A.

From the above analysis the reader will readily recognize the advantages of this classification whereby the interest obligation is included with the profit item instead of being left as a part of the operating costs.

Interest payment on borrowed capital for the thirteen companies varied considerably from company to company and within any one company from year to year but averaged roughly 0.8 per cent of sales receipts for the entire eleven-year period. Thus, the actual return to these companies in payment for their own capital invested and for risk and uncertainty connected with the business would be equal to the net operating profit less the amount of interest paid out for borrowed funds.

As already shown, profit is usually expressed in form of a per cent. We hear, for example, of a company making 10 per cent profit. Unfortunately, laymen as a rule do not stop to ask the meaning of the 10 per cent. For example, is it 10 per cent (1) of the total annual sales of the company, or (2) of the amount paid farmers for milk, or (3) of the total capital employed by the owners, or (4) of some other figure? In popular use and also too often in a more technical presentation, the word "profit" is so ill defined that even the critical reader may be unable to determine the significance of it.

The total amount of capital employed[2] by a milk-distributing

[2] Throughout this discussion we shall use the term "capital" in the meaning of the valuation of property in use. This is not to be confused with the specialized meaning employed by accountants in referring to a *capital* account in contrast with an *income* account.

company is almost always less than the total amount of the annual sales of the company. Therefore, if a given figure representing profits is divided by the smaller amount (capital invested) the per cent profit shown will be large as compared with a per cent profit when calculated by dividing this same profit figure by the larger amount, total annual sales.

Let us suppose, for instance, that a company buys $100,000 worth of milk from farmers during the year and sells $200,000 worth of milk at resale out of which operation he makes $10,000 operating profit. This $10,000 profit as a per cent of annual sales will be $10,000 divided by $200,000, or 0.05 (5 per cent). The profit as a per cent of amount paid farmers will be $10,000 divided by $100,000, or 0.10 (10 per cent). If the company had a capital investment of $50,000, its rate of return would be $10,000 divided by $50,000, or 20 per cent. Thus, if one calculates profit as a per cent of capital invested, the percentage will result in a large profit figure. If, on the contrary, he calculates profit as a per cent of sales receipts, the resulting percentage figure will be small. This is occasionally done with a foregoing knowledge that the profit figure obtained will be large or small, as those who calculate the figure choose to have it.

The reader may ask: "Which is the correct use of the word 'profit'?" The answer is that no one form is necessarily the correct one to use and the others incorrect. Any one of several forms of showing profits indicates something about the business. The form adopted is ordinarily determined in part by what appears to give the most meaningful figure under the conditions, and in part by what those who calculate the per cent of profit wish to have emphasized.

For instance, milk consumers may be anxious to know how much they might be able to save in the price of milk if no profits whatever were permitted but instead the entire amount of savings went to them in the form of lower prices of milk. This would be shown by a ratio between the total amount of profit and the total amount of sales (i.e., total profit divided by the total receipts from annual sales). If, on the other hand, the producers were interested in knowing how much a reduction or an elimination of profit would mean to them if the total amount of profit were turned back in the form of higher farm prices of milk, then the producer would want to calculate the ratio which total profits are to the amount of money paid for the milk purchased from farmers. We may properly refer to the above two classifications of profit by the term "margin of profit," the profit margin on the basis of sales and purchases, respectively, of milk distributors.

Again, if one were interested in showing the efficiency with which capital is employed, then the ratio between the total amount of

TABLE 14

NET PROFITS OF FIVE* LARGE MILK COMPANIES
CALCULATED ON THREE DIFFERENT BASES

Year	Net Profit as a Percentage of Sales Receipts (1)	Net Profit as a Percentage of Amount Paid Farmers (Cost of Goods Sold)† (2)	Net Profit as a Percentage of Capital Employed by Owners (3)
1927.........	5.5	10.3	13.1
1928.........	5.9	10.7	14.0
1929.........	6.9	12.8	16.7
1930.........	7.2	14.5	15.4
1931.........	5.8	13.5	10.0
1932.........	1.0	2.9	1.5
1933.........	0.5	1.0	0.5
1934.........	1.9	4.3	3.1
1935.........	1.7	3.4	2.5
1936.........	1.8	3.6	3.0
1937.........	2.5	4.7	4.6

* Four companies in 1927 and 1928.
† Footnote 3, p. 27, applies also to the figures in this column.

profit and the total amount of capital invested would give the proper ratio. This may be referred to as the "rate of profit."

Table 14 presents a comparison of figures on profits when expressed on different bases. The comparison virtually speaks for itself. Profits, when shown as a percentage of amount paid farmers, appear almost twice as larger as when shown in terms of the percentage of sales value (cf. cols. 1 and 2). When shown as a percentage of capital employed by owners, the figure is roughly two to three times as high as when shown in terms of sales receipts (cols. 1 and 3).

In this study more reliance has been placed on the profit figure stated as a percentage of sales than as a percentage of invested capital. There were two main reasons for this.

1. For most uses, profit shown as a percentage of sales is a more informative figure than when shown as a percentage of capital invested by the owners. Especially from a public point of view, it is more informative to know that out of every dollar of sales the profit to the seller is, say, 2 per cent, than it is to know that out of every dollar invested by the owner he obtains a profit of, say, 5 per cent. Put in another way, the buying public is especially interested in knowing how much out of every dollar which is paid for a product goes for profit.

2. The figure showing profit as a percentage of sales is generally more stable than one showing the profit as a percentage of invested capital. The following example will illustrate this point. In the milk-distribution business, as is the case with most businesses, the annual receipts from sales represent a larger amount of funds than does the figure representing capital invested by the owners. For example, on the basis of $250,000 sales and $100,000 capital invested, a change in profit of $2,000 would represent a 2 per cent change in rate of return on investment but only a 0.8 per cent change when calculated as a ratio of sales.[3]

EXTENT OF PROFITS

In Table 15 profits are shown in terms of a percentage of total receipts from annual sales by companies for thirteen Wisconsin milk-distributing companies covering an eleven-year period. Perhaps the two most outstanding characteristics of the profit figures as shown here are (1) the pronounced amount of variation from company to company and (2) the noticeable difference in the amount of profit during the first five years, 1927–31, inclusive, compared with that during the period 1932–37, inclusive. A few examples will show the differences between companies in the same year. In 1927 the highest profit was 10.3 per cent for Company E and the lowest a loss of 5.2 per cent for Company L. In 1930, the year of highest profit, the

[3] The term "pure profit" is taken to mean a final residual after a return equal to the normal interest rate on both owned and borrowed capital have been received. No attempt has been made to segregate this pure profit; instead, the entire amount has been carried as net operating profit.

profits ranged from a high of 13.4 per cent for Company G to a low of 0.4 per cent for Company K. Incidentally, this was the only year in which all these companies made a profit. In 1937 the highest profit was 4.2 per cent, while one company suffered a loss of 1.2 per cent.

If the companies are taken by years for the five-year period ending in 1931, records are shown for eight companies throughout

TABLE 15

NET OPERATING PROFIT SHOWN AS A PERCENTAGE OF TOTAL SALES BY COMPANIES, 1927–37, INCLUSIVE

(Arranged According to Size of Company)

Company	1927	1928	1929	1930	1931	1932	1933	1934	1935	1936	1937
A......	−0.4*	3.0	2.4	3.5	0.8	2.6	1.4	0.8	1.6	1.2	2.5†
B......	......	......	......	......	......	−0.3	0.1	0.0	−1.3	−0.3	1.7
C......	6.1	2.6	3.8	6.6	5.7	0.4	−1.1	0.8	2.2	1.5	3.8
D......	......	......	3.7	1.7	2.0	−2.8	−0.6	0.0	0.2	0.5	0.5
E......	10.3	11.7	14.8	10.6	9.2	3.1	0.2	5.4	0.1	1.4	1.4
F......	......	......	......	......	......	−4.0	−2.5	2.4	4.4	6.0	3.4
G......	6.0	6.3	9.8	13.4	11.3	1.8	2.4	2.6	4.2	4.5	4.2
H......	−0.5	2.6	5.4	8.7	6.3	−6.9	−12.9	−7.8	−2.7	−1.8	2.8
I......	......	......	5.0	3.1	0.2	−0.2	0.1	0.4	−0.2	0.7	0.9
J......	−0.1	−9.4	−6.5	4.9	3.8	−2.0	−1.0	0.0	1.6	−0.4	−1.2
K......	1.4	2.0	2.7	0.4	−0.3	0.4	−4.2	−2.9	0.1	0.3	1.3
L......	−5.2	−0.1	3.1	2.8	2.8	−0.7	0.2	0.1	1.2	0.4	−0.3
M......	......	......	7.3	7.2	2.6	0.5	2.3	4.5	−0.1	5.9	2.0

* Minus sign indicates loss.

† Figures representing profits as a percentage of capital invested by owners are about two to three times the size here shown (see Table 14, cols. 1 and 3).

that period, and for an additional three companies for the years 1929–31, inclusive, making a total of 49 items of profit or loss figures. These will be referred to as company years or "cases." Of these 49 cases, in only 7 of them (14 per cent) was a loss incurred, while in the other 42 (86 per cent) a profit was enjoyed. Briefly, in almost 9 cases out of 10 these companies were "operating in the black" during that period of years. For the six-year period 1932–37, inclusive, there were 78 cases, of which 54 made a profit and 24 took a loss.

Before 1932 practically all the cases which show a profit made a large enough amount to cover interest on capital employed with enough left for a final residual or pure profit. In that period operating profits were in general more than the amount necessary to attract the required capital to the industry. However, during the other years of the study, 1932–37, inclusive, it was only rarely that the operating profit was more than sufficient to cover interest on the capital invested. In fact, this was true in only about 16 of the 78 cases, or in 1 case out of about 5.[4]

In general, the larger companies had consistently higher profits than the smaller ones. This is indicated in Table 16. Taken as an average the "large" companies made a profit every year but one (1933), during which they just broke even. Out of the eleven years,

TABLE 16

Net Operating Profit Shown as Average of Four to Seven "Large" and Four to Six "Small" Milk-distributing Companies,* 1927–37, Inclusive

(Stated as a Percentage of Sales Receipts)

	1927	1928	1929	1930	1931	1932	1933	1934	1935	1936	1937
"Large" companies......	5.5	5.9	6.9	7.2	5.8	0.1	0.0	1.7	1.6	2.1	2.5
"Small" companies......	−1.2†	−1.2	2.8	4.5	2.6	−1.5	−2.6	−1.0	0.0	0.9	−0.3

* Number of large companies: four in 1927 and 1928; five in 1929–31, inclusive; seven thereafter; number of small companies: four in 1927 and 1928; six thereafter.
† Minus sign indicates loss.

on an average, the "small" companies suffered a loss during six of them. They just broke even one year and made a profit during four years only.

This contrast in profit between large and small companies is brought out with equal clarity in the more detailed Table 15. During the five years 1927–31, inclusive, there was only 1 case of the 23 cases where a "large" company (A–G, inclusive) incurred a loss compared with 7 cases in 33 for the small; almost 1 case in 4.

In the six years 1932–37, inclusive, in only 8 of the 42 cases did the seven "large" companies suffer an actual loss. In the other 34 cases (81 per cent) they made a profit which, in about half of the cases, was more than sufficient to pay interest on the employed capital. The smaller companies fared noticeably less well (see Com-

4 See n. †, Table 15, p. 97.

panies H–M for years 1932–37, inclusive). In 16 cases out of 36
they operated at a loss and in 1 case just broke even. Stated in another way, in slightly over half the cases the smaller companies
"operated in the black," while the other half failed to make sufficient return to cover even interest on the capital invested to say
nothing about having a pure profit left.

Some have argued that milk distributors should not be entitled
to a profit beyond the amount just necessary to pay interest at the
going rate on their investment of capital. Let us suppose that a
profit just sufficient to cover this amount had been allowed the
companies included in this study. If all profit above that amount
had gone to consumers in the form of lower milk prices, how much
would that have amounted to per quart of milk purchased? The
analysis of profits of these companies would seem to indicate that
such a question is largely without point, because in no year except
one (1930) could profits have been scaled down below what they
were without forcing some of the distributors into an actual loss.
During ten of the eleven years one or more of the companies studied
was operating at a loss (Table 15).

There were only three years out of the eleven when the "small"
distributors, taken as an average, made sufficient profit to return
anything above the interest on the capital employed (Table 16).
Taking the six-year period 1932–37, inclusive, on an average the
"small" companies obtained an operating profit only one year (1936)
of 0.9 per cent of sales value. This meant that the profit even then
was sufficient to pay only about 2 per cent interest on the capital
employed. During this whole six-year period any further squeezing
of distributors' margins, if long continued, would obviously have
forced some of these "small" distributors to the wall.

On the basis of the figures in column 3, Table 16, representing
averages of "large" companies only, it will be noticed that during the
five-year period ending in 1931 the profits were sufficiently attractive
so that, after allowing 5 per cent return on capital employed, there
would still have been left a handsome final residual or pure profit.

In fact, during those years, profits of the larger companies were
unduly high. For example, in 1929, after paying 5 per cent return
on the capital employed, there was still left what we have termed

a pure profit of 11.7 per cent (16.7 − 5.0 = 11.7). Of that five-year period, the year 1931 showed the lowest profit. Even that year, after 5 per cent return had been paid on capital, there was still a pure profit of 5 per cent. Thus, during those years, profits might have been reduced materially and still sufficient capital would have been attracted to maintain the industry.

However, as indicated earlier, the years after 1931 were much different from the earlier ones. Since then profits in the milk business have been conspicuously lacking. Only a few of the larger and more efficient companies appear to have made more than enough to pay a return on the employed capital. Indeed, there was only one year (1937) in which these larger companies, as an average, made sufficient income to bring a reasonable return on capital (Table 16).

On the basis of the data from this study, considering the six-year period 1932–37, inclusive, it seems clear that, if noticeable savings are to be made in the milk business under the present system of distribution, it would be necessary for the most part to look elsewhere than to reductions of profits.

However, if the present system of milk processing and distribution were replaced by a unified system, some of the operating profit now going to pay interest on capital employed could be saved. That is, to the extent that the total capital (including plant, equipment, and operating capital) could be reduced, the interest necessary to pay returns on this could also be reduced.

The capital invested in land, buildings, and equipment amounts to about 60 per cent of the total capital.[5] Suppose the investment

[5] Based on records of ten companies for representative years of the eleven-year period studied, the following figures show the percentage distribution of total capital employed:

Land............................	4	
Buildings...........................	21	
Total land and buildings................		25
Plant equipment (machinery).........	23	
Delivery equipment.................	12	
Miscellaneous......................	1	
Total equipment......................		36
Current and miscellaneous assets............		39
Total.............................		100

Figures from twenty-two New York companies (1931) show that 65 per cent of the total assets was land, buildings, and equipment as compared with 61 per cent for the in these items could be reduced by 30–40 per cent (see chap. iv), then, without changing the interest rates, the interest cost on them could be reduced a like proportion. A 30 per cent saving on this 60 per cent would mean a reduction of 18 per cent in total employed capital. Since the value of the annual sales is roughly two and one-half times the total capital employed, a 5 per cent profit (perhaps more accurately interest or return on capital) would be equivalent to 2 per cent of the amount of annual sales. If 18 per cent of this profit could be saved through a unified system, the saving as a percentage of sales would be 0.36 (0.18 × 0.02 = 0.0036 or 0.36 per cent). That is, on every dollar of sales 0.36 per cent, or 0.36 cent, would be saved. On a 10-cent quart of milk this saving would be 0.036 of a cent; at 12 cents the amount would be 0.0432 cent. It should again be pointed out that this "saving" is based upon the supposition that under the comparison being made the competitive system would be obtaining a return—or profit—sufficient to pay 5 per cent on the capital employed. The utility would find it necessary to pay interest on capital employed just as does private enterprise.

From the public point of view the only justification of a pure profit is that it enables a business to provide a reserve during good years from which to draw during adverse years. A business under public regulation should require no pure profit. If the regulating commission makes adjustments so that interest can always be returned on the capital employed, no losses will be incurred and hence there will be no need to provide a reserve. From this it follows that to the extent that there have been and still are pure profits in the milk business, that amount, in addition to the 0.04 cent per quart mentioned above, could presumably be saved under a unified regulated system of distribution.

Wisconsin companies. However, the investment in land and buildings was considerably higher proportionately, amounting to 40 per cent as compared with 25 per cent for the Wisconsin companies; land alone was 10 per cent as compared with 4 per cent for the Wisconsin companies. Current and miscellaneous assets amounted to 35 per cent of the total as compared with 39 per cent for the companies in Wisconsin (*Report of the Joint Legislative Committee To Investigate the Milk Industry, State of New York* [New York State Legislative Doc. 114 (Albany, 1933)], p. 183).

SUPPLEMENTARY INFORMATION ON PROFITS

Table 17 contains summary information for given years on profits for some 230 companies in markets other than those included in the

TABLE 17

OPERATING PROFITS OF MILK DISTRIBUTORS IN "OTHER" MARKETS
(Profits Expressed as a Percentage of Sales)

Location of Markets	Number of Companies	1927	1928	1929	1930	1931	1932	1933	1934	1935	1936	1937
New York*	14	....	....	....	....	....	....	....	....	....	4.46	2.88
New York City†	22–33	3.6	4.4	4.1	4.5	4.5	4.4	3.0	....	....	3.9	1.5
New York upstate‡	31–38	5.2	5.7	5.2	6.4	6.9	....	....	....	....	....	
New York upstate—large§	21	....	....	....	....	....	....	2.5	....	....	....	
New York upstate—small‖	7	....	....	....	....	....	....	3.4	....	....	....	
West Virginia¶	22	....	....	....	....	....	....	2.27	....	....	....	
Connecticut—large**	2– 4	....	....	....	4.5	7.1	6.2	2.8	2.0	....	....	
Connecticut —small**	5– 6	....	....	....	3.8	4.8	4.3	0.2	1.6	....	....	
Philadelphia—large††	3– 4	....	....	....	13.7	15.0	10.8	7.1	5.1	....	....	
Philadelphia—small††	3– 8	....	....	....	4.5	4.6	2.7	2.3	−1.1‡‡	....	....	
Connecticut§§	47	....	....	....	....	....	....	....	....	....	1.31	
Baltimore, St. Louis, Cincinnati, and Boston‖‖	11	....	....	....	6.8	....	....	4.5	1.4	2.6	....	
Milwaukee¶¶	3–20	....	0.73	2.73	4.61	3.34	3.23	−0.04	2.76	....	....	
Milwaukee, selected companies***	6	....	....	....	....	....	....	−0.04	....	....	....	
California†††	....	....	....	....	....	....	....	....	....	....	2.29	
Wisconsin supplementary companies‡‡‡	2– 3	....	....	....	....	1.4	− 5.6	0.4	1.2	1.6	1.1	0.5
Milwaukee§§§	5	....	....	....	....	....	....	....	....	....	....	1.54
Racine and Kenosha§§§	2	....	....	....	....	....	....	....	....	....	....	2.19
Madison§§§	2	....	....	....	....	....	....	....	....	....	....	0.1
Wisconsin—large‖‖‖		5.5	5.9	6.9	7.2	5.8	0.1	0.0	1.7	1.6	2.1	2.5
Wisconsin—small‖‖‖		−1.2	−1.2	2.8	4.5	2.6	− 1.5	−2.6	−1.0	0.0	0.9	−0.3

* *American Produce Review*, February 23, 1938, pp. 498–99. Audit of New York dealers by Ernst and Ernst. Figures for first nine months of 1937.

† *Report of the Joint Legislative Committee To Investigate the Milk Industry* (New York State Legislative Doc. 114 [Albany, 1933]), p. 182, for 1928–30; Leland Spencer, mimeographed publication "LS-38:361" (Ithaca, 1938), p. 9, for 1927, 1931–33, 1936, and 1937. The figures for 1937 are for nine months only.

‡ *Report of the Joint Legislative Committee To Investigate the Milk Industry*, p. 225.

§ Leland Spencer, "Costs and Profits of Milk Dealers in Upstate Cities, August, 1933" (Report to the New York State Milk Control Board, March 24, 1934), p. 3 (mimeographed). This figure included rent (0.3 per cent of sales) as an operating cost, but did not include federal income tax (0.3 per cent of sales) as a cost as was done in the Wisconsin study. The two adjustments thus offset each other.

‖ Leland Spencer, "Milk Distributors' Costs and Profits" (Preliminary Report to New York Milk Control Board, October 17, 1933), p. 8 (mimeographed). The data are for three months ending August 31 for each year. The distributors were located in cities of less than 50,000 population. Interest was included as an operating cost, and information was not available to exclude it; hence, on this point, there is not strict comparability with the other profit figures in this table. The adjustment for interest—as indicated where they have been made—would be, however, of only minor significance.

¶ R. O. Stelzer and L. M. Thurston, *Milk Distribution Costs in West Virginia* (West Virginia Bull. 266 [Morgantown, 1935]), p. 32. In order that the accounting procedure be comparable to that adopted in our Wisconsin study, the profit figure (2.27 per cent of sales) was the result of the inclusion of interest and rent as a part of the operating profit. The figure in the West Virginia study—exclusive of interest and rent— was 0.35 per cent of sales. Interest amounted to 1.23 per cent and rent to 0.69 per cent, resulting in a total operating profit of 2.27 per cent of sales.

** Federal Trade Commission, *Distribution and Sale of Milk and Milk Products: Philadelphia and Connecticut Milksheds* (House Document No. 387 [74th Cong.; 2d sess.] [Washington, 1936]), pp. 61–62). Data for 1934 are for six months. Federal income tax was not included as an operating cost in the Federal

[Footnotes to Table 17 continued on facing page]

earlier discussion. These markets are located in various sections of
the country and cover the same years as do the Wisconsin companies.
Information was available for only the years in which they are here
given. An examination of this table will show the same general picture with regard to profits as was true of the Wisconsin companies.
This is fundamentally significant. Note, for example, that the averages for the companies given in 1927, 1928, and 1929 are all within
the limits of the averages of the Wisconsin "large" and "small"

TABLE 18

PROFIT OR LOSS AS A PERCENTAGE OF SALES

	Loss	PROFIT (PERCENTAGE OF SALES)					
		0–1	1–2	2–3	3–4	4–5	Over 5
Number of times profit figures are within range shown..........	4	4	9	11	3	4	4

companies. In 1930 all except two figures were within the average
of Wisconsin companies. One Philadelphia company showed a profit
noticeably above any others. The Connecticut "small" companies
averaged a slightly lower profit than did those for Wisconsin—3.8
per cent compared with our 4.5 per cent of sales. If figures representing all the companies given in Table 17 for the six most recent and

Trade Commission studies (see *Report of the Federal Trade Commission on the Sale and Distribution of Milk: Connecticut and Philadelphia Milksheds* [House Document No. 152 (74th Cong.; 1st sess.)], p. 67).

†† *Ibid.*, pp. 67–68. Data for 1934 were for ten months.

‡‡ Minus sign denotes loss.

§§ S. McLean Buckingham, "Dealers' Spread in Connecticut" (Hartford, Conn., January, 1938), p. 2 (mimeographed). It was not possible to determine the procedure followed in arriving at the profit figure.

‖‖ *Report of the Federal Trade Commission on the Distribution and Sale of Milk and Milk Products* (House Document No. 501 [74th Cong.; 2d sess. (1936)], p. 148). The study included two Baltimore, four Cincinnati, three St. Louis, and two Boston companies.

¶¶ Agricultural Adjustment Administration, *A Survey of Milk Marketing in Milwaukee* ("U.S.D.A., Marketing Information Series," DM-1 [Washington, May, 1937]), p. 59. For the seven years from 1928 to 1934, inclusive, the number of companies included was as follows (in order of yearly sequence): 3, 4, 4, 7, 13, 16, 20. Data for 1934 were for four months.

*** *Ibid.*, p. 60. These six companies were included in the sixteen for that year in n. ¶¶ above.

††† J. M. Tinley, *Public Regulation of Milk Marketing in California* (Berkeley, 1936), pp. 130–31. The figure reported as profits (1.94 per cent of sales) was increased to 2.29 per cent of sales by the addition of rent (0.35 per cent of sales) to obtain the operating profit. The profit pertains to the sale and distribution of retail milk only.

‡‡‡ Data are for three Wisconsin companies not included in the thirteen for which detailed information has been given.

§§§ Unpublished data compiled by the Wisconsin Department of Agriculture and Markets. Figures for July and October, 1937, and July, 1938.

‖‖‖ From Table 16, p. 98.

less profitable years (1932–37, inclusive) are recorded, the frequency distribution shown in Table 18 will occur.

Of the 39 figures included in this grouping, 4 show a loss, 24 show a profit of from 0.1 to 3 per cent, another 7 figures vary from 3 to 5 per cent. The large Philadelphia and Connecticut companies, representing 4 figures in the table, show a profit over 5 per cent of sales. On the basis of the same relationship between capital employed and annual sales as was used earlier in the discussion, in only about 11 items out of the 39 was the profit figure sufficient to return a pure profit after interest due on capital had been met.

In general import the supplementary information on profits from more than two hundred milk-distributing companies clearly corroborates the information from the detailed study of the Wisconsin companies. All this should be sufficient evidence to show that the data and the sample upon which this study rests are sufficiently adequate and reliable to support the conclusions arrived at.

PART III
LEGAL CONSIDERATIONS OF CONTROL

CHAPTER VI

LEGAL ASPECTS OF MILK CONTROL[1]

T HE fundamental principle must be recognized that the constitutionality of laws is determined by the judicial branch of the American government. Consequently, the mere declaration by a state legislature, or by the United States Congress, that a particular kind of property or business is "affected with a public interest" does not give it ultimate power to determine the question of the constitutional validity. The right and duty of the United States Supreme Court to determine "whether or not an act of Congress was repugnant to the Constitution and therefore void was first decided in the early case of *Marbury* v. *Madison*, in which Chief Justice Marshall said: 'It is, emphatically, the province and duty of the judicial department to say what the law is.' "[2] This prerogative is imposed upon (or assumed by) the courts by reason of the limitations provided in the Fifth and the Fourteenth amendments.

A brief review of court decisions involving the regulation of fluid milk, especially those decisions handed down by the United States Supreme Court, will throw light on the trend which regulation has been taking in this field of activity during the last three decades or so. It may also provide some basis for determining the extent to which regulation may legally be extended. More specifically, such and analysis should furnish a basis upon which to determine whether or not the regulation may be carried to a point similar to that which is now imposed on the more commonly recognized public utilities.

[1] Much of this chapter has been published in the November, 1939, and the February, 1940, issues of the *Journal of Land and Public Utility Economics*. It is being published here with permission of that *Journal*.

[2] See *Constitution of the United States of America* (Senate Document No. 154 [68th Cong.; 1st sess.] [Washington, 1924]), p. 421; see also *Marbury* v. *Madison*, 1 Cranch 137 (1803), 368, 389.

COURT DECISIONS INVOLVING CONTROL OF HEALTH
AND SANITATION

Issues involving public health and welfare have ordinarily been subject to more rigid public control than purely economic issues.[3] Legal authority relative to these phases has been quite clearly defined.[4] Indeed the importance of obtaining supplies of pure and wholesome fluid milk for human consumption has been acknowledged almost universally, and the power of a municipality to pass ordinances requiring and enforcing regulation to this end has been recognized for more than a half-century[5] and has been common practice for more than a quarter of a century.[6] The power of a city to require the pasteurization of milk with the view of protecting public health was upheld by the Supreme Court of Wisconsin as early as 1920. This court held that such ordinance "is an appropriate and valid regulation for the protection of the people's health."[7]

In 1933 an important decision by the United States Supreme Court upheld an order of the state commissioner of agriculture in New York prohibiting cattle from being shipped into the state unless accompanied by an official certificate showing them to be free from Bang's disease, presumably the cause of undulant fever in humans.[8] Again the fundamental consideration was that of safeguarding the public health. Although other cases could be cited, these are rather typical and perhaps sufficient to indicate the power of the state to enforce legislation promoting sanitation and public health and welfare. Significantly, prior to about 1933 regulation in the dis-

[3] Those issues involving public morals are considered equally important, but they are seldom if ever involved in the phases of business which will be discussed in this treatise.

[4] For a more extended discussion of court decisions affecting milk control see James A. Tobey, *Legal Aspects of Milk Control* (Chicago: International Association of Milk Dealers, 1936) and *Federal and State Control of Milk Prices* (Chicago: International Association of Milk Dealers, 1937).

[5] In 1874 Massachusetts passed legislation prohibiting the sale of "diseased, corrupted, and unwholesome products" (*Massachusetts Laws, 1874,* c. 50).

[6] *State ex rel. Nowotny* v. *Milwaukee,* 140 Wis. 38 (1909).

[7] *Pfeffer* v. *Milwaukee,* 171 Wis. 514 (1920).

[8] *Mintz* v. *Baldwin,* 289 U.S. 346 (1933).

tribution and handling of milk centered almost entirely around questions of health and sanitation. There had been no important legislation involving control of prices or any of the more purely economic features.

DECISIONS INVOLVING MILK-PRICE CONTROL

Early in the 1930's, when some fifteen states and the federal government passed legislation setting up controls designed to fix prices and in general to stabilize the fluid-milk industry, new legal questions arose. The legislation was challenged, and court actions followed. The first important United States Supreme Court case involving the legality of the power of the state to fix prices became known as the Nebbia case (1934). The New York State Milk Control Board had been vested by the legislature with the duty and power to fix prices of milk. Under the Board's order milk was to be sold by retail stores at nine cents per quart. Nebbia, a grocery-store operator in Rochester, New York, violated the order by selling two quarts of milk and a five-cent loaf of bread for eighteen cents. This in reality meant a cutting of milk prices because it resulted in the giving of values above those specified in the order.

Associate Justice Roberts, who wrote the majority (five to four) opinion, held:

Under our form of government the use of property and the making of contracts are normally matters of private and not of public concern. The general rule is that both shall be free of governmental interference. But neither property rights[9] nor contract rights[10] are absolute; for government cannot exist if the citizen may at will use his property to the detriment of his fellows, or exercise his freedom of contract to work them harm. Equally fundamental with the private right is that of the public to regulate it in the common interest. . . . . Price control, like any form of regulation, is unconstitutional only if arbitrary, discriminatory, or demonstrably irrelevant to the policy the legislature is free to adopt, and hence an unnecessary and unwarranted interference with individual liberty.[11] The Fifth Amendment, in the field of federal activity,[12]

[9] *Munn* v. *Illinois*, 94 U.S. 113, 124, 125 (1876); *Orient Insurance Co.* v. *Daggs*, 172 U.S. 557, 566 (1899); *Northern Securities Co.* v. *United States*, 193 U.S. 197, 351 (1904).

[10] *Allgeyer* v. *Louisiana*, 165 U.S. 578, 591 (1897); *Atlantic Coast Line* v. *Riverside Mills*, 219 U.S. 186, 202 (1911); *Chicago B. & Q. R. Co.* v. *McGuire*, 219 U.S. 549, 567 (1911); *Stephenson* v. *Binford*, 287 U.S. 251, 274 (1932).

[11] *Nebbia* v. *New York*, 291 U.S. 502, 523, 539 (1934).

[12] *Addyston Pipe and Steel Co.* v. *United States*, 175 U.S. 211, 228–29 (1900).

and the Fourteenth, as respects state action,[13] do not prohibit governmental regulation for the public welfare. They merely condition the exertion of the admitted power, by securing that the end shall be accomplished by methods consistent with due process. And the guaranty of due process, as has often been held, demands only that the law shall not be unreasonable, arbitrary or capricious, and that the means selected shall have a real and substantial relation to the object sought to be attained. It results that a regulation valid for one sort of business, or in given circumstances, may be invalid for another sort, or for the same business under other circumstances, because the reasonableness of each regulation depends upon the relevant facts.[14]

The Court recognized:

We may as well say at once that the dairy industry is not, in the accepted sense of the phrase, a public utility. We think the appellant is also right in asserting that there is in this case no suggestion of any monopoly or monopolistic practice. It goes without saying that those engaged in the business are in no way dependent upon public grants or franchises for the privilege of conducting their activities. But if, as must be conceded, the industry is subject to regulation in the public interest, what constitutional principle bars the state from correcting existing maladjustments by legislation touching prices? We think there is no such principle. The due process clause makes no mention of sales or of prices any more than it speaks of business or contracts or buildings or other incidents of property.[15]

The language of the Court points out that regulation touching prices does not turn on the question as to whether the business is classed as a private enterprise or as a public utility. The Court made clear that a high degree of government regulation touching prices may be carried over into fields which have in the past been looked upon as purely private. This point was again emphasized in the United States Supreme Court case of the *West Coast Hotel* v. *Parrish*.[16]

Mr. Morris Duane, of the Pennsylvania bar, believes that the Nebbia decision "is important not because it enunciates new principles of constitutional law, but because it applies existing principles in a different way and marks distinctly a change from recent conceptions of due process. . . . . The decision marks the change from

[13] *Barbier* v. *Connolly*, 113 U.S. 27, 31 (1884); *Chicago B. & Q. R. Co.* v. *Drainage Comm'rs*, 200 U.S. 561, 592 (1906).

[14] *Nebbia* v. *New York*, 291 U.S. 525 (1934).

[15] *Ibid.*, p. 531.   [16] 300 U.S. 379, 398 (1936).

an era of laissez faire to an era of governmental regulation." The case "decided that for a business admittedly not a public utility the state legislature can enact laws authorizing the fixing of prices and other regulation of that industry, and that the courts will not set aside such laws or orders issued thereunder as denying due process unless they are 'arbitrary, disciminatory or demonstrably irrelevant to the policy the Legislature is free to adopt, and hence an unnecessary and unwarranted interference with individual liberty.' "[17]

The four justices dissenting in the Nebbia case insisted that the milk business is "essentially private in its nature" and that the fixing of prices in an ordinary business is beyond legislative power. "Rights shielded yesterday should remain indefeasible today and tomorrow. Certain fundamentals have been set beyond experimentation; the Constitution has released them from control of the state. Again and again this Court has so declared."[18]

Despite the long line of cases which may be cited in support of this position, a declaration that constitutional rights once shielded may never be rendered void will serve as a shock to many social scientists. Adoption of such a public policy would impose a rigidity upon a social order to the extent of making it impossible to meet the changing social and economic needs.

In his dissent, Mr. Justice McReynolds referred to the state control order upon which the case rested as "not merely unwise" but as "arbitrary and unduly oppressive." He questioned that the order would "accomplish the proposed end—increase of prices at the farm." The order was spoken of as taking away the liberty of twelve million consumers to buy a necessity of life in an open market. "It imposes direct and arbitrary burdens upon those already seriously impoverished with the alleged immediate design of affording special benefits to others." It would forbid one from selling the necessities of life at a price he is anxious to take and which buyers are willing

[17] Morris Duane, "Nebbia v. People: A Milestone," *University of Pennsylvania Law Review*, LXXXII, 619. Thus the Nebbia case, while consistent with the *Munn* v. *Illinois* case (1876) and with other cases of that period, it was not in line with the view held by the High Court in the 1920's, notably the Wolff Packing Company case in 1922, as we shall see later in the discussion.

[18] *Nebbia* v. *New York* (minority opinion), 291 U.S. 502, 541, 546 (1934).

to pay. Supplies of milk are plentiful, yet "no child can purchase from a willing storekeeper below the figure appointed by three men at headquarters."[19]

The dissenting opinion rested fundamentally upon a philosophy of abundance in production and consumption and argued against governmentally supported prices at a level above that which would otherwise exist.

Three years after the Nebbia case was decided the United States Supreme Court handed down another five-to-four decision in the Highland Farms case affirming the power of a state to fix resale prices for milk purchased within its borders.[20] Despite the five-to-four verdict in each of these milk cases, and the vigorous dissenting opinion of the minority which commonly has a strong influence in later court decisions, the re-emphasis in the West Coast Hotel case suggests that there should be no reason to expect a reversal from the Nebbia and Highland Farms decisions—at least in the immediate future.

It is to be noted that in the above cases the action centered on the power of the state to fix *resale prices.* Closely related to these cases was one in which the particular point of law involved the power of the Milk Control Board to *fix prices to be paid farmers* for milk to be resold for fluid use. By orders of the New York Milk Control Board the minimum price paid producers was fixed at five cents per quart for Grade B milk, the quality most common in the market. The Hegeman Farms, dealers in this class of milk, challenged the Board's power and purchased milk at prices below those fixed by law.[21] After a notice and hearing, this dealer's license was revoked by the Board to be reinstated only after the Hegeman Farms Company had paid producers the difference between prices actually paid those fixed by the Board. Back pay to producers amounting to some $23,000 was demanded by the Board. The case involved not only canceling the presumed amount owed to producers but also the exemption in the future from the requirement to

---

[19] *Ibid.,* pp. 557–58.

[20] *Highland Farms Dairy, Inc., et al.* v. *J. A. Agnew,* 300 U.S. 608 (1937). This case was appealed from the district court of Virginia.

[21] *Hegeman Farms Corp.* v. *Chas. H. Baldwin and Others,* 293 U.S. 163 (1934).

pay the fixed price. The language of the Court was unmistakable. To quote:

> True the appellant is losing money under the orders now in force. For anything there shown in the bill it was losing money before. For anything there shown other dealers at the same prices may now be earning profits; at all events they are content, or they would be led by self interest to raise the present level. We are unable to infer from these fragmentary data that there has been anything perverse or arbitrary in the action of the Board. To make the selling level higher might be unfair to the consumers; to make the purchasing level lower might bring ruin to producers. . . . . The Fourteenth Amendment does not protect a business against the hazards of competition. . . . . True, of course, it is that the weaker members of the group (the marginal operators or even others above the margin) may find themselves unable to keep pace with the stronger, but it is their comparative inefficiency, not tyrannical compulsion, that makes them laggards in the race.[22]

Thus this case seems to have established the right of the state to fix prices paid producers for milk.

These court decisions, however, clarified only a part of the question of price-fixing—that involving production within the borders of the state in question. Many fluid-milk markets are so located that a portion of their milk comes from other states. This raises the legal question of the power of a state to control prices for milk in interstate commerce. On this point the United States Supreme Court in a unanimous decision ruled that a state may not fix prices of milk coming from beyond its borders. The case at bar was *Seelig v. Baldwin*.[23] Seelig, a distributor selling milk in the city of New York, bought milk and cream in Vermont at prices lower than the minimum established by the New York Milk Control Board. The New York Commissioner of Farms and Markets refused to grant Seelig a license to transact business unless he entered into and conformed to an agreement not to sell within the state of New York milk which had been purchased beyond the borders of the state at prices below those fixed by the commission. Seelig declined to enter into such an agreement or conform to such a regulation. Court proceedings followed which were carried to the high judicial tribunal. The late Mr. Justice Cardozo delivered the opinion of the Court in language of telling finality.

[22] *Ibid.*, pp. 170–71.   [23] *G. A. Seelig, Inc.* v. *Baldwin*, 294 U.S. 511 (1935).

What is ultimate is the principle that one state in its dealings with another may not place itself in a position of economic isolation. Formulas and catchwords are subordinate to this overmastering requirement. Neither the power to tax nor the police power may be used by the state of destination with the aim and effect of establishing an economic barrier against competition with the products of another state or the labor of its residents. Restrictions so contrived are an unreasonable clog upon the mobility of commerce. They set up what is equivalent to a rampart of customs duties designed to neutralize advantages belonging to the place of origin.[24]

The decision of the United States Supreme Court in *Milk Control Board* v. *Eisenberg Co.*, involving the question of interstate commerce, seemingly contradicts the *Seelig* v. *Baldwin* case. In this instance the Court ruled that a state was within its legal right in prescribing minimum prices to be paid by milk dealers to producers even though the milk was shipped to and sold in another state. The fundamental distinction between this case and the *Seelig* v. *Baldwin* case was the importance of the interstate relative to the intrastate commerce.

Although Eisenberg, located in and purchasing his entire milk supply in Pennsylvania, sold all of it in New York, "only a small fraction of the milk produced by farmers in Pennsylvania is shipped out of the commonwealth." Approximately 10 per cent of the milk was apparently sold beyond the borders of the state. Because of the relatively small proportion of the total milk production entering into interstate commerce, such commerce was held to be incidental to that carried on within the borders of the state.

Every state police statute necessarily will affect interstate commerce in some degree, but such a statute does not run counter to the grant of Congressional power merely because it incidentally or indirectly involves or burdens interstate commerce. . . . .

The purpose of the statute under review obviously is to reach a domestic situation in the interest of the welfare of the producers and consumers of milk in Pennsylvania. Its provisions with respect to license, bond, and regulation of prices to be paid to producers are appropriate means to the ends in view. . . . . The Commonwealth does not essay to regulate or to restrain the shipment of the respondent's milk into New York or to regulate its sale or the price at which respondent may sell it in New York. If dealers conducting receiving stations in various localities in Pennsylvania were free to ignore the require-

[24] *Ibid.*, p. 527.

ments of the statute on the ground that all or a part of the milk they purchase is destined to another state the uniform operation of the statute locally would be crippled and might be impracticable.[25]

In the Court decisions discussed above the question did not arise as to whether a state legislature had the power to make a distinction between types of dealers and to fix one minimum price to be charged by one type of dealer and another price by a different type. Two cases involving this feature of price legislation were decided by the same high tribunal on February 10, 1936.[26] The New York Milk Control Act of 1933 and as amended in 1934 provided that dealers selling well-advertised brands of milk should charge one cent more per quart than those selling a similar but an unadvertised brand of milk. The Milk Control Board ruled that four milk dealers, including the Borden Company, should be classed as those selling advertised brands and therefore should be required to charge a cent more than the "independents." Prior to this act a one-cent differential between the two classes of dealers had apparently existed to such an extent that it was looked upon as more or less common practice. The purported reason for establishing this differential was (1) "the preservation of competitive opportunities among the dealers" and (2) the prevention of monopoly on the part of a few large distributors. The majority opinion (five to four) of the Supreme Court stated:

We hold that the fixing of the differential in favor of the sellers of milk not having a well-advertised trade name, in the situation exhibited by the findings, does not deny the appellant equal protection.[27] . . . . There was a plain reason for the classification. It was not merely that appellant had established good will; it was that there had resulted a balance between the advantage and the resulting disadvantage of the unadvertised dealers—a balance maintained by a price differential. To attempt the maintenance of that balance was to strive for equality of treatment, equality of burden, not to create inequality.[28]

On the day the above verdict was rendered another related case was also decided, known as *Mayflower* v. *Ten Eyck*. As stated above,

[25] *Milk Board* v. *Eisenberg Co.* (preliminary print), Vol. 306 U.S., No. 2, *Official Reports of the Supreme Court*, pp. 346, 351–53 (1939).

[26] *Borden's Farm Products Co., Inc.* v. *Ten Eyck*, 297 U.S. 251 (1936), and *Mayflower Farms, Inc.* v. *Ten Eyck*, 297 U.S. 266 (1936).

[27] *Borden's Co.* v. *Ten Eyck*, 257 U.S. 251 (1936).   [28] *Ibid.*, p. 262.

the New York milk control law as amended effective April 1, 1934, provided that dealers selling unadvertised brands who were in the market prior to a certain date (April 10, 1933) were permitted to sell milk at one cent per quart below the price fixed for dealers selling advertised brands. Paradoxically, the same law provided that dealers entering the market after that date would be denied the one-cent differential privilege. The Court held the latter discrimination to be arbitrary, unreasonable, and a violation of the equal-protection clause of the Fourteenth Amendment.

The Court pointed out that "one coming fresh into the field would not possess such a brand and clearly could not meet the competition of those having an established trade name and good will, unless he were allowed the same differential as others in his class. By denying him this advantage the law effectually barred him from the business."[29]

Clearly, the problem before the New York Legislature in providing for a price differential between established distributors and independents was that of passing an act and formulating a price structure which would bring about equality between two groups— those who sold well-advertised brands and independents whose product was not advertised. The Court took the position:

> In the light of the facts found the legislature might reasonably have thought trade conditions existed justifying the fixing of a differential. Judicial inquiry does not concern itself with the accuracy of the legislative finding, but only with the question whether it so lacks any reasonable basis as to be arbitrary.[30]

The facts before the Court in this case were such that a one-cent differential was found not to be arbitrary or discriminatory. According to the Court that difference, between the amount charged per quart by those distributors selling advertised brands and those selling unadvertised milk, brought about an economic balance between the two types of dealers. Suppose, however, that another act should be passed by the same or another state and that the legislature or the administrative board had fixed a two-cent differential (or any

---

[29] *Mayflower* v. *Ten Eyck*, 297 U.S. 266, 273 (1936).

[30] *Borden's Co.* v. *Ten Eyck*, 257 U.S. 251, 263 (1936).

other amount) between the two types of dealers, would that have been adjudged by the Court as arbitrary?[31]

The larger the price differential between the two groups of dealers, the greater would be the opportunity of those who sell unadvertised brands to build up their business at the expense of the purveyors of well-advertised products. Moreover, since new distributors are permitted to enter the market with the privilege of a like differential, then the dealers handling advertised brands would suffer loss of volume of sale at the hands of both. This loss of business would increase their unit cost of distribution because of (1) increased overhead or fixed cost in proportion to volume—and value—of sales and (2) greater distance of travel per unit of product disposed of on resale routes and with the consequent increased unit cost of delivery.

The effect of the two decisions was thus to encourage an increase of an already extremely competitive condition with its resultant waste of duplication rather than to discourage it. True, emphasis was placed upon the fact that the then existing regulation of prices was intended by the statutes to be of a temporary nature only; hence the Court believed the aim should be to return the milk business to a competitive condition similar to that which existed prior to the event of the price-control measures set up in 1933–34. Nevertheless, it would seem that the two decisions tend to bring added confusion into an already bad situation. Such differential price privileges not only encourage new distributors to enter the market, thus tending to aggravate an already inefficient system of milk distribution, but will also encourage companies who regularly sell advertised brands to form subsidiaries (independents) which may take advantage of this price differential as a means of obtaining new business.

Among the greatest hazards of any business is the loss of volume of sale in an industry where capital equipment and cost of operation are relatively fixed, as they are in milk distribution. A policy whereby some distributors are compelled by law to charge prices above those of their competitors, thereby virtually stopping the former

[31] It is recognized, of course, that an important reason for the Court's decision of the one-cent differential as not being arbitrary was due to the fact that such a differential had existed between the classes of dealers before the time of the Control Act, and apparently had become a more or less established part of the price structure of the market.

from obtaining new business or even holding the established business, strikes one as a sanction of a type of legislation which will result in, or actually force, inefficiencies in the market structure and discourage business enterprise from seeking to create good will for its product or to build up a favorable reputation with its customers. Such a court decision may have in it a grain of justification supporting temporary legislation, but, in the long run, effects are likely to be more harmful than helpful. A market structure such as was sanctioned by this court action may decrease the tendency toward monopoly, but it will also, with just as much certainty, decrease the possibilities of efficiency of distribution.

FEDERAL PRICE-FIXING IN INTERSTATE COMMERCE

The cases so far mentioned involved the power of the state to regulate prices. More recently (June, 1939), two companion cases involving the power of the federal government to fix milk prices were decided by the United States Supreme Court.

Under the authority and following the provisions of the Federal Agricultural Marketing Agreement Act of 1937 the Secretary of Agriculture entered into milk-marketing agreements with milk producers and others engaged in handling milk, or issued milk-marketing orders in various milk markets of the United States. Controversy arose over the validity of the orders in the New York and Boston milk-marketing areas, and appeals were made through the courts. The cases reached the United States Supreme Court and were decided June 5, 1939.[32]

Issues other than the specific question of the power of the federal government to fix minimum prices were also involved, namely, unconstitutional discrimination because of (1) exemption of producer co-operatives from the payment of uniform price required of proprietary handlers; (2) limiting minimum prices to that milk "sold in the marketing area or which passes through a plant in the marketing area"; (3) provision of price differentials between territories located favorably and unfavorably to the market area; (4) the validity of the referendum; and (5) the violation of the order.

[32] *United States* v. *Royal Cooperative, Inc., et al., Supreme Court Reporter,* LIX, No. 15 (June 15, 1939), 993; *H. P. Hood and Sons, Inc., et al.* v. *United States et al., ibid.,* p. 1019.

These, however, may be said to be secondary to the more fundamental question of the power of the federal government to fix minimum producer prices for milk entering into interstate commerce.
On this question the Court ruled that "where commodities are
bought for use beyond state lines, the sale is part of interstate
commerce."[33]

This power over commerce when it exists is complete and perfect. It has
been exercised to fix a wage scale for a limited period, railroad tariffs and fees
and charges for live-stock exchanges. The authority of the Federal government
over interstate commerce does not differ in extent or character from that retained by the states over intrastate commerce. . . . . . Recently, upon a re-exami-
nation of the grounds of state power over prices, that power was phrased by
this Court to mean that "upon proper occasion and by appropriate measures
the state may regulate a business in any of its aspects, including the prices to
be charged for the products or commodities it sells."[34]

REGULATION OF LEGALIZED MONOPOLY

Up to the present time all the legislative acts passed concerning
milk-price regulation and the litigation which followed as a result
of the challenge of their legality involved only the power of the state
to fix prices under a condition in which competition was fostered.
None of the cases involved the question of monopoly. So far as is
known to the writer no state legislative acts have been passed and
set into operation which were designed to make milk a public utility
in the ordinary meaning of the term—that is, where one company,
or a very small number, was granted exclusive license or franchise
to perform all the services in the market.

Assuming that in the future the United States Supreme Court
does not reverse the position held in the court cases cited above, will
these cases serve as a basis to settle the question as to whether the
business of processing and distributing milk may be operated as a
public utility under an exclusive license or franchise? Since the
legality of a controlled monopoly was not at issue, we will need to
go beyond these cases for the necessary information. Perhaps a
brief outline of the historical events in the larger field of regulation
as it has manifested itself primarily in the field of the more typical

[33] *United States* v. *Royal Cooperative, op. cit.*, pp. 993, 1010.

[34] *Ibid.*, p. 1011 (phrase from the Nebbia case).

public utilities will assist us in an attempt to foretell the position courts may take. Unfortunately, there is no single index by which one can distinguish between a private and a public calling. The courts have consistently avoided laying down a blanket test by which one may judge whether a particular business would be classed as one or the other.

The American public seems always to have had confidence that the force of competition would bring about a supply of commodities and services at reasonable prices and rates. It was assumed that the "natural law of supply and demand" could be depended upon to protect the public welfare. Formerly this faith in competition existed not only in the case of those businesses which were distinctly private in their nature and which were operated as small business units, but until about the beginning of the present century it appeared as well in the operation of those businesses which have since been set up and operated as regulated monopolies—public utilities under legislative grants. As an example, for a considerable period of years after electric light and the gas used for heating and lighting purposes were in common use, the public continued to foster competition among several companies operating in one city. In 1887, for instance, New York City granted franchises to six electric-light companies to operate at the same time. Indeed, the granting of franchises to operate competing utility companies was a common practice everywhere. Competition in this latter group of businesses with its duplication of capital and effort proved, however, to be wasteful and expensive. If competitive forces did eliminate all but the most efficient company—or the one which for other reasons was able to outlive the rest in a struggle for existence—the result was an unregulated or at best an improperly regulated monopoly. "Experience convinced nearly every community, sooner or later, that the beneficent results usually attributed to competition were not being realized."[35] The fact finally became obvious that better services could be obtained through a system of monopolies regulated by the public for the common benefit.

If a state passed legislation declaring the business of processing

[35] Eliot Jones and Truman Bigham, *Principles of Public Utilities* (New York, 1931), p. 68; see also pp. 14 and 57.

and distributing milk to be a public utility and then imposed the appropriate control measures, what would be the legal issues involved and what would be the likelihood that the courts would hold such legislation to be within the proper exercise of the police power of the state? In an attempt to foretell what position the courts may take, it will be necessary to reason almost entirely by analogy. Accordingly, care must be exercised to avoid erroneous conclusions since there is no way of knowing the conditions under which the litigation will come before the courts or the factual materials which will be contained in the briefs and records.

The Sherman Anti-trust Act, passed July 2, 1890, was designed with a view to breaking down certain monopolies which had developed because of the economic and social conditions favoring them. They were usually the result of a combination of several competing businesses into one giant monopoly, either entirely unregulated or inadequately regulated from the public point of view.

For example, prior to the passage of the Sherman Act, the American Tobacco Company and the Standard Oil Company of New Jersey were almost complete monopolies. "By order of the courts, the American Tobacco Company was divided into four large competing concerns."[36] The oil company was ordered broken down in a similar manner. Albeit sections 1 and 2 of the Sherman Anti-trust Act make the restraint of trade and monopoly, respectively, illegal, it was not intended to destroy monopolies created by legislative grants. This fact was settled in a circuit court case in which the court emphasized:

In construing the federal and state statutes, we exclude from consideration all monopolies which exist by legislative grant; for we think the word "monopolize" cannot be intended to be used with reference to the acquisition of exclusive rights under government concession, but that the law-maker has used the word to mean "to aggregate" or "concentrate" in the hands of a few, practically and, as a matter of fact, according to the known results of human action to the exclusion of others; to accomplish this end by what, in popular language, is expressed in the word "pooling," which may be defined to be an aggregation of property or capital belonging to different persons, with a view to common liabilities and profits.[37]

[36] Sumner H. Slichter, *Modern Economic Society* (New York, 1931), p. 359.

[37] *American Biscuit and Manufacturing Co.* v. *Klotz*, 44 Fed. 721, 724 (1891).

From this it follows that the distribution of milk by a company which had gained monopoly control of a market through a normal trend of business, by forcing its competitors to the wall or by buying them out, could legally be broken down into competing units in accordance with the provisions of the Sherman Act. But if that same company had been granted a monopoly through legislative action, its operation would be legally permitted under the act.[38]

Leaving out of consideration for the moment the question of municipal or city ownership of the milk-distributing business, the question concerning the legality of public utility control—a controlled monopoly—will turn mainly on one of two considerations: (1) Will the United States Supreme Court rule that the business of processing and distributing milk is so distinctly a private competitive business—a common calling—that it cannot constitutionally be subjected to the complete public regulation generally imposed over the typical public utilities? or (2) will it hold as it has in the more recent cases that there is no closed class or category of business "affected with a public interest"?

In a modern economy, especially as it manifests itself in the complex relationships of industry and trade, can businesses by their nature be classified into those which are strictly private and those which are sufficiently clothed with a public interest to require substantially complete social and economic regulation? It is obvious that any attempt at such classification into clear-cut categories would place courts in an extremely untenable position sooner or later. In the Nebbia case for the first time the Supreme Court took the position that rigid categories of this nature cannot be so established. Such a position would seem to fit much more closely the everyday business conditions in a complex society than would the other point of view. Hence, there seems good reason to believe that this position will prevail in court decisions involving future issues of public regulation. One should, however, not be too certain in his prediction because decisions sometimes emanate from the United States Supreme Court which are puzzling to the laity and to the economists as well.

[38] Actually the company is granted an exclusive franchise by the city or municipality. The right of granting this monopoly is conferred upon these units of government by the state.

In a case somewhat analogous to those which might test the validity of milk as a public utility, the United States Supreme Court did not uphold such control. In 1925 the Oklahoma legislature declared the manufacture of ice for sale and distribution to be a "public business," or public utility. Powers of regulation similar to those customarily exercised over public utilities were conferred upon the State Corporation Commission.[39] For a period of five years the act remained unchallenged, and there was little competition in the ice industry in that state. One-third of the ice plants were owned and operated by public service corporations which conducted the ice business in connection with their public utility business.

Under the provisions of the act, before obtaining a license to operate, an applicant was required to show a public necessity for a new company entering into the manufacture and sale of ice in the community in which he proposed to operate. The legal procedure called for a hearing held by the Corporation Commission, the state body in charge, for the purpose of receiving applications and hearing the testimony of prospective ice distributors and others concerned. If, at the close of the hearing, the Commission decided that the public needs were already being served adequately, it could deny the applicant a license.

In spite of the law a Mr. Liebmann had engaged in the ice business without obtaining a license. A competitor, the New State Ice Company, which had been engaged in manufacturing and selling ice under a license, brought suit against Liebmann for operating without the required license.

Liebmann contended that the business of manufacturing ice for sale was not a public business but instead a private business and a common calling, and the right to engage in a common calling is one of the fundamental liberties guaranteed by the due-process clause. To make the right to engage in a common calling dependent upon the finding of a public necessity deprived him of liberty and property in violation of the Fourteenth Amendment.

The case reached the United States Supreme Court, which declared the Oklahoma law unconstitutional and ruled that "all businesses are subject to some measure of public regulation . . . . but the

[39] *Oklahoma Session Laws, 1925*, c. 147.

question here is whether the business is so charged with a public use as to justify the particular restriction above stated."[40] On the most salient point of the case the court spoke with positiveness:

> Here we are dealing with an ordinary business, not with a paramount industry upon which the prosperity of the entire state in a large measure depends. It is a business as essentially private in its nature as the businesses of the grocer, the dairyman, the butcher, the baker, the shoemaker, or the tailor, each of whom performs a service which, to a greater or lesser extent, the community is dependent upon and is interested in having maintained; but which bears no such relation to the public as to warrant its inclusion in the category of businesses charged with a public use. . . . .[41]

> There is nothing in the product that we can perceive on which to rest a distinction, in respect to this attempted control, from other products in common use which enter into free competition, subject, of course, to reasonable regulations prescribed for the protection of the public and applied with appropriate impartiality.[42]

One who reads only the above majority opinion in that case is rather impressed by the finality of the language of the court, but he will be equally impressed by the vigorous and heavily documented dissenting opinion written by Mr. Justice Brandeis and concurred in by Mr. Justice Stone. This minority opinion seems to have carried much weight in decisions on subsequent cases involving public regulation.

Mr. Brandeis' most telling argument was directed to the point that the power to determine how far public regulation should be extended into the various fields of business enterprise should be left to the discretion of the legislature.

> Whether the local conditions are such as to justify converting a private business into a public one is a matter primarily for the determination of the state legislature. Its determination is subject to judicial review; but the usual presumption of validity attends the enactment. . . . . [43]

> In my opinion, the true principle is that the State's power extends to every regulation of any business reasonably required and appropriate for the public protection. . . . . Moreover, the Constitution does not require that every calling

[40] *New State Ice Company* v. *Liebmann*, 285 U.S. 262, 273 (1932).

[41] *Ibid.*, p. 277.

[42] *Ibid.*, p. 279.

[43] *New State Ice Company* v. *Liebmann* (minority opinion), 285 U.S. 262, 284 (1932).

which has been common shall ever remain so. The liberty to engage in a common calling, like other liberties, may be limited to the exercise of the police power.[44]

He went on to show that in the past businesses which had been common callings have later been declared public businesses by legislatures.

The general import of the minority opinion of Brandeis in 1932 became the majority opinion in the Nebbia case four years later. In fact, in the latter case the Court was even more sweeping in its language, saying: "So far as the requirement of due process is concerned, and in the absence of other constitutional restriction, *a state is free to adopt whatever policy may reasonably be deemed to promote public welfare and to enforce that policy by legislation adopted for its purpose.*"[45]

If this edict of the United States Supreme Court is to be interpreted literally, what constitutional limitation would estop a state— or a municipality which is a "department of a state"—from adopting a unified system of distributing fluid milk, either municipally owned or privately owned but municipally controlled? It would require no undue strain on the imagination to see that increased milk consumption resulting from lower consumer prices, possible under a unified system of distribution, would contribute to the health and vigor of the race.

Several United States Supreme Court cases, one dating back more than sixty years, have helped lay the foundation which is still serving as a guide to the courts in determining the basis for public regulation. Three of these cases—*Munn* v. *Illinois*, the Wolff Packing Company case, and the West Coast Hotel case—will be summarized briefly. (The Nebbia case has already been discussed.) First, the Munn case.

In 1870 the state of Illinois passed legislation declaring all grain elevators and storehouses where grain is stored for compensation to be public warehouses. It was also required that persons operating such businesses must procure a license from the proper state authorities and submit to regulation of rates to be charged for storage.

[44] *Ibid.*, pp. 302–3.

[45] *Nebbia* v. *New York*, 291 U.S. 502, 537 (1934). (Italics mine.)

Munn and Scott, managers of a type of warehouse falling under the above designation, violated the law by operating without a license. They were drawn into court, the litigation being carried to the United States Supreme Court and decided in 1876. The Court (seven to two) upheld the regulation as being a proper exercise of the police power of the state. Here the basic question at bar was apparently not that of the power of the state to require a license to operate; that power seems to have been assumed. The issue was rather whether the limitation upon the legislative power of the state as imposed by the Constitution of the United States was such as to release from the state the right to fix maximum charges for the storage of grain. Mr. Chief Justice Waite pointed out that the very essence of government suggests

the power to govern men and things.[46] . . . . Every statute is presumed to be constitutional. The courts ought not to declare one to be unconstitutional, unless it is clearly so. If there is doubt, the expressed will of the legislature should be sustained.[47]

The concept "affected with a public interest" was the structural foundation upon which the Court rested this case and many others involving the power of a state to regulate business. To quote:

Property does become clothed with a public interest when used in a manner to make it of public consequence, and affect the community at large. When, therefore, one devotes his property to a use in which the public has an interest, he, in effect, grants to the public an interest in that use, and must submit to be controlled by the public for the common good, to the extent of the interest he has thus created. He may withdraw his grant by discontinuing the use; but, so long as he maintains the use, he must submit to the control.[48]

This concept of businesses being divided into two categories—public and private—was discarded in the Nebbia case, as already mentioned. The Court apparently recognized that, as society increases in complexity, clear-cut division into these categories becomes more and more unworkable in practice and, accordingly, more and more unsatisfactory as a legalistic classification.

In attempting to draw an analogy between the Munn case and the power of the state to make milk a public utility, it should

[46] *Munn* v. *Illinois*, 94 U.S. 113, 125 (1876).

[47] *Ibid.*, p. 123.   [48] *Ibid.*, p. 126.

be recalled that in the Munn case the Court placed some emphasis upon the existence of a "virtual monopoly" in the elevator business under consideration. This monopoly was not granted by legislature or regulated by the state for the common benefit and hence should not be confused with a monopoly existing through legislative grant. The latter type of monopoly is in no way repugnant to the Constitution, since its purpose is to serve the public better than it can be served through a competitive system. Under the circumstances which existed in the Munn case the Court found:

Under such circumstances it is difficult to see why, if the common carrier, or the miller, or the ferryman, or the innkeeper, or the wharfinger, or the baker, or the cartman, or the hackney-coachman, pursues a public employment and exercises "a sort of public office," these plaintiffs in error do not. They stand, to use the language of their counsel, in the "very gateway of commerce," and take toll from all who pass. Their business most certainly "tends to a common charge, and is become a thing of public interest and use."[49]

Two justices presented a long and emphatic dissent, holding that powers as contemplated according to the act were clearly beyond the exercise of legislative authority.

In the second case, the Wolff Packing Company case—as in the New State Ice Company case previously mentioned—the court denied the right of control which was specified in the legislative enactment. The Kansas legislature passed an act in 1920[50] declaring the following enterprises to be affected with a public interest:

First, manufacture and preparation of food for human consumption; second, manufacture of clothing for human wear; third, production of any substance in common use for fuel; fourth, transportation of the foregoing; fifth, public utilities and common carriers.[51]

The legislation was challenged, and the case carried to the high tribunal.

At the outset the Court classified those businesses clothed with a public interest and over which there may be imposed regulation of varying degrees of completeness, namely: (1) Those occupations recognized from earliest times as being exceptional in that a public interest was attached to them. Included in these occupations are inns, cabs, grist mills, etc., which were regulated by colonial legisla-

[49] *Ibid.*, pp. 131 and 132.

[50] *Kansas Laws of 1920, Special Session*, c. 29.   [51] *Ibid.*

tures. (2) Those occupations which operate under authority of a public grant giving them special privileges and requiring, in turn, that they render service requested by any member of the public. These include the common carriers and our more typical public utilities. (3) Those businesses which have developed such a peculiar relationship to society that, from the public point of view, regulation of them has become desirable or necessary. The last group is more distinctly a product of our complex society than are those in Classes 1 and 2. In this group would be included the regulation of hours and wages; health and sanitary regulations; regulation of monopolies including those involving regulation of margins to be charged by commission companies and brokers; the present type of regulation of fluid-milk prices; and a host of others.[52]

Here again the Court mentioned:

That the mere declaration by a legislature that a business is affected with a public interest is not conclusive of the question whether its attempted regulation on that ground is justified. . . . . In a sense, the public is concerned about all lawful business because it contributes to the prosperity and well being of the people. The public may suffer from high prices or strikes in many trades, but the expression "clothed with a public interest," as applied to business, means more than that the public welfare is affected by continuity or by the price at which a commodity is sold or a service rendered.[53]

The sharp contrast between the language of the majority opinion in the Wolff Packing Company case and that of the Nebbia case twelve years later is at first glance so decided that a reader is inclined to ask what was responsible for the change in the philosophy of the Court. (However, one must recognize that, whereas the point of view of the Court may have changed, the import of the two acts was in equally sharp contrast.) The decision in the Wolff Packing Company case turned largely on legalistic interpretation, the concept of public welfare being relegated to the background. In the Nebbia case the relative importance given to the two concepts was reversed. The Court in the Wolff Packing Company case made the historical observation:

It has never been supposed, since the adoption of the Constitution, that the business of the butcher, or the baker, the tailor, the wood chopper, the mining

52 Cf. *Wolff Packing Co.* v. *Industrial Court*, 262 U.S. 522, 535 (1922).
53 *Ibid.*, p. 536.

operator or the miner was clothed with such public interest that the price of his product or his wages could be fixed by State regulation. It is true that in the days of the early common law an omnipotent Parliament did regulate prices and wages as it chose, and occasionally a Colonial legislature sought to exercise the same power; but nowadays one does not devote one's property or business to the public use or clothe it with a public interest merely because one makes commodities for, and sells to, the public in common callings of which those above mentioned are instances. . . . .[54]

If, as, in effect, contended by counsel for the State, the common callings are clothed with a public interest by a mere legislative declaration, which necessarily authorizes full and comprehensive regulation within legislative discretion, there must be a revolution in the relation of government to general business. This will be running the public interest into the ground, to use a phrase of Mr. Justice Bradley when characterizing a similarly extreme contention (Civil Rights Cases, 109 U.S. 3, 24). It will be impossible to reconcile such results with the freedom of contract and of labor secured by the Fourteenth Amendment.[55]

Among recent cases the statement of the United States Supreme Court in the West Coast Hotel case (1936) is highly significant. The Court reiterated the position it had taken in the Nebbia case two years earlier, calling attention to the fact that

the general subject of the regulation of the use of private property and of the making of private contracts received an exhaustive examination [in the Nebbia case], and we again declared that if such laws "have a reasonable relation to a proper legislative purpose and are neither arbitrary nor discriminatory, the requirements of due process are satisfied"; that "with the wisdom of the policy adopted with the adequacy or practicability of the law enacted to forward it, the courts are both incompetent and unauthorized to deal"; that "times without number we have said that the Legislature is primarily the judge of the necessity of such an enactment, that every possible presumption is in favor of its validity, and that though the court may hold views inconsistent with the wisdom of the law, it may not be annulled unless palpably in excess of legislative power."[56]

[54] *Ibid.*, p. 537.

[55] *Ibid.*, p. 539; see also Charles Bunn, "Public Price Fixing and Due Process," *Annals of the American Academy of Political and Social Science*, January, 1938, Supplement, p. 46.

[56] *West Coast Hotel Co.* v. *Parrish*, 300 U.S. 379, 398 (1936). For a discussion on the Federal Agricultural Marketing Agreement Act, especially as it effects milk regulation, see *New York University Law Quarterly Review*, Vol. XVII, No. 1 (November, 1939). Also see an interesting article, "Recent Trends in Public Utility Control," *American Economic Review*, Vol. XXIX, No. 4 (December, 1939).

In deciding this case, the Court relied mainly upon the Munn case of sixty years standing.[57]

Neither the Nebbia case nor the West Coast Hotel case was decided on the basis of an existing economic emergency requiring temporary legislation. The decisions rested, instead, largely upon the principle of public purpose and public welfare. As long as the existing philosophy of the Court toward public regulation continues, these two cases will have a profound influence in future Court decisions concerning the right of the state to enact and carry out legislation involving "public regulation for the common good."

When and if a case comes before the United States Supreme Court involving the regulation of milk under public utility control, including the exclusive-franchise feature, the question of the legality of the franchise will probably turn on the degree of public interest involved. Specifically, in the opinion of the Court will the fostering of competition or of monopoly best promote the public welfare? On the basis of recent decisions the likelihood would seem strong that the present personnel of the United States Supreme Court would sanction regulation under a legislatively created monopoly. For example, in the West Coast Hotel case (1936) the Court was clear in its position:

> There is no absolute freedom to do as one wills or to contract as one chooses. . . . . Liberty implies the absence of arbitrary restraint, not immunity from reasonable regulations and prohibitions imposed in the interest of the community. . . . .[58]
> But the liberty safeguarded is liberty in a social organization which requires the protection of law against the evils which menace the health, safety, morals, and welfare of the people.[59]

On the basis of the position taken in the above case, and others adhering to the same philosophy in which the public welfare received major emphasis, the Court could logically rule that the law governing the distribution of milk as a public utility would also turn on the question of public welfare. Accordingly, if it can be shown that excessive waste inherent in the existing competitive system redounds to the public disadvantage, the economic outcome

[57] *Munn* v. *Illinois*, 94 U.S. 113 (1876).

[58] *West Coast Hotel Co.* v. *Parrish*, 300 U.S. 379, 392 (1936).   [59] *Ibid.*, p. 391.

is similar to that which would prevail if a virtual monopoly existed. Either is contrary to the public interest. From a purely economic point of view it matters little whether the high price paid by milk consumers, in relation to that received by those who produce that same milk, is the result of unduly wasteful competitive methods of distribution or of unduly large monopoly profits. May there not be the same justification to protect the public against competitive waste as against monopoly profits? The courts have concerned themselves with the latter but have not been required to give major attention on questions involving competitive waste. Summarily, assuming the legality will turn on the question of public welfare, then the issue will become primarily one as to the possible economic saving of public utility operation.

In several United States Supreme Court cases reference was made to the idea of monopoly, but in none of the cases does a direct distinction appear to have been made between regulation permitting an exclusive franchise and a provision for a license to operate with no specified number of businesses permitted in an area. In the New State Ice Company case, for example, reference was made to the condition of monopoly, though the case cannot be said to have turned on that point. It does, however, give sufficient warning that a proposal to limit the number of concerns permitted to enter a field in the so-called common callings may encounter serious objections by the courts. To be sure, regulation, with or without the exclusive franchise, comprises the license feature which, on the face of it, presumably involves the power of the regulatory body to decline the granting of a license to a prospective operator or to revoke the license from an actual operator in event of violation of the provisions set down by the legislative act.

If the distinction between operation under regulated competition and regulated monopoly involves form or method of operation rather than legal principle, then, since the first method of regulation is not repugnant to the Constitution, on the basis of the Nebbia and the West Coast Hotel cases, the legality of a regulated monopoly could be logically defended as coming within the same rule. There would seem to be no difference in the fundamental principle involved in the two.

In the legislative acts of the states which the writer reviewed, a license was required of all milk distributors in the field, although the intent of the acts seems not to have been a limitation of distributors to any particular number. There was, however, nothing which the writer was able to interpret to the effect that licenses must be granted to all who applied.

Provisions for the revoking of licenses may vary with the method of control and the language of the act, but some provision for the revocation in the case of noncompliance is in reality the heart of the purpose of this kind of license feature.

INTERPRETATION OF THE CONSTITUTION BY THE COURTS

Two overmastering bases of interpretation, or measuring sticks, have guided the United States Supreme Court in arriving at its decisions in cases involving public regulation to be imposed upon business, industry, and trade: (1) a purely literal, legalistic interpretation of the Constitution in which the Court has relied rather heavily upon former cases in support of the conclusion and (2) a less literal interpretation with greater emphasis upon the concept of public purpose and public welfare, the assumption being that the writers of the Constitution intended it to be an instrument under which society would be permitted to meet gradual or violent social and economic adjustments.

Under the first interpretation, the Constitution and amendments are assumed to be documents fixed and unchangeable; under the second, a living instrument. The assumption of a judicial fixity in a dynamic social order, when carried to its logical end, will eventually be all but sure to lead to economic chaos. If the Constitution is to be so interpreted that a society is estopped from adjusting itself to conditions arising out of the increasing social and economic complexities, then by the same process a democracy may fix itself in a judicial strait jacket which will sooner or later lead to governmental strangulation.

This should, however, not be construed as a defense of judicial sanction of all new and experimental legislation. Legislation always carries with it the dangers of being entirely ill conceived, economically unwise, or poorly adapted to meet existing conditions. To the extent that this is so it will bring about maladjustment and discontent among individuals and among social and economic groups. Add to this the resistance on the part of some who are adversely affected by legislation involving control and by others who continue to cling to the idea that they have an inherent right to unqualified freedom of action, then one may appreciate the shortcomings attached to a philosophy whereby the judiciary takes the unequivocal position that "a state is free to adopt whatever policy may reasonably be deemed to promote public welfare and to enforce that policy by legislation adapted to its purpose."[60] Although rigid fixity of government may prove unworkable, a certain stability and continuity of public purpose would seem essential. From the standpoint of public policy and public welfare, even the courts may waver too far toward one extreme of a static state or toward the other of ratifying every legislative whim that may appeal to the fancy of legislators.

Speaking generally, there can be but little doubt that the realist will be more favorably impressed with the concept of the Constitution as a living document than with that of a historical conceptualistic monument.[61] In one of his dissenting opinions, Mr. Justice Brandeis suggested:

There must be power in the states and the nation to remould, through experimentation, our economic practices and institutions to meet changing social and economic needs. I cannot believe that the framers of the Fourteenth Amendment, or the states which ratified it, intended to deprive us of the power to correct the evils of technological unemployment and excess productive capacity which have attended progress in the useful arts.[62]

Charles A. Beard founded his argument upon the following proposition:

Since most of the words and phrases dealing with the powers and the limits of government are vague and must in practice be interpreted by human beings, it follows that the Constitution as practice is a living thing. . . . . From the records of history we can get some idea of past practices under the instrument. But what the Constitution as practice is today is what citizens, judges, ad-

---

[60] *Nebbia* v. *New York*, 291 U.S. 502, 536 (1934).

[61] See Thomas P. Hartman, "Public Utilities—a Quest for a Concept," *West Virginia Law Quarterly*, XXXVII, 250, and references there cited.

[62] *New State Ice Co.* v. *Liebmann* (minority opinion), 285 U.S. 262, 311 (1932).

ministrators, law makers, and those concerned with the execution of the laws, do in bringing about changes in the relations of persons and property in the United States or in preserving existing relations. The Constitution as practice is thus the contemporary thought and action of citizens and authorities operating under it.[63]

Continuing, Beard stresses the fact that "surely no one means by the term 'Constitution' merely the engrossed copy—the original parchment deposited in the National archives in Washington."[64]

The late Mr. Justice Cardozo in speaking of fundamental judicial conceptions and justice calls attention to the conflicting principles with which courts are faced.

One principle or precedent, pushed to the limit in its logic, may point to one conclusion; another principle or precedent, followed with like logic, may point with equal certainty to another. In this conflict, we must choose between two paths, selecting one or other, or perhaps striking out upon a third, which will be the resultant of two forces in combination, or will represent the mean between extremes.[65]

Referring to a particular case, Cardozo summarized his philosophy by saying, "In the end, the principle that was thought to be most fundamental, to represent the larger and deeper social interest, put its competitors to flight. I am not greatly concerned about the particular formula through which justice was attained."[66] In his opinion a purely legalistic interpretation of the Constitution as it applied to everyday problems was virtually impossible. "There is," he said, "in each of us a stream of tendency, whether we choose to call it philosophy or not, which gives coherence and direction to thought and action. Judges cannot escape that current any more than other mortals."[67]

All historians, jurists, and philosophers by no means concur in this point of view. Charles Beard, in the above article, pointedly emphasizes the popularity of the opposite point of view:

It seems absurd to have to mention the fact. Yet there is a deep-rooted tradition in the United States to the effect that the Constitution, from the

[63] Charles A. Beard, "The Living Constitution," *Annals of the American Academy of Political and Social Science*, May, 1936, p. 31.

[64] *Ibid.*

[65] Benjamin N. Cardozo, *The Nature of the Judicial Process* (New Haven: Yale University Press, 1937), p. 40.

[66] *Ibid.*, p. 42.   [67] *Ibid.*, p. 12.

Preamble to the last word of the latest amendment, is so clear, positive, and unequivocal that even the wayfaring man cannot err in understanding and expounding its command. "Great constitutional lawyers," eminent politicians, leaders of the bar, columnists, editors, and thousands who ought to know better talk that way. They claim to "know" the Constitution. They can tell us just "what it is." They can give the "right" interpretation, and disclose with infallibility just wherein any opposing interpretation is "wrong."[68]

So run the arguments. On these issues references presenting various points of view could be cited without end, but the above are perhaps sufficient to set forth the general idea of the conflict of opinion.[69]

The discussion to this point suggests that probably a more accurate prediction could be made by knowing the members of the Court than by knowing in detail all the history of similar Court decisions. In the words of Mr. Chief Justice Hughes prior to his appointment to the Supreme bench, "We are under a Constitution, but the Constitution is what the judges say it is."[70]

Although the courts can find both legal precedence and logic for supporting legislation which would make milk a public utility operated as a unified system under an exclusive franchise, they will not be unmindful of the practical limitations and difficulties of this type of control and of the repercussions of legal sanction of such legislation. For example, producers' co-operative groups and producers individually have generally taken the position that milk distribution operated as a public utility would redound to their disadvantage because of a loss of bargaining position. Accordingly, they can be expected to exercise all possible influence against this method of distribution. Many producer-distributors will insist upon their constitutional right to sell the product of their toil in a free and open market. Even though consumers have an opportunity for real gains through unification, many of them will resent a requirement that they purchase exclusively through a legislatively created monopoly.

[68] *Op. cit.*, p. 30.

[69] The reader is referred to a lengthy bibliography entitled "The Constitution of the United States," in *Annals of the American Academy of Political and Social Science,* May, 1936, p. 190.

[70] Edwin S. Corwin, *The Twilight of the Supreme Court* (New Haven: Yale University Press, 1934), p. 181; see also Charles Evans Hughes, *Addresses* (New York, 1908), p. 139.

Especially in the smaller towns and cities they would insist upon their right to deal with individual distributors in obtaining their milk supply.

Those associated with the existing milk-distributing system, including organized labor, can naturally be expected to exert all their individual and organized effort against a new and different system. And who would blame them? The competitive form of business activity is pretty firmly rooted in the American philosophy. That philosophy permeates the courts as well as the American public and will have a decided influence upon the action of the courts in rendering their decision as to the legality of such legislation.

To summarize the legal phases, so far the United States Supreme Court has not ruled upon the legality of a type of control in the milk business involving the exclusive-franchise feature, although such rulings have been made in the accepted public utility field. Court decisions to which one must look for precedence are not such as will provide a dependable indication of what position the United States Supreme Court may take regarding the exclusive-franchise feature of control of milk distribution. Nevertheless, there would seem to be sufficient legal precedence for the position that the legislatures have power either to grant an exclusive franchise to a private corporation for processing and distributing milk or to delegate to the city or municipality the power to perform the function through municipal ownership. The outcome of the decision will depend largely upon the particular case brought before the Supreme Court and upon the philosophy of the majority of the Court at the time the case appears for decision. In the final analysis the outcome will doubtless turn mainly upon the question of whether the costs of inherent competitive wastes are serious enough so that in the opinion of the United States Supreme Court the public welfare of the people in a city will be improved through control and unification of the milk distribution system. If the Court favors a philosophy of increased social control in the interest of public welfare, it can with consistency reach a decision supporting a legislative act imposing control similar to that now in force in the more typical public utility fields.

CHAPTER VII

PUBLIC OWNERSHIP AND PUBLIC CONTROL

GENERAL AND LEGAL CONSIDERATIONS

PUBLIC ownership, as the term is commonly employed, refers to ownership and operation by the federal, state, municipal, or any other unit of government. Of these forms, municipal ownership is by far the most common in America. Experiences in federal ownership, covering a long period, are extremely limited. They include enterprises such as the United States Post Office; a few dams for irrigation, flood control, and power purposes; the Panama Canal and railroad; the Alaska railroad; the Mississippi barge; and certain enterprises involving in part considerations of military significance. Here and there states have embarked upon undertakings of state ownership of hydroelectric systems, grain elevators, flour mills, etc., but relatively these businesses are of no outstanding economic significance.[1] Not only is state and federal ownership relatively limited, but also the type of the business in which they have been engaged is such that it furnishes little information applicable to the enterprise of processing and distributing fluid milk.

In our attempt to point out the advantages and disadvantages of a publicly owned enterprise as compared with a public utility (a privately owned monopoly under public regulation) we shall, therefore, be obliged to rely largely upon such information as we are able to glean from municipal ownership of waterworks, the light and power enterprises, and, to a lesser extent, the gas systems. In these enterprises city ownership is by no means an untried venture. Over three-fourths of the city waterworks, one-half of the city electric-light and power establishments,[2] one-twentieth of the gas plants, and a few street railway companies are municipally owned.

[1] Educational and police systems, highways, streets, and other forms of public enterprise not primarily economic in character will be left out of consideration.

[2] The percentage of the number of light and power establishments overemphasizes the number of kilowatt hours involved because (a) the city-owned plants are often the

If the milk business were publicly owned, the ownership would likely center largely in the municipality; consequently, facts concerning municipal ownership would apply more directly to the milk business than would ownership by the state or federal governments. We shall, therefore, employ the term "public ownership" to mean ownership and control by the municipality unless otherwise stated. The more common term "municipal ownership" will be used synonymously with the term "public ownership." The term "public utility" will have reference to a privately owned monopoly under public regulation.

Legally there would be less restriction to public ownership than to operation as a public utility. The federal Constitution gives the state the right to own and operate virtually any private enterprise. On this point the United States Supreme Court, commenting upon the power of the state to tax, has ruled that "the use to which the tax is laid may be any purpose in which the state may engage, and this covers almost any private business, if the state legislature thinks the state's engagement in it will help the general public and is willing to pay the cost of the plant and incur the expense of operation."[3] A few state constitutions forbid the state to "engage in works of internal improvement." Various other limitations are imposed by state constitutions which may give rise to legal complications; the fact that virtually all states have some type of publicly owned enterprises, however, suggests that state ownership is legally possible. It is not the intent of the federal Constitution to impose restrictions upon the state if it "sees fit to enter upon such enterprises."[4] Likewise, there is reason to believe that municipal ownership is constitutionally possible the same as is state ownership because the state may delegate such powers to the municipality through the state-granted charter or through legislative action. "A municipality is merely a department of the State, and the State may withhold, grant or withdraw powers and privileges as it sees fit."[5]

---

smaller ones and (b) they not uncommonly purchase their power at "wholesale" from large private utilities and become only distributors of the electric energy.

[3] *Wolff Packing Co.* v. *Court of Industrial Relations*, 262 U.S. 522, 537 (1923).

[4] *Green* v. *Frazer*, 253 U.S. 233, 243 (1920); also *Jones* v. *City of Portland*, 245 U.S. 217 (1917).

[5] *Trenton* v. *New Jersey*, 262 U.S. 182, 187 (1923).

Even though these governmental units are not expressly endowed with the power to engage in the business of distributing fluid milk, such power may be implied from similar powers specifically granted. While, offhand, it would seem that legal obstructions to the municipalization of the milk business could be overcome with little difficulty, nevertheless before a municipality or a state attempts operation of the milk business as a publicly owned enterprise, or as a public utility, the state constitutional limitations as well as any which may be imposed upon the municipality by the state will need to be fully explored along with federally imposed legal limitations.[6]

There can be little doubt but that, where a government unit enters business to the exclusion of private enterprise, payment would have to be made for tangible and intangible property and going-concern value to all those private concerns directly affected thereby, since the taking-away of their business would have effects similar to those of taking away the actual property. The Fifth Amendment provides that private property may not be taken for public use without just compensation. In this respect, municipal ownership and public utility operation would be faced with a similar issue. Under public utility operation the utility would probably purchase the private competing companies, while under public ownership the governmental unit would make the purchase.

ECONOMY OF MANAGEMENT

In comparing economy of operation of a privately owned publicly controlled utility with that of a publicly owned enterprise, the relative effectiveness of management is an important factor. From a standpoint of efficiency of operation, privately owned utilities have, by and large, made a good record. Most students of public utility economics agree that private management has been more effective than has public management in developing vigor and enthusiasm

[6] For a discussion on public ownership see Martin G. Glaeser, *Outlines of Public Utility Economics* (New York, 1927), chap. xxxi; and Eliot Jones and Truman C. Bigham, *Principles of Public Utilities* (New York, 1931), chaps. xiv and xv and the references cited therein; see also references at close of article written by Felix Frankfurter and Henry M. Hart, Jr., in *Encyclopaedia of the Social Sciences*, XIII, 42; and another by Stacy May in *ibid.*, VII, 119. For an exhaustive study of municipal corporations see Eugene McQuillin, *The Law of Municipal Corporations* (2d ed.; Callaghan, Chicago, 1937).

of personnel. It has been more free to adopt sound and up-to-date business principles and quicker to adopt money-saving and time-saving equipment and methods. It has followed a more rigid policy of keeping down costs and of discouraging laxity on the part of employees than has public management.

It is unfortunate, but too often true, that municipally owned enterprises are under the control of ill-informed and even disinterested voters, and sometimes operated by poorly qualified managers and employees. Even worse, the executive officers directing the affairs may be chosen on the basis of political considerations rather than qualification and capacity. Once appointed they are often more keenly interested in adopting a short-time policy which will win current support rather than a long-time policy with the view of building up a sound business concern.[7] The general opposition toward paying attractive salaries often tends to exclude superior directors and managers from associating themselves with public enterprises.

While the public utilities generally have been operated efficiently, as to whether the owners of the public utilities have always operated the business in the public interest is quite another question. On this point there is much doubt. It may be, however, that the method of controlling these utilities has been at fault as much as have owners and officials of the utilities. It is only natural that owners of utilities like owners of competitive enterprises attempt to operate the business mainly for their own benefit. The main difference between a

---

[7] "Private corporations, under the spur of profits, are eager to anticipate the future and to preempt all opportunities for profit; whereas governments are essentially conservative, and hesitate to make improvements that necessitate the scrapping of expensive plant and equipment. Although economical in the long run, the scrapping of equipment that is more or less obsolete involves an immediate outlay, which calls for an increase in indebtedness or the postponement of rate reductions that might otherwise have been possible. Few of the economies eventually to be realized through costly improvements would be realized during the term of office of a particular representative or councilman; and therefore these functionaries are more interested in reducing rates or showing a profit, or making improvements for which there is less need, but which bring results with sufficient promptness to redound to their credit while they are still in office. It is much easier to convince a group of stockholders (or the directors chosen by them) that a certain improvement is desirable than it is to convince the voters (or the representatives chosen by them)" (Jones and Bigham, *op. cit.*, p. 753).

utility and a competitive business is the monopoly element connected with the former which, if unregulated, permits opportunity to
work a hardship on the public.

If the owners of a public utility had a public point of view and would
attempt to operate the utility in such a way that the public interest
is given first consideration, and the owners secondary, then such a
utility would likely make a better showing than one publicly owned
and operated. Unfortunately, utility owners have seemingly not yet
attained this point of view; consequently, it has been, and still is,
necessary to provide control to protect the public interest. The
necessary regulation can be enforced only after information has been
gathered, plans and operating policies scrutinized, and charges of
the utility reviewed. In extreme cases the job of regulation may
necessitate detail and thoroughness to the point where the personnel
required involves a virtual duplication of management. Should the
control machinery reach such proportions, then the government unit
might almost as well actually operate the enterprise and save the
expense of regulation.

COST OF CAPITAL FOR FINANCING MILK-DISTRIBUTION SYSTEM

Advocates of public ownership argue that, in those fields of endeavor where it is difficult or impossible to obtain sufficient capital
through private channels, government ownership has not only an
advantage but becomes virtually essential. Under the competitive—
largely unregulated—milk-distribution system of the past there has
been no apparent lack of capital, but whether that condition would
obtain if milk were made a public utility cannot be foretold. True,
public utilities have never gone begging for capital, although the
rate of interest or dividend has consistently been higher than the
rate paid by municipalities—or by states.[8]

Until public utility operation in the milk business moved beyond
the experimental stage, one would not expect capital to flow into
the enterprise except under the inducement of a relatively favorable
rate of return. The fact must also be conceded that, if the municipality were to float bonds for that enterprise alone, it might be

---

[8] The most common difference has been from 1 to 1½ per cent.

required to pay a higher rate of interest than is customary for other bonds; especially would that be true if the amount of this bond issue was substantial. While the city's power to impose taxes for the purpose of meeting payments of these bonds is no different from that of taxing for other purposes, many prospective buyers might look askance upon the project and set up a sales resistance against the bonds which were to furnish capital for its initiation.

The argument that municipal ownership would bring about substantial savings due to lower cost of capital may easily be overemphasized. The savings, if there be any in this item, may be so small per quart of milk handled as to be imperceptible. An example will assist in giving an idea of the possible savings due to lower cost of capital. According to a study made of the Milwaukee milk market by the dairy section of the Agricultural Adjustment Administration, the estimated capital expenditures of a proposed central plant and unified milk-distribution system would be roughly $5,100,000 (based on May, 1934, costs).[9] Their findings showed a daily per capita consumption of fluid milk (including light cream) of about 0.37 quart. Let us assume for the sake of argument that it would be possible to save 2 per cent interest or divident paid on capital. On the basis of the data of this study, the difference of 2 per cent would amount to a little over one-tenth of a cent per quart of milk handled. This would mean a saving of about thirteen cents annually per capita, or roughly of about fifty cents per family on a fifty-dollar yearly milk bill.

In public ownership certain legal technicalities in financing would need to be met. For example, in forty-five states a limit is placed upon the amount of bonded indebtedness which a municipality may carry.[10] In some of these states this limitation has been partly nullified by permitting municipalities to issue "revenue bonds" which represent a charge only against the properties or revenues, thus falling outside the statutory definition of indebtedness. Regardless of whether or not legal limitations exist, many cities would find it no

[9] Agricultural Adjustment Administration, *A Survey of Milk Marketing in Milwaukee* ("U.S.D.A. Marketing Information Series," DM-1 [Washington, 1937]).

[10] See Jones and Bigham, *op. cit.*, p. 720 and references there cited.

easy matter to provide the necessary funds to purchase the private milk-distributing companies and also finance a unified milk-distribution system.

VALUATION FOR RATE-MAKING PURPOSES

Agreement as to what constitutes a fair rate of return to a utility has generally been reached with little difficulty, but the question of a fair valuation or "rate base" has always raised issues leading to a disquieting condition, if not a nightmare. So long as utilities are able to obtain a return on the basis of their capitalized value, it is to their advantage to hold this value as high as possible. Indeed, they are tempted to overcapitalize, often carrying what is known as "watered stock," when possible to do so in order to realize the extra income. The United States Supreme Court (referring to a railroad corporation) has held that "what the company is entitled to ask is a fair return upon the value of that which it employs for the public convenience."[11] Even with this statement to serve as a guide, the legal question of valuation for rate- or price-making purposes has by no means been settled.[12] There is almost certainty that it would arise if milk were made a public utility.

Difficulties of establishing valuation for price-making purposes would be eliminated by public ownership because under that method of operation the profit motive is removed, the purpose of the enterprise being to maintain itself on a continuing basis. If a finanical balance were left at the end of the accounting period, it may be used for accumulating a reserve or pooled with the general tax fund. Likewise, should the enterprise be faced with a deficit, the project might be reimbursed from the general fund.

POLITICAL ACTIVITIES OF EMPLOYEES AND LABOR EFFICIENCY

It has often been alleged that, under municipal ownership, employees will be in a stronger position to take an active part in politics and accordingly to exert undue political influence. For example, they would be in position to maintain unduly high wage levels, to limit the size load of milk to be delivered on the resale routes, and

[11] *Smith* v. *Ames*, 169 U.S. 466, 547 (1898).

[12] It is assumed that, if a unified system either publicly or privately owned were established, it would make use of the adaptable capital equipment of the existing system.

to dictate policies regarding the number of employees to be maintained for other specific duties. A public utility, it is argued, would be in a stronger position than a publicly owned business to force labor efficiencies and thereby to reduce the labor load and the wage bill.

EFFECT ON LARGE-SCALE OPERATION.

Up to the limits of the market area within a municipality the savings due to economies of large-scale operation would be made possible whether the milk business was municipally owned or was operated as a privately owned public utility. However, beyond the area of the municipality, this situation would be quite different. Indeed, one of the greatest handicaps of public ownership would be that the political area—the municipality—may not be identical with the economic area—the total area over which a unified milk-distributing system would operate with the highest economic efficiency. In many of the densely populated sections of the country two or more cities or towns are located sufficiently close together so that at least the larger milk distributors are able to increase their efficiency of operation by distributing milk in more than one municipality. Under municipal ownership it might become awkward if not governmentally impractical for the enterprise to expand operations beyond the legal limits of the municipality. Especially in cities of medium or small size, such limitation would prohibit the expansion of the market to the point of greatest operating economy. A public utility would not suffer this handicap because, even though it were operating with headquarters in one municipality, it might encounter no difficulties in obtaining from a neighboring municipality an exclusive franchise to process, sell, and deliver milk. Thus, it would be in a position to avail itself of large-scale operation through an indefinite enlargement of the market area.

PRIDE, EDUCATION, AND DEMOCRACY

Idealistic statesmen may argue (1) that a city does, and rightly should, take a pride in "owning its own business," including those businesses which have ordinarily been operated as public utilities and those other businesses which can advantageously be operated as such, and (2) that the responsibility of such operation leads to a highly educated citizenry and with it an advanced form of democracy.

To these arguments realistic businessmen answer (1) that the mere gratification of such pride renders little lasting satisfaction if municipal ownership proves to be less practicable than operation as a privately owned utility, or under a private competitive system, and (2) that a definition of "a higher education and a greater advancement of democracy" of a citizenry has little tangible meaning unless consideration is given to the question as to whether or not the ventures which prompt this higher education and advanced democracy are demonstrably feasible from an economic point of view.

INTEREST IN MUNICIPAL OWNERSHIP BY LEGISLATIVE BODIES

Interest in public ownership of the business of processing and distributing milk, although not widespread, has been given some legislative consideration. For example, there was presented before the 1935 session, and again before the 1937 session, of the Wisconsin legislature a bill to create a section of the statutes providing that the cities be permitted to distribute fluid milk to the exclusion of private enterprise. In the 1935 session the bill passed the assembly and lost in the senate by only five votes. The 1937 bill was designed to accomplish the same purpose but was prepared in more detail than the former one. The latter bill was recommended for passage by the committee on agriculture but failed, along with numerous other bills, to appear before either house because of sine die adjournment of the legislature. There is reason to believe, however, that similar legislation will be presented in the future.

The 1937 bill[13] was promulgated on the basis of increased efficiency of milk distribution, declaring that

the supply of these products [milk and dairy products] to metropolitan centers has been impaired by the present methods of distribution and that such condition cannot be remedied by the ordinary operation of private enterprise, and that the providing of a safe, sanitary and economical supply of milk in such metropolitan centers is a public use and purpose for which public money may be

[13] State of Wisconsin, "A Bill To Create Section 100.30 of the Statutes, Providing for the Establishment, Organization, Operation and Dissolution of Municipal Milk and Dairy Distributing Authorities," No. 334 A (February 25, 1937).

spent and private property acquired; . . . . [and] that such supply in the interest of both the producer and consumer should not be subject to duplication and waste in the delivery service in order that the producer may receive the highest returns for his product and the consumer receive the same at the lowest rate. . . . .[14]

The proposal of the bill was, briefly, to create—upon a resolution passed by a majority vote of the members of the city council—a municipal milk authority composed of five members responsible to the city mayor, which shall assume responsibility for operation of the fluid-milk business of the city, including the hiring of all employees, technical experts, etc. Under the conditions of the bill the authority

(1) May obtain from the city such sums of money as are necessary to acquire real and personal property, the payments of expenses, etc.;
(2) Is granted (a) the exclusive privilege by the acquiring, through purchase, gift or condemnation, of the distribution plants actually engaged in the pasteurization, sale and distribution of all grades of milk and cream distributed for consumption to the residents of such city, but not including milk or cream used for manufacturing purposes; and (b) the "sole and exclusive privilege of conducting and carrying on the pasteurization, distribution and sale of milk and cream, other than manufactured milk or cream, within the territory of the municipality. . . . .[15]

Further, the authority is privileged to engage in the marketing, processing, manufacturing, and buying or selling of all other dairy products or commodities, and to receive grants made by a federal, state, county, municipal, or any other, source.

It thus appears that according to this bill the authority would become a complete legal entity having exclusive power to conduct the milk business of a city and such functions as are allied thereto; it would in reality become a quasi-municipal corporation.

Provisions were made in the bill to grant the State Department of Agriculture and Markets the power to fix the price of milk and cream to producers, but the authority was to have full power to fix prices to the city consumers. Either the authority or the city had the privilege under the bill to apply to the circuit court for an order dissolving the authority. Upon dissolution the property of the authority would be transferred to the city.

[14] *Ibid.*   [15] *Ibid.*

PART IV

METHODS AND DIFFICULTIES OF REGULATION

CHAPTER VIII

METHODS AND DIFFICULTIES OF PUBLIC UTILITY CONTROL OF MILK DISTRIBUTION

THE discussion up to this point has centered mainly upon two questions: (1) the possible economic savings resulting from unification of the milk-distributing system and (2) the legal aspects. In chapter iv we arrived at the inescapable conclusion that noticeable savings could be attained through unification of milk distribution. Indeed, from the purely economic point of view, the plan would seem to be highly feasible. On the basis of the United States Supreme Court decisions, such a system should have much more than an even chance of being legally possible. If unification be economically advantageous, it would by the same token be socially desirable.

The principal objections to the new method would arise because of conflicting interests between groups and individuals and because of political barriers, not because of fundamental obstacles inherent in the system. Stated in another way, the stumbling blocks would be laid by those individuals and groups who are concerned with safeguarding their own interests at the cost of social welfare as a whole.

In general, the American public does not look askance upon the public utility as an institution any more than it does upon private enterprise, especially upon those private businesses operated as large units. The public utility is an institution of recognized standing just as is the purely private enterprise or the producers' or the consumers' co-operative. It has found an important place in our American economy. Privately owned public utilities supply manufactured gas, electricity, telephones, and street railways. These represent a capital investment of twenty-four billion dollars in the United States. Publicly owned utilities, the most important of which are the city water systems, represent an added six billion dollars. This combined investment of roughly thirty billion dollars accounts for approximately 10 per cent of the national wealth.[1]

[1] Data for 1932 obtained from *Encyclopaedia of the Social Sciences*, XII, 667.

The public has accepted the idea of control over certain enterprises where unregulated conditions would permit of unduly high profits or salaries. From a purely economic point of view it makes no difference whether the high price of a product is due to excessive profits and salaries or to operating inefficiencies of the existing competitive system which could be remedied under a unified system. Thus, it would seem that public utility operation may very properly be urged in any enterprises where it can reasonably be shown that such operation will redound to the public welfare, present or future, and it should definitely be urged where the competitive system leads to practices detrimental to the public. Detrimental practices may include such considerations as large profits, high salaries of executives, or remediable inefficiencies of operation. The very structure of the competitive system in certain industries may be such that the inherent inefficiencies and economic wastes cannot be reduced to a point as low as might be done under a unified system operated as a controlled monopoly.

There should be no need to present a case for or against the public utility as such. Rather, it should be the purpose to present an analysis showing the extent to which the mode of operation typical of our established public utilities may be successful when applied to an enterprise which has previously been operated largely as a private industry. Public control of the milk business under unification would not necessarily be an innovation. It would merely be an extension of an already established trend. As society has grown more and more complex and hence has become more dependent upon certain services, the trend has been to extend public regulation over those certain services for the common benefit. Indeed, public regulation is a part and parcel of a complex economy, and the public utility is the product of regulation as it applies in the more complete and direct form. Regulation would be carried out mainly through the legal instrument, the franchise, and a regulating commission.

THE FRANCHISE

Any one of several types of franchises may be granted, but experience in other utilities has proved rather conclusively that the so-called indeterminate franchise (more clearly a terminable franchise) has been the most successful. Under the provisions of this type of franchise the municipality may terminate it at any time, or after a stated period, and purchase the utility. Such a provision serves to stimulate the owners of the utility to render at all times satisfactory services at reasonable rates or prices.

Utilities are generally staffed with highly trained and capable engineers, attorneys, and managers who counsel with and assist the owners in anticipating legal, technical, and business problems. There are reasons to believe that this same situation would hold true in a privately owned, publicly controlled milk utility. A well-trained legal staff of the utility might outargue the city officials with whom negotiations relating to the terms of the franchise would be made. Accordingly, the utility might secure an advantage in drawing up the franchise; and the more rigid and specific the terms, the greater this advantage would prove to be. For that reason (and others not mentioned here) the city would no doubt strengthen its long-run position by adopting a franchise with broad general terms and allowing for considerable flexibility. The direct control and supervision of policies under such a plan would be delegated to a commission responsible for protecting the public interest.

THE REGULATING COMMISSION

Regulation of the new utility would divide itself into two categories: (1) establishing valuations of the utility for purposes of allowing it reasonable returns and (2) establishing prices, especially those to be paid milk producers. The first type would be designed to protect the general public—producers and consumers—but mainly consumers. The second type would be designed to protect the producers against either the public utility or the consumers.

Inasmuch as regulation would likely have two distinct objectives, it might prove more workable to have two separate commissions, each responsible for its own specific task but co-operating to obtain a general unity of purpose. The commission charged with the responsibility of fixing prices to be paid farmers should logically be responsible to the state department of agriculture (or whatever the specific designation of that department may be), or it should consist of members from this department designated as a commission for that purpose. The other commission might be created either by the state or by the city in question. Except for the larger cities, a state commission might be more satisfactory than one responsible to the city alone. Perhaps the state commission which is already responsible for regulating other utilities may increase its personnel and be authorized to regulate the milk business also. For the want of better names, we shall designate these as the "agricultural commission" and the "public utility commission." Markets or market areas which involve two or more states would probably find it necessary to rely, in part at least, upon a federal commission to determine producer prices. Exact arrangements would necessarily have to fit local conditions and hence would vary from state to state and even from market to market. Flexibility in control and direction would be more important in the milk business than in the more common public utilities for reasons which we shall presently point out.

DIFFICULTIES IN INSTITUTING THE PLAN

It must be recognized that, inasmuch as some individuals and groups will be ill affected by a change from a competitive to a unified system of milk distribution, they will oppose the plan as soon as it comes up for serious public discussion. We must take people as they are and acknowledge the fact that individual and group pressure against a proposed enterprise, especially if that effort is effectively organized, will have a dominant influence in determining whether or not the undertaking will be instituted and if it will be successful. Such adverse action may have a decided influence even though a relatively small number of individuals are actively supporting it. The public does not always distinguish between the number of the voices and the volume of the sound. Those who are operating the present milk-distributing companies, including the owners, officers, managers, and many of the employees, can be expected to oppose any movement to change the system. Even if this opposition were overcome, all the difficulties would not be solved.

An equally important question is whether those political units which assume responsibility for the operation and management of the new enterprise will rise to their responsibilities or whether they will permit political considerations and other unfortunate influences

to come into play and thereby tend to render the enterprise unworkable. No amount of economic analysis can answer these questions. Unfortunately, political considerations are all too commonly
mixed with economic ones.

To use a specific example, suppose that one or more candidates
for city alderman who had been elected on a platform of "lower
milk prices to our city consumers" had been able to carry through the
procedure necessary to make milk a public utility. Then suppose
that it was discovered that efficiency in the new plan as it then
operated could not be brought to the point of fulfilling their promises
to reduce milk prices. What methods would they adopt in order to
make good their promises? After a brief unsuccessful attempt to
reduce resale milk prices through high efficiency in distribution,
would they attempt to lower resale prices by hammering down producer prices? Or would they, for example, endeavor to convince the
public that the existing rigid sanitation requirements are a "farce"
and that milk prices could be decreased by dispensing with them?
Would they be successful in carrying through a program for discontinuing milk inspection, pasteurization, and other precautions
against infected milk? If so, would not the net effect be to disturb
the general program for maintaining and improving the quality and
sanitation of milk which has been in progress for decades?

There is always danger that the public may become overcredulous
in its acceptance of statements of those who assume themselves
capable of directing public policy. Statements of political office-
seekers or office-holders involving purely economic issues might
well be accepted with caution, but those issues involving sanitation
and health have an even greater public concern. Surely questions
pertaining to the omission of sanitary precautions, with its danger
of inviting milk-borne disease epidemics, should not be determined
on the basis of economic savings.

POLICY TOWARD CO-OPERATIVES

This treatise has not set forth a separate discussion of individual
producer-distributors or of either producer or consumer distributing
co-operatives (as distinct from producers' bargaining associations).
Scattered illustrations of outstanding success could be cited, but,

for the most part, the distributing co-operative has had substantially the same influence in the market as a private distributor. The presence of such a co-operative means one more distributor in a market with its added duplication of effort. To date these co-operatives have made no decided impression upon the fluid-milk industry in the United States. Not until they become a real influence toward greater efficiency in distributing milk will they be a potential factor for improving the market structure. Co-operatives, as well as the producer-distributors, however, do carry a public significance different from that of the private company. They are not uncommonly held in a higher general public esteem than are private businesses. From the standpoint of determining public policy, it is a matter of indifference whether the distinction between private business and the co-operative has an economic or a sentimental basis. Many individuals who might approve of excluding privately operated companies from the market would not favor the exclusion of co-operatives.

This immediately raises the question whether or not special consideration should be given to distributing co-operatives. Suppose a franchise were granted to only one distributing agency or to a limited number, or that the city was granted the power to operate the milk business to the exclusion of private enterprise. Should the distributing co-operative, whether producer or consumer controlled, also be denied entrance into the market or should compromises be permitted on this point? In case of such compromises, it should be made clear at the outset that the economic advantages of a unified milk-distribution system would be reduced by such duplication.

DIFFICULTIES IN REGULATING THE UTILITY

Difficulties of public utility control would not be limited to those manifested in political issues and political pressure referred to above. The task of regulating utilities carries its own anguish.

Operated as a public utility, the milk business would be subject to the general conditions specified in the legislative grant. Presumably it would operate under an exclusive franchise, permit, or license issued by the municipality granting it a monopoly to operate in a specified area. A monopoly is always in a strategic position to work hardship upon the public unless effectively regulated for the public benefit.

While some information can be gained from the experiences of the more common utilities, the problems of these utilities are not strictly comparable to those which would exist in a unified milk-distributing system.

City gas and electric systems may operate for relatively long periods of time with little or no change in the rate structure, in the method of operation, or in the labor policies. Wages for labor do not bulk a large part of the total expense. Hence, even though wage rates must be adjusted from time to time, it is not essential to make correspondingly frequent and major changes in (a) rate schedules, (b) laborsaving devices (together with the consequent reduction of the labor load and the resulting protest from the wage-earners involved), or (c) general labor policies. Techniques have been quite definitely established, sources of supplies are relatively continuous, and costs are reasonably stable. Compared with these enterprises, the fluid-milk business is intensely dynamic. For this reason a system of public control and direction would need to be sufficiently flexible and adjustable to meet the rapidly changing situations as they arise. In milk control the producers, a group not involved in the ordinary public utility regulation, would come into the picture. Accordingly, a commission to protect their interests would also be necessary.

The main features of regulation of the milk business as a public utility would be divided into three categories: (a) establishing valuation of the properties "purchased" from the existing system; (b) establishing valuations of the new utility for the purpose of providing a reasonable, and only a reasonable, rate of return to the enterprise, and perhaps also for assisting in establishing wage rates and salaries; and (c) establishing prices to be paid by consumers and to be paid to producers of milk.

A. ESTABLISHING PURCHASE VALUE OF EXISTING PROPERTIES

The establishment of valuations of property owned by the existing companies for the purpose of "purchase" by the new utility or by the city would be aside from the function of regulating the utility

which would
be more than
they have

itself. Once these properties were "purchased" that question would be settled. However, acquisition of plants, equipment, and other property from the existing milk distributors would of necessity be made at terms satisfactory to the parties concerned, or litigation would incite discussion and ill feeling within the municipality with the consequent resistance against the new undertaking.

B. ESTABLISHING VALUATIONS FOR PURPOSES OF PROVIDING REASONABLE RETURNS TO THE ENTERPRISE

Determination of valuations to provide reasonable returns would automatically fix the margin to be retained by the milk utility. This would be analogous to that of determining valuations for rate-making purposes in the common public utilities and would be regulated by the public utility commission.

After more than two decades of experience, no entirely satisfactory basis of valuation of public utility properties has been established for rate-making purposes. Thus the regulating commission of the milk utility would have insufficient usable experience upon which to make decisions. The new commission would doubtless find it necessary to rely largely upon the rule laid down by the United States Supreme Court in the *Smyth* v. *Ames* case (1898)—namely, that rates (returns) are reasonable when the utility is permitted to earn a fair rate of return on a fair value of the property actually used for the service of the public. According to this same court case, valuations cannot be arrived at through a fixed formula.

In order to ascertain such valuations, a commission would need to give attention to at least six different factors: "(1) the original cost of construction, (2) the amount expended in permanent improvements, (3) the amount and market value of its bonds and stock, (4) the present as compared with the original cost of construction, (5) the probable earning capacity of the property under particular rates prescribed by statute, and (6) the sum required to meet operating expenses." Each of these factors is "to be given such weight as may be just and right in each case."[2] Indeed, the Court pointed out that, in addition to the above, there may be still other factors to be regarded in establishing the value of utility property.

From the consumers' point of view, they are entitled to adequate

[2] *Smyth* v. *Ames*, 169 U.S. 466, 546–47 (1898). Numerals in parentheses are mine.

and continuous service at reasonable costs. Consequently, returns to the utility must be sufficient so that the capital necessary to provide such service will be attracted to the industry. It should hardly be necessary to point out that reasonable rates, or margins in case of milk distribution, would need to cover all operating expenses, including insurance and taxes, and, in addition, leave a fair return on the "rate base."[3]

We shall discuss briefly what appear to be the two most important of the six items listed by the Court in the above case—namely, (1) original cost and (4) the comparison between present and original costs—and then touch upon a few of the more general difficulties of regulation. The reader is referred to the textbooks previously cited for a treatment of the other four points.

Original cost.—The amount of money actually, prudently, and honestly invested is recognized by public utility economists and the courts as an important if not the most important factor in determining the value, or rate base, of a public utility for rate-making purposes. This is referred to by some as *original-cost theory* and by others as *prudent-investment theory*. In reality, it is a combination of both, being the amount originally and prudently invested.[4] Obtaining this cost is an exceedingly complicated undertaking if the utility has been in operation for a considerable time before cost determinations are made. On the other hand, if a well-qualified commission responsible for making those determinations is in existence before the utility is started and has authority over setting up the accounts involving building and equipment costs, then the task becomes much less knotty. Thus, if legislation were passed making milk a public utility, provisions should be made simultaneously to establish a regulating commission. Even under these more favorable conditions the established valuations are only close approximations, especially when it is considered that they are to be used not at one point of time only but that they are to form the basis for valuation

---

[3] In this case the purpose is not to seek a value for which the utility might be exchanged—an exchange value—but rather a value upon which "fair returns" would be made. To distinguish between these two concepts of value, the term "rate base" instead of the term "value" has been suggested by the United States Supreme Court.

[4] It must be emphasized that, if this investment is imprudently or dishonestly made, the original-cost concept has little value as a measure for establishing the rate base.

from year to year. The establishment of valuations in reality becomes a continuous process.

Even though the investment be prudently and honestly made, there is still the question of arranging depreciation schedules of buildings, equipment, machines, and appliances necessary for conducting the business. Depreciation which is due to deterioration—actual wear from use or an impairment resulting from the elements—can be determined with reasonable ease and accuracy, but that depreciation which is due to obsolescence is not so easy to forecast. No one can foretell when new inventions may appear on the market. Inventions may be in the form of new and more efficient equipment, new machines, or improved processes which will presumably bring about a saving in labor. Any new invention will likely necessitate replacement of equipment, machines, or appliances prior to the anticipated life-limits of these assets, thus upsetting former depreciation schedules.

Present and original cost compared.—Conditions which make changes or replacements necessary at a more (or less) rapid rate than was forecast will require revaluations from time to time. For such revaluations things other than, or at least things in addition to, the original cost will need to be considered. Perhaps the most important of those mentioned by the Court in the *Smyth* v. *Ames* case is "the present as compared with original cost of construction." The difference between the "present" and "original" costs of construction will be great or small depending upon the amount of price change through time. If price changes are relatively rapid, the difference between the two figures will be relatively large. If prices remain constant, the difference will be nil.

There is encouragement in the fact that, even though exact valuations cannot be maintained from year to year, they can be kept up to date with reasonable accuracy through a carefully kept accounting system in which all investments for new property, additions, or replacements, as well as the decreased value of the old equipment, are recorded. New accounting practices and systems are becoming increasingly important in public utility regulation.[5] While

[5] G. Lloyd Wilson and Joseph R. Rose, "Recent Trends in Public Utility Regulation," *American Economic Review*, Vol. XXIX, No. 4 (December, 1939); see also

it may still be necessary to go back to all six items referred to in the *Smyth* v. *Ames* case in order to establish valuation, an increasing emphasis is being placed upon the original (prudent) investment basis. The question has recently been raised "whether more states may not in the near future accept 'prudent investment,' or some basis approximately the same, as the rate base." The writer of the above statement observed that "the Court in an opinion by Chief Justice Hughes carefully analyzed the evidence bearing on fair value and concluded that the amount of the rate-base as determined on the basis of prudent investment was substantially the same as the amount that would have been arrived at on the basis of fair value."[6]

The principal reason why the courts have in the past played such an important role in determining the basis of valuation for public utilities has been because (*a*) legislatures have not expressed a clear-cut basis, or bases, for such determinations and (*b*) the regulation has been such that the utility or the public has had a just cause for judicial action. "Rate-making," said the Supreme Court in 1922, "is no function of the courts and should not be attempted either directly or indirectly."[7] Would it not be a move in the right direction for a legislature to direct specifically that the original (prudent) investment should form the basis of valuation for rate- (or price-) making purposes? This would greatly simplify the task of a regulating commission. Such an experiment might well be carried out when a new type of utility, as, for example, the business of processing and distributing milk, was being established.

General difficulties of regulation.—The impression should by no means be conveyed that the complexities of regulation would be solved with such improvement in legislative acts. Students in the field realize the obstacles associated with all public utility regulation. For example, Felix Frankfurter, now United States Supreme Court

---

E. W. Morehouse, "Innovations in Public Utility Accounting Regulation," *Yale Law Journal*, XLVI, 955.

[6] Wilson and Rose, *op. cit.*, p. 746.

[7] *Newton* v. *Consolidated Gas Co.*, 258 U.S. 165, 177 (1922); see also *Pacific Gas Co.* v. *San Francisco*, 265 U.S. 403 (1924), and *St. Louis and O'Fallon R. Co.* v. *United States*, 279 U.S. 461 (1929).

Justice, and Henry M. Hart, Jr., made the following comment on rate regulation:

In a wide variety of concrete instances the machinery of utility regulation has shown increasing strain. Revealed shortcomings in administration and legislation and in the judicial doctrines to which they are required to conform have been accentuated by the stress of new economic forces and by the ingenuity of the utilities in devising unanticipated means of eluding effective control. Beyond question successful regulation cannot be achieved upon a permanently unstable and incalculable rate base.

The difficulties inherent in the methods imposed by the judiciary upon administrative agencies have been intensified by the quality of their personnel. Almost everywhere the commissions have been inadequately staffed, overburdened by detail, denied necessary technical aid, dependent on meager salaries and without security of tenure.[8]

Too many appointments have been made on the basis of political considerations. Unattractive salaries in many states have induced many appointees to look upon the opportunity "not as a means for solving difficult problems of government but as a step toward political advancement or more profitable future associations with the utilities."[9]

Even though it is assumed that the public is entitled to efficient service, it is almost impossible for a commission to determine whether or not the utility is actually being operated under maximum efficiency. Indeed it is even more difficult to compel the utility management to operate at a high degree of efficiency if that management lacks inclination and capacity for such operation. The extent of efficiency is dependent largely upon the capability of the management. After a management has become established, the capacity of the individuals comprising it is not easily changed, nor are managers easily and quickly removed from their position. Lack of sufficient and capable personnel making up the commission imposes limits in submitting and enforcing suggestions for pronounced improvements in the efficiency of utility operation.

An equally important problem is to determine whether expenditures have been honestly and prudently made. Records and accounts, if properly set up and kept by the utility and carefully audi-

[8] *Encyclopaedia of the Social Sciences*, XIII, 111.
[9] *Ibid.*

ted by the commission, may help to detect *dishonest* expenditures, but it is not so easy to determine whether expenditures have been *prudently* made. Often an imprudent expenditure does not manifest itself until after it has become a "sunken," irretrievable cost.

Needless to say, these same shortcomings of regulation would manifest themselves if the milk business were operated under similar conditions. Along with the question of reasonable returns to the utility arises the question of returns to labor. In most fluid-milk markets the labor costs are from two-fifths to one-half of the total expense of processing and distributing milk. The largest amount of this labor is involved in delivering the milk to consumers. Milk deliverymen are in an exceedingly strategic position because they are quite completely unionized in many markets and because they have a sufficiently direct contact with the consumers to influence their thinking, to solicit, and often to win, their support for higher wages and improved working conditions. This direct consumer contact is, of course, more effective under a competitive system of milk distribution than it would be under a unified system because an employee who is displeased with his employer or is dissatisfied in any way may be in a position to obtain employment with another distributor and to induce many of his customers to shift their patronage with him. Under a unified system, deliverymen would not have the opportunity to secure employment with other distributors in the same city. Even so, one has reason to expect that questions of wage rates and labor policies would be a subject of many headaches under a unified distribution system.[10]

Another problem would be that of dealing with the utility holding company. Before the depression the fluid-milk industry in many parts of the country tended toward concentration into large—in some cases nation-wide—units not greatly dissimilar from those of large public utilities with holding companies. This rather suggests that if the distribution of milk were operated as a public utility, under public regulation, but with private ownership, holding companies might follow as a more or less natural development because of the opportunity for economies which they permit.

[10] It is recognized, of course, that the state and federal labor relations boards would also play an important part in settling labor disputes.

Suppose the distribution of milk were operated as a privately owned public utility with an exclusive franchise. Would the size of a utility be limited (1) to a single city, (2) to two or three adjacent cities located in a common milkshed, or (3) would the utility extend itself beyond those limits into several cities?

Many students of public utility operation argue that properly organized and administered holding companies make for efficiency of operation. If milk distribution were operated as a public utility, a holding company might assist the operating company in the following ways:

1. To assist financially the operating utility
2. To furnish guidance in constructing plants, in purchasing operating facilities, and in giving general counsel on planning and operating the business
3. To assist in working out satisfactory policies with labor and to aid in establishing a general price structure

If those in control of the holding company have a public-spirited point of view, these advantages may easily redound in large measure to the benefit of the public—consumers and producers. On the other hand, if those in control use these advantages for their own selfish purposes, the result may lead to no end of difficulty and detriment to the public. A review of the difficulties in which holding companies have been involved during the past decade suggests this as a danger.

Among the criticisms which have been leveled at utility holding companies are:

1. A tendency on the part of some utilities to overemphasize the opportunity for profits to the promoters, especially in floating security issues, often at excessive prices
2. The danger that accounts of subsidiaries may be manipulated in such a way as to enable insiders to secure undue advantage in purchasing or selling securities at prices other than those which would prevail if all the facts were generally known
3. The placing of charges on the operating company beyond those justifiable on the basis of service rendered
4. The concentration of control and power into the hands of a few individuals who may use it to the disadvantage of the public

C. ESTABLISHING PRICES TO PRODUCERS AND CONSUMERS

The regulations just discussed resolve themselves into a fixing of the margin retained by the milk utility in payment for the func-

The elasticity of cream might be force or to have a very
low price and make it up on milk and still return
more to the producer.
METHODS AND DIFFICULTIES   163

tions of processing and distribution. The amount of the margin
merely determines the relationship between prices received by the
producers and those paid by the consumers. A given margin of distribution might be established with high or low farm and resale milk
prices.

The question of fixing the prices to be paid to producers—and in
turn paid by consumers—involves a different consideration. In
many ways this is likely to become a more vexing problem than that
of establishing valuations of the utility, for reasons which we shall
soon see. The hardest problem will be that of establishing the prices
to be paid milk producers. When the producers' price and the margin of distribution have been fixed, the resale price will automatically
be established except for price adjustments of the various kinds of
dairy products, such as milk, coffee cream, and whipping cream.

For the past decade or more producers have maintained effective
bargaining organizations in a large proportion of the fluid-milk
markets. As expressed in the bylaws of these organizations, the
purposes are many, but actually almost the entire emphasis has
been placed directly or indirectly upon the improvement of producer prices.[11] Under the public utility system, producers would
continue to maintain effective bargaining organizations in an attempt to bargain with the utility for favorable prices. No franchise,
regardless of how carefully worded, could fully anticipate the problems and questions which might arise between the utility and the
producers. A regulating commission would be essential to bring
about necessary compromises. It is here that the agricultural commission would function. In many ways it would carry a more difficult task than would the public utility commission.

The basic considerations in fixing the farm price would be similar
to those now being followed in state and federal price-fixing of fluid
milk. Under the present system of milk-price regulation the state
milk control board (or commission) is either attached to the state
department of agriculture—or agriculture and markets—or composed of the identical individuals who direct this department. This

[11] Although producers' associations bargain only for their own members, the prices
established become uniform for all producers, members, and nonmembers who sell to
distributors adhering to the price schedule of the association.

type of organizational setup naturally leads to a policy of protecting the interest of milk producers, especially the organized milk producers, giving only secondary consideration to the interest of consumers. These boards have not uncommonly favored producers by establishing prices which are noticeably high in relation to those received in contiguous areas for milk going for manufactured uses. In fact, they have frequently shown a willingness to fix prices at the relatively favorable level requested by the producers' associations.

Although these favorable prices have also tended to maintain relatively high resale milk prices in many instances, it has brought virtually no organized repercussion from consumers. It has, however, brought complaints from those milk producers who furnish milk to creameries, condenseries, and cheese factories for manufactured uses at prices that were not regulated. These producers have alleged that in some milk markets the control boards have been a party to the maintenance of prices of fluid milk considerably above those which local and general economic conditions would appear to warrant. That is, the prices are said to have been out of line with those of the milk manufactured into butter, cheese, or evaporated milk. Producers of manufactured dairy products have argued that this relatively high farm price obtained by city milk producers encourages them to increase their milk production and makes higher resale prices and consequently lower fluid consumption. The combined influence of increased production and reduced consumption, they argue, brings about a surplus of fluid milk in the city markets which must be sold in competition with manufactured dairy products, with its depressing effect on manufactured dairy prices.

This tendency on the part of the control board to cater to the interests of organized groups of producers is to be expected and may not result in a policy to be feared greatly or condemned. The fact must be acknowledged, however, that it tends to shift the emphasis of the milk producers' association from its original purpose, that of being primarily a co-operative designed to bargain with dealers' prices, to that of a political pressure group.

Consumers have little influence in establishing prices. To be sure, it has been the common practice to hold a public hearing in a market before an order to establish and regulate prices is enforced.[12] At these hearings milk producers, distributors, and consumers are given the opportunity to present their views. Naturally, however, representatives from organized groups of producers are usually given greater consideration by the state regulating commissioners conducting the hearings than are individuals representing themselves only. Consumers generally do not attend these hearings, and, when they do, they seldom appeal in any vigorous manner for consideration in fixing prices.

It is always difficult to determine at what level prices should be established. Even among city-milk producers, views differ as to what is a proper or a "fair" price. Many argue for higher prices on the basis that their production expenses are high; others, usually a minority, argue that prices which are noticeably above those paid farmers for milk going to cheese, butter, or evaporated milk will invite too much milk to the fluid market.

The regulating board finding itself torn between these conflicts of interests must attempt to distinguish between that which is fair and unfair, that which is reasonable and unreasonable, that which is equitable and arbitrary, and, unfortunately, that which is politically expedient and that which may mean political suicide.[13]

A policy of sanctioning a wide price differential between similar products produced by two groups of dairy farmers—those who produce for the city markets and those who produce for the manufactured markets—is by no means one which can recommend itself from a public point of view.

Despite the fact that producers of cheese, butter, and evaporated milk have been profuse in their criticism of the wide farm price differential which exists between the fluid and the manufactured market, and the policy of a state regulating body in upholding it,

[12] This practice is also followed by the dairy section of the Agricultural Adjustment Administration, although the emphasis placed upon the hearings may be somewhat different than in the state control boards.

[13] It is significant that Mr. Arthur H. Lauterback, manager of the Pure Milk Association of Chicago, after several years' observation of the present system of milk-price control, believes that "price fixing to both producers and consumers may eventually lead to forcing milk distribution into a public utility" ("What Is Wrong with the Milk Industry," *Pure Milk Association News Release*, September 27, 1937, p. 10).

their lack of organization as well as the lack of a common program and policy has made them ineffective in forcing a change. The complaints seem, however, to be receiving more and more public consideration, and, if they are not heeded by the control boards, some day recourse will surely be taken through legislation.

Thus, it can be seen that the upper limit which city milk producers have been able to obtain with the present type of control has been determined very largely by the prices received by producers for milk sold to creameries, condenseries, and cheese factories and not by the upper limit which might be obtained from milk distributors. Milk distributors are often inclined to accept the high producer prices and pass the higher price on to the consumer, who registers little or no effective complaint. This situation would probably not be changed much, if any, under public utility operation. Consumers would gain the advantage of lower prices through the increased efficiencies of operation, not through hammering down producer prices.

The desirability or necessity of the government considering cooperatives only as a part of the larger group of milk producers and not distinct from them has apparently been recognized more clearly by the Agricultural Adjustment Administration than by state regulatory boards. H. R. Tolley, assistant administrator, said in 1934:

The Agricultural Adjustment Administration is obliged to look at the cooperative picture and the farm picture as a national one, not as a regional or local one exclusively. We are concerned with *all* milk producers and their problems, irrespective of whether they are selling milk to city markets or to manufactured milk plants. . . . . We wish to be fair and helpful to the producer-distributor as well as to the man who ships his milk to a pasteurizing plant at wholesale prices. . . . . I know that many of the cooperative leaders understand the necessities of our position. . . . . Any Federal agency must follow the principle of working together for the sound betterment of milk producers of the land.[14]

Unfortunate though it may be from the point of view of all milk producers, it has not been politically feasible for the price-determining bodies to carry out their policies under the hypothesis that in practice the organized producers may be considered as, and only as, a portion of all milk producers. Direct and indirect political

[14] In an address given before the American Institute of Cooperation, July 9, 1934.

pressure has made such an approach unworkable. The whole question of determining the price relationship to be maintained between milk going to fluid use and to manufactured uses will likely become one of the more if not the most difficult of all problems with which a regulatory body must grapple. Under public utility operation these problems would still exist. Consumers, represented through the public utility commission, would likely be given somewhat more consideration than is the case at present.

In summary, while the difficulties of regulation would serve as a constant deterrent to outstanding success, they would not seem to be insurmountable. Opponents of public utility operation emphasize that, after an experience of more than a third of a century, regulation of the established American public utilities with their holding companies has been more or less unsatisfactory from the public point of view. That in itself, they say, strongly suggests the likelihood that the regulation of the milk business under public utility control might be at best only moderately satisfactory. They pointedly emphasize that milk consumers and producers will not wait quietly for a third, or even a tenth, of a century for similar regulatory bodies to work out plans and principles whereby fluid milk may be handled satisfactorily under a system of public utility.

Advocates of public utility operation answer that the existing lack of satisfactory public control over utilities may easily be overstressed. They suggest that one must consider that almost the entire growth, at least the great expansion, of the types of utilities which are now of the greatest importance dates back only about thirty to thirty-five years—a relatively short time. The experiences of a third of a century, they say, have been of too short duration for Congress, the legislatures, the courts, and public regulating commissions to lay hold of the principles and practices necessary for properly regulating utilities in a dynamic world. Now that many of these principles have been formulated, the rate of advancement will be much more rapid than formerly, and the milk business, if operated as a utility, will share in this advancement. They insist that any plan which has reasonable assurance of improving the standard of living and which is essentially evolutionary in its procedure can by that token be classed as typically American. America's tradition, they urge, was never intended to stand in the way of progress.

It would seem that an educated public should not be deterred by a mere statement that certain enterprises may be labeled by some as being "socialistic." The fundamental question is: "How will those concerned be affected by the change?" If it is economically advantageous to the public to operate the milk-distributing business under more complete control than it has been under in the past, then it is not only a public privilege but also a public responsibility of the state or municipality. With all the probable shortcomings of regulation, they may not be so grave but that both milk producers and consumers would be better off under a publicly controlled unified system than under a competitive system with no regulation whatever or under a system of regulation now in operation in several states.

It is important to re-emphasize that, if pitfalls are to be avoided, the probable advantage of such control should be reasonably well established before moves are made which will involve large public expenditures as well as radical changes in methods of operating a business as important as that of distributing milk.

ALTERNATIVES OF PUBLIC CONTROL

The public has three alternatives and perhaps variations of any one of them: (1) free and unhampered competition, (2) regulation of the type of milk business now operating in a few states, and (3) public utility operation and regulation. Each has its advantages; each, its shortcomings.

The free and unhampered competitive system has carried with it pronounced inefficiencies. The costs of these are ordinarily reflected forward to consumers, who have no recourse but to reduce milk consumption. Moreover, complete lack of regulation leaves too much opportunity for price wars among distributors and between distributors and producers. The effects of these price wars are often reflected back to milk producers who may have inadequate means of self-protection.

The system of regulation now operating in a number of states, including Wisconsin, which resulted from legislation inaugurated in 1933–34 and re-enacted at subsequent sessions of legislatures, serve at best only to calm a troubled situation. By many it is characterized as only a makeshift. Judging by the present trend of events, the lack of public support, and open criticisms, it is likely that some states will either abandon these efforts or materially change the type of approach. Violations have been and still are numerous, and the financial gains resulting from them are sufficient so that those who actually abide by the regulation often suffer serious financial losses at the hands of violators.

Public utility regulation with its admitted shortcomings does afford an opportunity for at least reasonably effective regulation. The fundamental principle must be recognized that regulation of one distributor—the utility—would obviously be less complex and less difficult than the regulation of a large number of competitive distributors. Distribution of milk operated as a unified system under public utility control may easily prove to be more satisfactory or less unsatisfactory than the present system (or lack of system) of regulation now applied to the milk business, or better than a condition of free and unhampered competition. On the other hand, it will not perform miracles, nor will it likely be as successful as enthusiastic supporters of the idea anticipate.

PART V
ECONOMIC EFFECTS OF REGULATION

CHAPTER IX

WHAT GROUPS WOULD GAIN UNDER A UNIFIED DISTRIBUTION SYSTEM?

ASSUMING that under a unified milk-distributing system the margin of distribution could be reduced, who would benefit by the reduction? Would this advantage be passed on entirely to the consumer or back to the producer, or would it be shared jointly by the two? Under what conditions may other groups, such as salary- or wage-receiving employees, gain or lose by such a change? The fact should be made clear, of course, that if, for any reason, the new system is not operated so as to bring about the possible efficiencies in processing and distributing milk, both consumers and producers might be in a less fortunate position than they would be under a competitive system where the forces of competition tend to maintain at least a reasonable degree of efficiency.

As far as producers and consumers are concerned, this question involves two separate considerations: First, the gain to consumers or producers resulting from the possible reduction of the margins of processing and distributing milk; second, the loss which producers may suffer as a result of a diminishing of the bargaining strength of the producers' association under the new method of distribution. No one positive and final answer to these questions would necessarily hold for both short-run and long-run periods, nor would it hold for all conditions. It would, however, seem clear that the short-run effect will be to pass any savings resulting from a decrease of the distributor's margins on to the consumer. Moreover, there is no reason to believe that they would not continue to hold at least a major portion of this benefit. Ordinarily the purpose of establishing a public utility with its proper regulation in the more common public utility field is to protect the consumer.

The relative gain of each of the two groups resulting from a change in the bargaining position will depend in no small part upon the

173

effectiveness with which individuals comprising each group can, and will, form and maintain a unity of action among themselves, as well as their ability to muster public support or public pressure to attain its goals. For every producer there are seventy-five to a hundred and fifty consumers, the number varying greatly from market to market. This ratio, however, has little significance as long as consumers continue to manifest an apparent indifference to moderate price changes. In the past their main response has been to purchase slightly less milk when prices rise and somewhat more when they fall. The demand for fluid milk is relatively inelastic. At least, in the short-run period, a comparatively high resale price will bring a larger total amount of money from the milk-consuming public than will a lower price. The aggressive milk producers' price-bargaining associations have capitalized upon this principle and, accordingly, have followed a policy of maintaining a relatively high price of Class I and Class II milk (milk utilized as fluid milk and cream, respectively), which high price has been largely passed on to the consumer.[1]

In the state-regulated markets as well as those without regulation, consumer interest and influence have been decidedly lacking, especially in comparison with that of producers. Here and there consumer representatives have appeared at public hearings which were held by the public milk control boards, but, in general, direct consumer influence in determining public policy in milk price-fixing has been virtually nil.

Leaving labor out of consideration for the moment, if milk were operated as a public utility, would the interest of the consumer still continue to be passive and that of the producer continue to be the dominant influence in price determination? Presumably not. For the most part, a unified system of milk distribution would be formulated by consumers in their interest and dominated by them. It is almost inconceivable that consumers of a city would delegate the control of the system to the producers. If consumers are sufficiently interested to reorganize the milk-distribution system, one would expect that their interest would also be extended to the point of exer-

[1] This is no reflection against the milk distributors. Except as they are able to cut costs (or profits), no other alternative is open to them if they are to continue operation.

cising a price-bargaining influence. That is, consumer representatives would bargain with producer representatives directly or indirectly through the public utility commission for farm prices to be paid for milk going to fluid-milk and cream consumption. Most of the direct price negotiation will, however, be carried on between the public utility commission and the agricultural commission, the latter of which would protect the interest of producers (see chap. viii).

In general, fluid-milk distributors have made no vigorous and persistent attempts to obtain milk from beyond the established milkshed, even when they have been obliged to pay a price seemingly out of line with the price of manufactured milk in the same or in contiguous areas.[2] There is some reason to believe that representatives purchasing milk for a unified, publicly controlled system would be more aggressive in this respect than distributors have been. The more aggressive producers' associations are now exercising a relatively powerful bargaining influence and could hardly expect to strengthen it. The less active associations might actually be stimulated to strengthen their association as a result of a greater need for such action. The dominant bargaining position which the more active associations now hold might be shared in part by the consumers. At least there is no evident reason why the consumers would, or should, sanction turning over much if any of the savings of distribution to the producers. This is particularly true in those markets where the present producer price for Class I and Class II milk is already so high, relative to prices paid in alternative markets, that appreciably more milk is now being supplied than is used for fluid-milk and cream purposes.

Under the present competitive system of milk distribution (without support of public regulation or even with the support of public regulation), to what extent can producers' associations continue to maintain as dominant a position in the market and as high a price differential between Class I and manufactured milk as has existed

---

[2] The strength of the producers' association and the general price structure in many markets have been such that, if distributors obtained any considerable amount of "unorganized" milk, such procedure might create a market disturbance even to the point of generating a price war, with its resulting loss to all parties concerned, including themselves. Hence, distributors have generally refrained from the practice.

in some of the organized markets during the last five to ten years? Past experiences do not supply information from which to provide a general answer. In some markets a relatively wide price differential has existed for several years with no clear evidence that the position of the producers' association has been weakened seriously as a result. In other markets where the Class I price paid producers has been appreciably out of line with prices of milk going to manufactured uses, there has been a gradually increasing proportion of the total market receipts sold as "surplus." Increased production of those producers regularly supplying the market, coupled with "new" milk coming from beyond the established milkshed, has set up a condition which suggests clearly that the price differential between Class I and manufactured milk must be decreased if those producers who now supply the market are to continue to hold it.

Thus, regardless of whether milk is distributed through a competitive or through a unified system, the producers in these markets would eventually be forced to reduce the price differential between Class I and manufactured milk. The amount of such reduction would be determined by conditions characterizing the particular market. In general, it would be reduced to or near the point where the average price paid city producers for their total milk production would be above the price paid in competing markets by an amount necessary to compensate for the added cost and inconvenience of meeting such factors as city health and sanitation requirements and uniform production.

Summarily, it is *only in those markets where the producers' association could continue to maintain its present dominant position in price bargaining (and hence its relatively favorable Class I and Class II prices) under the present competitive system, but lose it under a unified system, that producers would be definitely better off under a competitive than under an efficiently operated unified system of milk distribution.* Even though producers might lose some of their bargaining effectiveness under the new system, they certainly would not lose it entirely. Of course, conditions might arise where consumer representatives would decline to bargain with producer associations for prices but instead would attempt to obtain milk from "unorganized" sources. They might even satisfy themselves with milk from farms which have not met city inspection. Under any new type of organization, one may expect unusual things to happen. However, the opportunity for consumers to "run wild" would be lessened or virtually stopped by the commissions responsible for regulation.

The fact must not be overlooked that lower resale prices made possible by economies of processing and distribution under unification will tend to increase fluid-milk and cream consumption. The effects of increased consumption will be reflected back to the advantage of the producer through a larger portion of his production being sold at the higher fluid prices (Class I, fluid milk, and Class II, cream)[3] and a lower proportion as surplus (manufactured uses).

Present trends are by no means encouraging for producers in all the milksheds. During recent years there has been in many markets a gradually decreasing proportion of the market milk going into the fluid-milk and cream consumption and a correspondingly increased proportion going to manufactured uses. Thus, even though the Class I price has been relatively favorable, the average or blended price received for the total milk production has been less so. Per capita milk and cream consumption in cities and villages has barely held its own during the last ten years, and in some markets it has decreased noticeably.

Briefly, the present trends in many milk markets may be characterized by (1) increasing resale milk prices in relation to the resale prices of those products which can, and do, replace fresh milk and cream (notably evaporated milk),[4] (2) decreasing or barely maintaining fluid-milk and cream per capita consumption, (3) gradually widening margins of milk distribution (Table 11), and (4) increasing milk surpluses. Such trends seem destined to lead to a situation

---

[3] While no study of the elasticity of demand for fluid cream has proven that cream consumption would increase materially with a lowering of cream prices, there is clear evidence that the demand for cream has greater elasticity than does the demand for fluid milk. Inasmuch as cream deliveries are made to those doorsteps where, and usually only where, fluid-milk deliveries are also made, the cost which can be logically allocated directly to cream delivery is relatively low. For these reasons it would likely pay the milk distributors as well as the milk producers in many markets to adjust the fluid-cream resale prices so that it will be lower in relation to that of fluid milk than is now the case (March, 1939).

[4] See Appen. C.

which will eventually work to the distinct disadvantage of city-milk producers.

Turning our attention again to the unified system of milk distribution, let us suppose that all the gains of the increased efficiency went to consumers. Would the producers necessarily lose because the consumers gained? Contrary to common opinion among many producers, they also might actually gain. Increased fluid-milk consumption in response to lower resale prices, made possible through an increased efficiency of distribution, would bring about a larger proportion of the total city milk receipts consumed as fluid milk and cream. If the producers lost none of their bargaining power, this increase in fluid consumption might easily result in a net gain to producers because a larger proportion of their production would be sold as fluid milk and cream, bringing the higher Class I and Class II prices. The average price of their total production relative to the Class I price would thus be increased.

Even if producers found it necessary to accept slightly lower Class I and Class II prices, it is not unlikely that there would still be a net gain to them. Diminished distributors' margins would reduce resale prices vastly more than farm prices, thereby encouraging consumption without a price loss to producers. That is, the retail price drop would be primarily the outcome of increased efficiency of distribution, not the result of a like drop in the farm price of Class I and Class II milk. Let us suppose that, before the change from a competitive to a unified system, fluid milk was selling at eleven cents per quart at retail, of which the farmer got five cents and the distributor a margin of six cents. A reduction of the distributor's margin to four cents instead of six cents as before would bring the retail price down to nine cents. If the producers were forced to reduce their Class I price from the five-cent level to four cents, and pass this reduction on to the consumers, the retail price would fall to eight cents. Under this condition the retail price would be lowered three cents, three times as much as the drop in the Class I producer price. Put in other words, the consumption increase would be in response to the three-cent fall in price of which the producer was assuming only one cent. The proportionate consumption increase in response to the 27 per cent drop in price (three-elevenths of 100 per cent = 27 per cent), would be sufficient to absorb a considerable amount of the regular surplus milk into fluid-milk and cream uses. This, in turn, would place more of the producers' milk in the higher Class I (and Class II) price instead of the surplus price, thus tending to bolster up the average producer price.

Producers' associations in some markets, under pressure of reduced fluid-milk consumption together with competition from outside milk, have recently debated whether it might not pay them to reduce Class I and Class II prices (even though distributors' margins remained unchanged, or changed only slightly) and pass this price reduction on to the consumers with the view to increase fluid consumption. Other associations have already reduced retail prices, absorbing most of the reduction themselves. In addition to increasing consumption, the reduction of the farm price would, of course, also tend to discourage the entrance of additional new milk. A reduction of the retail price of one cent, say, from eleven cents to ten cents (9 per cent), would be relatively ineffective as a stimulus to a consumption increase compared with a 27 per cent retail price reduction as cited above.

The effect in relative changes in producer and consumer prices resulting from a savings of distribution, coupled with a reduction, in the farm price, may be illustrated by an example:

Condition A.—Unified system in which two cents were saved in distributors' margins and, in addition, producers took a one-cent cut

Consumer price reduction from eleven to eight cents, or 27 per cent

Producer price reduction from five to four cents, or 20 per cent

Condition B.—Competitive system in which distributors' margins could not be reduced but producers took a one-cent cut as before

Consumer price reduction from eleven to ten cents, or 9 per cent

Producer price reduction from five to four cents, or 20 per cent

To summarize, at the inception of a unified milk-distribution system, producer prices would either be unaffected or they would be somewhat depressed because of lessened bargaining influence of the producers' associations. Through time, except for possible continued weakened bargaining position, producers would be as well or even better off under an efficiently operated unified milk-distribution system as under a competitive one. A unified system would permit of decreased costs of distributing milk, hence lower resale prices with a resultant increased fluid-milk and cream consumption. *The key question with regard to both producer and consumer benefits depends largely upon whether the unified system would be operated with the high efficiency which such a setup makes possible.*

The present labor policies on the part of those employed in the milk-distribution business, especially milk deliverymen, are such that many people are apprehensive that the gains of efficiency of milk distribution would go to labor in the form of higher wage rates, shorter hours, smaller loads delivered, etc., rather than to either producers or consumers. There are some grounds for such apprehension. The fact should, however, be pointed out that part of the present apparent strength of organized labor in this field is due to the competitive condition existing in the milk business. If a certain distributor fails to meet the demands of labor, his business may be seriously injured through threatened or actual strike of his employees, picketing, and all manner of adverse publicity. Milk distributors have been known to lose as much as half of their business in a relatively few weeks as a result of such labor activities. Under those conditions the employer has little choice but to yield to the demands of labor whether or not those demands may seem justifiable.

Under a unified system of milk distribution, where one employer (milk distributor) could not be pitted against another, organized labor would be in a less strategic position; consequently labor leaders would probably be less likely to make demands of a type which, from the public point of view, may appear unwarranted or unreasonable. No one should deny the employee reasonable wage rates, hours, and working conditions. Neither should milk producers or consumers sanction or permit wage rates noticeably out of line with the effort, responsibility, and training involved any more than they should permit unnecessarily large salaries of managers and officers or profits of distributors.

To the extent that milk processing and distribution could be carried on with less labor and management under a unified system than under the present competitive one, those who may find it necessary to obtain less desirable employment elsewhere will, of course, suffer a loss. Even though it can be shown that a unified milk-distribution system will make for lower prices to consumers, any program which noticeably reduces the number of people employed in the industry, whether wage-earners or salary-earners, cannot be expected to meet with enthusiastic public support during times when large numbers are already unemployed.

CHAPTER X

CONCLUSIONS AND OUTLOOK

ATTENTION has been centered mainly upon milk distribution in cities of 100,000 or less population. On the basis of the findings, the purely technical phases involving increased efficiencies in the operation of a unified system of milk distribution, and the possible economies resulting, permit of rather definite measurements and conclusions. These conclusions leave little doubt that, under the conditions which prevailed during the period covered in the study, and for the size and type of markets included (about 10,000–100,000 population in east north central United States, particularly in Wisconsin), an efficiently operated, unified system of milk distribution could bring about a reduction of milk-distribution costs by amounts varying from, say, $1\frac{1}{2}$ to 2 cents or perhaps even $2\frac{1}{4}$ cents per quart of milk handled. However, even though it can be shown that such savings could be brought about, there is no proof or certainty that they would be carried out if unification in milk distribution were put into effect.

When one leaves the purely technical phases of the investigation and attempts to analyze the social implications involved, the problems become much more complex and less tangible or predictable. If it were certain that those who are given responsibility for the government of a city—or state—were always thoroughly qualified to direct this new business and that, in addition to such qualifications, they could also be depended upon to see that it was operated strictly in the public interest, with no personal or political considerations or favors, then it would be a relatively easy and simple matter to predict the extent of savings which would actually be effected.

But can we always be confident that such conditions will be carried out? On this point there are doubts. An undertaking such as the distribution of milk under public utility control will be a pronounced success to the extent, and only to the extent, that those

concerned—producers, consumers, and city and state officials—have
the will and the capacity to make it succeed.

The possible savings which, according to our analysis, could be
brought about are predicated upon the following assumptions.

1. That the investment in land, plant, and equipment for the
new system would be prudently and honestly made—more specifically, that all the units of the plant and the equipment would be of
such size, construction, type, and quality as to permit of relatively
high efficiency and corresponding low cost of operation; and that
the prices for which these were purchased represent economic values
void of all semblance of favors, bribes, excessive profit, or graft.

2. That the management of the new system would maintain substantially the same degree of efficiency permitted in the operation
of that system as is now being maintained by each of the milk distributors under the competitive system.

3. That the enterprise will be free from political influence in deciding policies to be established, in the appointments of management,
in the prices to be paid and received for milk, and in the standard and
type of services rendered in the operation of the enterprise.

The reader will recognize these as fundamental issues in determining the success or failure of such an enterprise. Will the city mayor,
the councilmen, and others responsible for carrying on city government, and the residents of a city have the foresight, the courage, and
the public point of view to adopt and carry out rigidly those policies
which are essential for success? The challenge is a real one.

Even though public utility operation of milk distribution may
permit of economies, what is the likelihood that such a system will
be generally adopted in the near future? The rate of progress of
such a movement will depend partly upon the amount of public
criticism of the existing system but more upon economic conditions
in cities. The greater the pressure upon consumer budgets, the more
rapidly can changes be expected in that direction. The agitation for
such a system will come mainly from consumers; perhaps somewhat
from interested groups such as manufacturers of milk-processing
machinery and equipment, who will stand to gain as a result of increased sales of these machines when new milk-distribution plants
are put in; or from candidates for public office.

It would seem that major changes of this nature should move slowly, perhaps starting as experiments in a few markets where existing distribution costs are relatively high or services unusually poor. If a reasonable degree of success can be achieved under such circumstances, then the experiment will furnish valuable information for other cities to follow. In cities where there exists a combination of competent public officials, a healthy budget, and a population which would support this type of enterprise—there the conditions would be ideal for such an experiment. If the plan were adopted in a few cities and made a favorable showing, the movement would gather rapid momentum. If, on the other hand, the first attempts proved failures or were only moderately successful, the more general movement would be delayed.

When the public believes profits and salaries to be unduly high under the existing system, and that these are important factors in bringing about a wide price margin between the farmers who produce the milk and the consumers who use it, then it will be relatively easy to obtain wide public support for more control in milk distribution or support for a complete change in the distribution system.

Even though many consumers may insist that the margin of distribution is too wide, it will be less easy to bring about a change, and presumably an improvement, where the wide margin is due to the wastes of competition than where it is due to high salaries, profits, or graft. If the latter condition were shown to exist and were publicized, then emotion could be fanned into action rather quickly—but apparently, even though they may pay for it, not many people worry about competitive waste.

Judging by recent trends in legal decisions on public regulation, it appears that there is much more than an even chance that the legality of public utility control would be upheld by the courts. To be sure, a few years would be required to clear up all the legal rights and powers of a city to control or to operate the milk-distribution system to the exclusion of private enterprise. In the meantime, litigation would hamper the free operation of the plan and produce delay, uncertainties, irritation, and expense. Milk distributors, and the laborers associated with them, can be expected to oppose any movement in the direction of public utility control. Milk producers are not likely to lend support to this type of distribution. Instead, they will probably bend their efforts in the direction of price improvement by strengthening their bargaining position with the existing milk-distributing system and by continuing state and federal price-control measures under the competitive system of distribution.

In the past, producers' co-operative bargaining associations have opposed any movement toward public utility operation, believing they would be likely to suffer because of a loss in bargaining power under such a system. In this view they may be partly correct, but it is equally true that they may be overlooking opportunities which would be to their own advantage by narrowing of the margin of distribution through a unified system.

From the standpoint of a disinterested observer the case for milk distribution under a unified system is very strong, and likewise from that of the consumer the case for such a system is clear cut. On the other hand, from the standpoint of the distributor and of organized labor the opposition will be powerful, while the producers, especially the organized producers, will not favor the change although they may be converted.

APPENDIXES

APPENDIX A

DIVISION OF COSTS OF MILK DISTRIBUTION

TABLE A

DIVISION OF OPERATING COST INTO VARIOUS ITEMS BY INDIVIDUAL COMPANY* ARRANGED IN DESCENDING ORDER OF SIZE, BY YEARS, 1927–37, INCLUSIVE

(Expressed as a Percentage of Total Operating Cost)

Operating Cost	1927	1928	1929	1930	1931	1932	1933	1934	1935	1936	1937
						Company A					
Salaries	2.3	1.9	1.7	1.6	1.5	1.7	1.7	1.6	2.2	1.8	1.8
Wages	56.6	54.9	56.1	55.6	54.0	52.1	51.4	51.7	54.0	55.7	57.0
Total labor	58.9	56.8	57.8	57.2	55.5	53.8	53.1	53.3	56.2	57.5	58.8
Depreciation	6.4	5.7	7.1	8.5	9.0	10.1	10.1	8.4	7.1	5.2	3.7
Bad Debts	0.4	0.7	0.7	0.8	1.4	6.1	3.2	3.9	1.1	1.4	0.8
Taxes	0.5	1.4	1.4	1.7	1.1	1.5	2.1	1.7	1.5	2.0	1.7
Insurance	1.2	1.0	1.5	1.4	1.1	1.6	2.0	2.3	2.9	0.6	0.9
Advertising	3.3	2.8	3.1	2.7	2.4	1.5	2.0	1.9	2.7	3.7	5.2
Repairs	2.8	5.7	3.3	3.3	3.5	3.6	3.7	3.5	3.9	3.9	3.1
Power, light, and water	....	....	2.7	2.7	3.1	3.1	3.5	2.9	2.9	2.8	2.3
All other	26.5	25.9	22.4	21.7	22.9	18.7	20.3	22.1	21.7	22.9	23.5
Total operating cost	100.0	100.0	100.0	100.0	100.0	100.0	100.0	100.0	100.0	100.0	100.0

* Companies A to G, inclusive, are those included as "large" companies in the study, while those designated as H to M, inclusive, are included as "small" companies. Grouping into the two sizes was made on the bases of the amount of sales. Included in the list of large companies are the seven whose sales were greater than $100,000 in 1932. The small companies had sales below this amount. In that year (1932) sales of six of the seven large companies varied from $107,000 to $199,000. One was appreciably larger with sales of $425,000. Sales of the small companies varied from $73,000 to $97,000 the same year.

Operating Cost	1927	1928	1929	1930	1931	1932	1933	1934	1935	1936	1937
Company B											
Salaries	......	......	......	......	......	14.3	19.5	20.1	14.0	11.8	9.8
Wages	......	......	......	......	......	34.2	37.6	40.2	42.1	44.0	46.9
Total labor						48.5	57.1	60.3	56.1	55.8	56.7
Depreciation						6.4	6.5	5.3	4.5	4.8	4.3
Bad debts						18.4	5.5	3.2	3.4	0.8	1.0
Taxes						0.3	0.5	0.5	0.6	0.7	0.7
Insurance						0.8	2.5	1.8	2.3	1.5	3.0
Advertising						3.4	3.2	3.2	4.7	3.8	3.0
Repairs						2.3	1.5	0.7	1.6	2.0	1.9
Power, light, and water											2.9†
All other						19.9	23.2	25.0	26.8	30.6	26.5
Total operating cost						100.0	100.0	100.0	100.0	100.0	100.0
Company C											
Salaries	8.0	9.7	11.2	11.9	13.5	13.3	13.9	12.4	11.8	12.8	12.8
Wages	35.5	35.8	35.2	35.0	35.3	36.2	35.8	33.7	33.2	31.9	34.8
Total labor	43.5	45.5	46.4	46.9	48.8	49.5	49.7	46.1	45.0	44.7	47.6
Depreciation	17.1	16.3	16.4	13.9	10.6	8.1	9.5	11.7	13.6	12.4	10.3
Bad debts	0.2	2.3	1.8	1.8	0.7	0.3	1.3	2.3	1.0	2.5	0.5
Taxes	2.4	3.3	2.4	2.4	3.0	3.7	2.5	1.3	1.3	1.7	2.3
Insurance	1.7	1.7	1.6	1.4	1.3	2.2	1.8	2.2	2.4	1.6	1.5
Advertising	6.2	5.2	5.1	4.7	6.6	4.7	3.6	3.3	4.2	4.6	4.1
Repairs											4.4
Power, light, and water	4.2	3.7	3.8	3.8	3.6	3.8	4.2	3.7	3.7	3.2	3.5
All other	24.7	22.0	22.5	25.1	25.4	27.7	27.4	29.4	28.8	29.3	25.8
Total operating cost	100.0	100.0	100.0	100.0	100.0	100.0	100.0	100.0	100.0	100.0	100.0

† Heat, light, and power.

TABLE A—Continued

Company D

Operating Cost	1927	1928	1929	1930	1931	1932	1933	1934	1935	1936	1937
Salaries	....	....	15.5	15.1	15.1	16.6	17.4	16.4	16.8	16.4	10.0
Wages	....	....	46.3	45.4	47.5	49.0	50.8	49.7	50.2	45.7	51.2
Total labor	....	....	61.8	60.5	62.6	65.6	68.2	66.1	67.0	62.1	61.2
Depreciation	....	....	13.5	11.2	12.4	7.6	11.0	11.0	9.5	11.5	10.4
Bad debts	....	....	1.1	0.8	1.2	1.4	2.0	3.5	0.7	1.7	1.0
Taxes	....	....	2.1	2.8	2.3	1.5	2.5	2.6	2.6	2.1	2.2
Insurance	....	....	2.1	1.3	1.5	2.8	2.2	2.1	2.6	2.1	2.1
Advertising	....	....	2.5	5.1	2.3	3.5	0.3	2.5	2.2	2.9	3.3
Repairs	....	....	4.9	6.9	7.0	5.8	4.8	3.8	6.3	6.3	5.6
Power, light, and water	....	....	3.9	3.5	3.1	3.7	4.3	3.9	3.2	3.1	3.1
All other	....	....	8.1	7.9	7.6	8.1	4.7	4.5	5.9	8.2	11.1
Total operating cost	....	....	100.0	100.0	100.0	100.0	100.0	100.0	100.0	100.0	100.0

Company E

Operating Cost	1927	1928	1929	1930	1931	1932	1933	1934	1935	1936	1937
Salaries	12.8	14.9	14.5	16.2	17.5	19.2	16.0	13.8	14.1	14.4	13.1
Wages	28.3	29.7	30.0	28.8	30.9	32.5	33.3	33.7	33.2	32.0	33.7
Total labor	41.1	44.6	44.5	45.0	48.4	51.7	49.3	47.5	47.3	46.4	46.8
Depreciation	8.6	7.2	7.0	6.2	6.9	8.5	8.2	7.4	7.3	7.2	6.9
Bad debts	2.3	1.1	1.1	2.3	2.3	1.0	1.0	1.8	0.7	1.7	2.5
Taxes	7.5	8.3	8.8	9.2	8.4	7.6	6.4	3.5	4.5	3.2	4.0
Insurance	2.3	1.5	1.5	1.6	1.7	2.2	2.4	2.4	2.8	2.3	3.0
Advertising	1.8	1.8	1.8	1.7	2.5	2.3	2.1	1.5	1.2	0.9	....
Repairs	3.9	5.4	4.3	5.1	5.2	2.2	3.8	3.4	4.3	3.1	4.4
Power, light, and water	....	....	....	....	....	....	....	....	....	....	3.3
All other	32.5	30.1	31.0	30.2	25.6	24.3	26.8	32.5	31.5	34.3	29.1
Total operating cost	100.0	100.0	100.0	100.0	100.0	100.0	100.0	100.0	100.0	100.0	100.0

TABLE A—Continued

Operating Cost	1927	1928	1929	1930	1931	1932	1933	1934	1935	1936	1937
Company F											
Salaries........						3.4	3.6	3.7	3.5	3.5	2.9
Wages..........						39.9	40.9	45.9	43.1	44.2	39.8
Total labor...						43.3	44.5	49.6	46.6	47.7	42.7
Depreciation..						8.5	9.6	7.2	6.7	6.3	4.9
Bad debts.....						3.8	3.9	3.8	3.5	2.0	2.1
Taxes.........											
Insurance.....											
Advertising...						7.5	4.5	4.6	7.2	8.1	12.6
Repairs........						3.2	3.4	3.9	3.8	4.2	6.5
Power, light, and water...						4.1	4.8	4.4	3.8	3.7	3.0
All other.....						29.6	29.3	26.5	28.4	28.0	28.2
Total operating cost...						100.0	100.0	100.0	100.0	100.0	100.0
Company G											
Salaries........	33.3	29.6	23.3	22.2	21.2	21.3	22.1	20.2	19.0	18.1	17.2
Wages..........	22.8	23.4	25.6	27.3	28.1	29.2	32.9	33.2	36.1	36.6	37.8
Total labor...	56.1	53.0	48.9	49.5	49.3	50.5	55.0	53.4	55.1	54.7	55.0
Depreciation..	6.2	7.5	10.1	9.8	9.4	9.5	8.7	6.7	6.6	7.3	6.5
Bad debts.....	1.6	1.7	1.7	0.4	0.8	1.3	2.0	1.2	1.3	1.2	3.9
Taxes.........	4.1	4.1	5.7	6.0	7.5	7.3	5.4	4.1	4.2	4.4	4.5
Insurance.....		1.1	1.1	0.8	1.4	1.7	1.3	1.4	2.0	1.4	1.6
Advertising...		4.2	4.1	4.7	5.4	4.9	3.3	3.1	3.2	3.2	3.2
Repairs........		1.5	1.3	2.0	1.7	1.7	1.8	1.7	1.9	0.3	3.0
Power, light, and water...		1.8	2.5	2.6	2.7	2.5	2.6	2.6	2.7	2.5	2.7
All other.....	32.0	25.1	24.6	24.2	21.8	20.6	19.9	25.8	23.0	25.0	19.6
Total operating cost...	100.0	100.0	100.0	100.0	100.0	100.0	100.0	100.0	100.0	100.0	100.0

TABLE A—Continued

Company H

Operating Cost	1927	1928	1929	1930	1931	1932	1933	1934	1935	1936	1937
Salaries	7.4	7.0	6.3	6.8	6.7	7.6	8.2	7.7	7.7	7.3	7.0
Wages	44.2	44.6	45.4	50.5	45.7	45.0	42.2	45.1	45.4	46.8	49.5
Total labor	51.6	51.6	51.7	57.3	52.4	52.6	50.4	52.8	53.1	54.1	56.5
Depreciation	5.6	4.5	5.7	7.3	9.9	14.1	17.1	15.2	12.5	8.9	7.0
Bad debts	0.4	1.8	0.0	0.2	1.5	0.0	0.2	0.0	0.0	0.4	1.0
Taxes	1.4	2.6	1.3	1.1	4.3	4.2	4.0	2.9	2.7	2.5	3.6
Insurance	2.5	2.8	2.4	0.5	2.1	3.6	3.9	3.7	4.8	4.9	5.0
Advertising	2.6	1.6	2.5	1.1	2.0	4.1	1.7	1.6	2.4	2.8	2.7
Repairs	2.9	2.9	5.2	3.2	2.2	3.2	3.4	4.0	3.6	5.9	4.2
Power, light, and water						3.4	4.2	3.8	4.0	3.9	3.6
All other	33.0	32.2	31.2	29.3	25.6	14.8	15.1	16.0	16.9	16.6	17.4
Total operating cost	100.0	100.0	100.0	100.0	100.0	100.0	100.0	100.0	100.0	100.0	100.0

Company I

Operating Cost	1927	1928	1929	1930	1931	1932	1933	1934	1935	1936	1937
Salaries			11.4	17.8	22.3	11.2	13.2	15.3	13.4	17.5	15.8
Wages			39.0	35.3	34.9	36.7	41.3	39.1	39.5	41.5	38.8
Total labor			50.4	53.1	57.2	47.9	54.5	54.4	52.9	59.0	54.6
Depreciation			8.9	7.0	7.4	9.0	10.7	6.2	4.5	6.3	7.5
Bad debts				3.0	0.2	7.4	4.0	2.9	3.9	0.8	1.2
Taxes			1.8	1.2	1.3	1.5	1.1	1.0	1.1	1.3	1.0
Insurance			1.0	1.3	1.3	1.7	1.7	2.5	2.5	2.8	1.4
Advertising			9.3	3.3	2.8	3.0	3.6	3.5	4.8	3.5	5.4
Repairs			6.9	4.4	11.0	7.5	4.7	4.4	5.0	8.3	10.3
Power, light, and water			2.7	2.2	2.3	2.9	2.9	2.5	2.5	3.0	3.2
All other			19.0	24.0	16.5	19.1	16.8	22.6	22.8	15.0	15.4
Total operating cost	100.0	100.0	100.0	100.0	100.0	100.0	100.0	100.0	100.0	100.0	100.0

TABLE A—Continued

Company J

Operating Cost	1927	1928	1929	1930	1931	1932	1933	1934	1935	1936	1937
Salaries	5.6	8.4	8.3	12.7	6.7	7.7	8.8	13.4	9.4	6.0	5.8
Wages	57.8	39.9	49.7	49.8	56.5	57.5	51.5	45.8	51.7	47.4	54.1
Total labor	63.4	48.3	58.0	62.5	63.2	65.2	60.3	59.2	61.1	53.4	59.9
Depreciation	4.2	11.5	8.1	6.4	6.5	7.4	6.6	6.2	7.2	7.1	7.1
Bad debts	0.9		2.3	5.4	4.3	4.2	3.8	4.0	1.1	2.6	3.5
Taxes	0.9		0.5	0.8	1.0	1.0	1.6	1.3	1.3	2.3	2.9
Insurance	1.4	3.6	2.0	2.3	1.0	1.6	4.0	2.3	1.3	3.5	1.4
Advertising	2.2	7.3	2.2	0.9	0.9	1.1	0.7	1.7	2.4	2.0	1.4
Repairs	2.2										3.1
Power, light, and water	2.2	2.4	3.5	3.0	3.1	3.0	3.3	3.5	3.5	3.1	3.0
All other	22.6	26.9	23.4	18.7	19.8	16.5	19.7	21.8	22.1	25.9	17.7
Total operating cost	100.0	100.0	100.0	100.0	100.0	100.0	100.0	100.0	100.0	100.0	100.0

Company K

Operating Cost	1927	1928	1929	1930	1931	1932	1933	1934	1935	1936	1937
Salaries	14.8	20.5	28.4	25.6	32.2	13.9	16.6	17.1	15.4	20.2	18.1
Wages	40.2	37.7	36.7	36.5	38.8	44.5	49.2	51.3	49.3	47.9	46.1
Total labor	55.0	58.2	65.1	62.1	71.0	58.4	65.8	68.4	64.7	68.1	64.2
Depreciation	6.5	4.8	6.4	6.0	6.8	8.3	6.6	5.2	5.1	4.2	4.4
Bad debts	1.0	1.1	1.1	1.6	0.4	5.7	0.0	0.0	0.9	1.2	4.8
Taxes	2.6	2.0	1.7	2.1	1.2	1.1	1.3	1.5	1.6	1.6	1.5
Insurance	1.7	1.8	1.0	2.6	0.6	2.7	2.4	2.8	3.4	3.3	3.9
Advertising	1.4	0.9	0.5	4.5	1.4	2.2	1.7	0.7	1.9	2.0	2.6
Repairs	3.8	1.4	6.2	4.4	2.0	1.8	1.4	1.0	0.6	1.4	1.2
Power, light, and water	4.7	2.8	2.4	2.8	3.3	3.8	4.3	4.3	4.2	3.4	3.1
All other	23.3	27.0	15.6	13.9	13.3	16.0	16.5	16.1	17.6	14.8	14.3
Total operating cost	100.0	100.0	100.0	100.0	100.0	100.0	100.0	100.0	100.0	100.0	100.0

Company L

Operating Cost	1927	1928	1929	1930	1931	1932	1933	1934	1935	1936	1937
Salaries	10.5	15.9	13.5	13.8	13.7	14.0	12.5	15.1	18.6	21.4	26.1
Wages	54.7	44.3	46.0	46.1	44.4	44.4	43.4	38.1	36.6	33.3	33.2
Total labor	65.2	60.2	59.5	59.9	58.1	58.4	55.9	53.2	55.2	54.7	59.3
Depreciation	3.9	6.4	5.9	4.8	5.6	7.4	8.7	8.1	7.1	6.8	6.0
Bad debts	0.6	....	1.1	1.3	1.1	1.3	2.0	3.2	1.6	0.9	0.5
Taxes	0.5	0.5	0.4	1.3	1.1	1.3	1.8	1.6	1.6	2.5	2.3
Insurance	0.2	0.2	0.2	0.9	1.2	0.8	1.2	1.4	2.4	2.6	2.4
Advertising	2.4	3.0	2.2	3.1	2.5	2.9	3.0	2.8	2.9	3.0	2.0
Repairs	1.2	1.7	2.8	2.4	3.0	2.2	2.1	2.4	3.0	3.2	2.8
Power, light, and water	2.2	2.5	2.8	3.2	3.1	2.5	2.7	2.3	2.3	2.1	1.8
All other	23.8	25.5	25.1	23.1	24.3	23.2	22.6	25.0	23.9	24.2	22.9
Total operating cost	100.0	100.0	100.0	100.0	100.0	100.0	100.0	100.0	100.0	100.0	100.0

Company M

Operating Cost	1927	1928	1929	1930	1931	1932	1933	1934	1935	1936	1937
Salaries	....	....	9.1	9.5	9.0	8.2	9.3	7.6	5.5	5.2	4.8
Wages	....	....	38.9	45.0	45.8	42.3	44.6	44.0	41.6	44.6	44.1
Total labor	....	....	48.0	54.5	54.8	50.5	53.9	51.6	47.1	49.8	48.9
Depreciation	....	....	8.1	10.4	12.0	14.1	11.6	10.4	7.8	8.4	7.7
Bad debts	....	....	....	....	0.3	2.0	2.4	2.2	1.5	2.1	3.9
Taxes	....	....	....	1.2	2.2	3.0	3.1	2.3	2.4	1.0	4.2
Insurance	....	....	3.9	2.9	1.6	2.8	2.5	2.7	3.5	1.6	1.6
Advertising	....	....	3.0	3.2	3.3	3.0	2.0	2.4	1.6	1.6	1.6
Repairs	....	....	....	....	....	....	....	....	7.6	6.0	8.3
Power, light, and water	....	....	5.7	5.2	....	....	....	....	4.4	4.0	3.6
All other	....	....	31.3	22.6	25.8	24.6	24.5	28.4	24.1	24.6	20.0
Total operating cost			100.0	100.0	100.0	100.0	100.0	100.0	100.0	100.0	100.0

195

TABLE B

STANDARD ERROR OF THE MEANS OF EACH OF THE COST ITEMS GIVEN IN TEXT TABLE 2,* 1930–37, INCLUSIVE

Cost Item	1930	1931	1932	1933	1934	1935	1936	1937	Average†
Total labor.......	±5.8	±6.7	±6.4	±6.3	±6.4	±6.6	±6.2	±6.2	±6.3
Depreciation.....	0.8	0.7	0.9	0.8	0.8	0.8	0.7	0.6	0.8
Bad debts........	0.5	0.4	1.4	0.4	0.4	0.3	0.2	0.4	0.5
Taxes...........	0.8	0.8	0.7	0.5	0.3	0.3	0.3	0.4	0.5
Insurance........	0.2	0.1	0.2	0.3	0.2	0.2	0.3	0.3	0.2
Advertising.......	0.4	0.5	0.5	0.3	0.3	0.5	0.5	0.8	0.5
Repairs..........	0.6	1.1	0.6	0.4	0.4	0.6	0.7	0.8	0.6
Power, light, and water..........	±0.3	±0.1	±0.2	±0.2	±0.2	±0.2	±0.2	±0.1	±0.2

* Detailed data contained in Table A; salaries and wages combined into total labor.

† Simple average of the eight annual standard errors. For a discussion on the interpretation of the standard error see G. Udny Yule and M. G. Kendall, *An Introduction to the Theory of Statistics* (London: Charles Griffin & Co., Ltd., 1937), pp. 353 and 386 and index references; cf. also Mordecai Ezekiel, *Methods of Correlation Analysis* (New York: John Wiley & Sons, Inc., 1930).

APPENDIX B

SUPPLEMENTARY INFORMATION ON DELIVERY

I. DISCUSSION OF DELIVERY LABOR

In addition to wages paid milk deliverymen, there are other costs of selling and delivering such as that part of managerial expense involved in obtaining new business, including the direction of salesmen, of competitive advertising, and the costs associated with all delivery equipment, including such items as repairs, depreciation, taxes, and insurance. In the records of only a few of the Wisconsin companies studied were costs segregated in such a way that the total costs of selling and delivering could be obtained. Such information as was secured indicated that this total cost amounted to about 50–60 per cent of the total cost of processing and distribution. In order to check our information with that from other studies, such information as was available to the writer was tabulated in summary form (Table C). The figures in column 5 of this table show that total selling and delivery expense (except for the wholesale or "largely wholesale" routes) varies from about 52 to 68 per cent of the total operating costs of milk distribution. Virtually all the figures fall within a range of 55–65 per cent of total cost. Since so large a proportion of the total cost of milk distribution goes for sales and delivery, it is clear that in those functions we must look for the major savings under a unified system of operation. If a significant percentage reduction can be brought about in these functions, then the reduction of cost per quart of milk handled will be considerable.

II. GLIMPSES OF INFORMATION CONCERNING URBAN MAIL DELIVERY-MEN AND GARBAGE COLLECTORS

Because comparisons are often made between the relative efficiencies of milk and mail delivery systems, some information will be presented on this point. In the same city for which the detailed milk-route survey was made, certain information was also obtained concerning the United States mail delivery. In the residential area the mailmen delivered on an average of 110 pounds of mail daily, consisting of 1,249 pieces (in addition to 56 pounds of mail "relayed"). On the routes (virtually the entire residential area of the city) where two deliveries were made daily deliverymen averaged 437 "possible delivery stops." That is, as an average, each mailman stood ready to serve 437 "patrons" twice daily. Not all individuals received mail twice a day, but it was estimated that about 75 per cent of them did receive mail once daily and about 50 per cent of them twice daily. In any event, virtually the entire route

197

TABLE C

RELATIONSHIP OF DELIVERY AND SELLING COSTS TO TOTAL OPERATING
COSTS OF MILK-DISTRIBUTING COMPANIES IN VARIOUS MARKETS

(Expressed as a Percentage of Total Operating Cost)

Market	No. of Cos.	Year	Delivery	Selling	Total Selling and De-livery*
	(1)	(2)	(3)	(4)	(5)
Philadelphia†	6	1930–33	47.6	19.1	66.7
Connecticut‡	9	1931–33	47.4	10.2	57.6
Baltimore, St. Louis, etc.§	11	1930–33–35	61.7	6.9	68.6
Milwaukee‖	⎧ 3–20	1928–34	51.7	5.0	56.7
	⎨ 3–7	1928–31	47.7	4.9	52.6
	⎩ 14–20	1932–34	56.0	4.9	60.9
Milwaukee¶	6	1933	56.6	5.1	61.7
California**	12	1936	W56.9††	W1.4	W58.3
			R67.5††	R1.4	R68.9
San Francisco‡‡	14	1932	W35.5	W7.3	W42.8
			R63.7	R3.2	R66.9
New York City§§	19	1933	....	....	65.1
New York upstate, large‖‖	21	1933	....	....	55.2
New York upstate, small¶¶	7	1932–33	....	....	52.0
Illinois***	....	1925–26	....	....	62.8
New York City†††	⎧ 14	1936	⎫	....	⎧ 62.8
	⎩ 14	1937	⎭		⎩ 62.7
West Virginia (largely whole-sale)‡‡‡	22	1933	....	....	40.0

* The two items (delivery and selling) have been separated in those cases where the information made such separation possible. However, it should be borne in mind that the divisions are not always on a strictly comparable basis as between markets. For that reason, more reliable comparability is obtained by comparing the total selling and delivery cost (col. 5) with that of total operating cost than by comparing either delivery (col. 3) or selling (col. 4) with the total operating cost.

† Federal Trade Commission, *Distribution and Sale of Milk and Milk Products: Philadelphia and Connecticut Milksheds* (House Document No. 387 [74th Cong.; 2d sess.] [Washington, 1936]), p. 70.

‡ *Ibid.*, p. 65.

§ Federal Trade Commission, *Distribution and Sale of Milk and Milk Products* (Boston, Baltimore, Cincinnati, and St. Louis) (House Document No. 501 [74th Cong.; 2d sess.] [Washington, 1936]), p. 148.

‖ Agricultural Adjustment Administration, *A Survey of Milk Marketing in Milwaukee* ("U.S.D.A. Marketing Information Series," DM-1 [Washington, 1937]), p. 56.

¶ *Ibid.*, p. 60.

** J. M. Tinley, *Public Regulation of Milk Marketing in California* (Berkeley, 1938), pp. 125–26.

†† W = wholesale; R = retail.

‡‡ John Marshall, Jr., "Cost of Distributing Market Milk in San Francisco" (State Department of Agriculture, Division of Markets [Sacramento, Calif., 1932]), Table 2 (mimeographed). Wholesale business 63.5 per cent of total.

§§ Leland Spencer, "Costs and Profits of Milk Dealers in New York City, August, 1933"(Albany: State Department of Agriculture and Markets, 1934), p. 3 (mimeographed). Transportation not included as a cost.

‖‖ Leland Spencer, "Costs and Profits of Milk Dealers in Upstate Cities, August, 1933" (Report to the New York State Milk Control Board, March 24, 1934), p. 3 (mimeographed).

¶¶ Leland Spencer, "Milk Distributors' Costs and Profits" (Preliminary Report to the New York State Milk Control Board, October 17, 1933), p. 13 (mimeographed).

*** C. A. Brown, *Costs and Margins and Other Related Factors in the Distribution of Fluid Milk in Four Illinois Market Areas* (University of Illinois Bull. 318 [Urbana, 1929]), p. 255. Markets included are Chicago, Peoria, Quincy, and St. Louis.

††† "The Milk Audit," in the *American Produce Review*, February 23, 1938, p. 498.

‡‡‡ R. O. Stelzer and L. M. Thurston, *Milk Distribution Costs in West Virginia* (West Virginia Bull. 266 [Morgantown, 1935]), p. 12. Records of a majority of the plants indicate that business was about 70 per cent wholesale.

must be traveled twice per day.[1] If these estimates are correct, the mailman would make a total of 550 delivery stops during an eight-hour day, of which six hours are spent on the route and the other two in the office.

Information was also obtained in the same city concerning the number of "pickups" by garbage trucks manned by three men—a driver who picked up garbage only occasionally, and two men devoting their entire time to picking up garbage. A "pickup" was defined as the collection of any garbage, whether the amount was small or large. The average number of pickups per truck under

[1] The standard deviation and the coefficient of variation from the averages were noticeably larger for the mail deliverymen than for the garbage collectors. Tables I and II, below, show the variation which exists between different routes for mailmen and for garbage collectors, respectively.

TABLE I

ARITHMETIC MEAN, STANDARD DEVIATION, AND COEFFICIENT OF
VARIATION BETWEEN MAIL-DELIVERY ROUTES

	Arithmetic Mean	Standard Deviation	Coefficient of Variation
Total weight of mail (lb.)	110.5	26.5	24.0
Length of route (miles).............	6.5	2.0	30.1
Average number of pieces handled..	1,248.6	342.4	27.4
Number of "possible" stops........	436.6	199.7	45.7
		106.6*	27.0*

* Figure which would have existed if two routes had been edited out. These two had an abnormally large number of stops because they were located in apartment-house areas. For the two routes edited out, both having more than twice the average number of possible stops, the total weight of all mail as well as the number of pieces handled was less than the average of all routes. This indicates that not only are the stops closer together but that the stops in apartment areas (smaller families and less permanent residents) receive much less mail than the average.

TABLE II

ARITHMETIC MEAN, STANDARD DEVIATION, AND COEFFICIENT OF
VARIATION BETWEEN GARBAGE-COLLECTION TRUCKS
(Average for Five Trucks)

	Arithmetic Mean	Standard Deviation	Coefficient of Variation
Total miles traveled per eight-hour day..........................	40.5	4.22*	10.4*
Total pickups per eight-hour day...	1,019	70	6.8
Average minutes per pickup.......	0.37	0.034*	9.2*
Total pickups, Monday to Friday, inclusive, for each of five trucks†..	988	117.1	11.9

* Standard deviation and coefficient of variation indicate the variation between trucks when calculated from weekly averages.

† Figures are calculated on the basis of five trucks for each of five days, i.e., $n = 25$, not five, as in the above three cases. The number of pickups per hour was greater on Saturday (a four-hour day) than on the other days. This accounts for the relatively larger mean of total pickups when Saturday is included.

this system was 1,019 per day for five trucks which collected virtually all the garbage from the residential area of the city of about 70,000 population. This would be an average of more than 340 pickups per man daily. In many cases milk deliverymen must deliver milk at the back door, and in practically all cases garbage must be collected from that point. The time required to remove garbage from the household receptacles and transfer it to the carrying pails certainly would be no less than the time required to set down the full bottles and pick up the empties. The fact should be noted that the number of pickups made per man is greater than the number that is suggested for a milk delivery-man under a unified system—a possible 330 customers served as compared with 340 pickups made in eight hours.

APPENDIX C

THE EFFECT OF PRICE UPON THE CONSUMP-
TION OF FRESH AND EVAPORATED MILK

At the end of chapter iv it was shown that an efficiently operated unified system of milk distribution could effect a possible annual saving in a family's milk bill of from $4.50 to as much as $22.00 annually. Anything approaching the latter amount cannot be dismissed as unimportant to a large family with small or medium income. The alert housewife is ever weighing one value against another in purchasing daily food items. If the price of one product is high in relation to another product which can be used in its stead, the less expensive one is often purchased. To use the more common expression, the consumer substitutes one product for another. Such substitution is usually partial rather than complete. Suppose, for example, that a housewife believes that the price of fresh fluid milk is disproportionately high as compared with evaporated milk. She merely reduces the amount of fresh milk taken and replaces it in part with evaporated milk, which she may use, let us say, for cooking and baking purposes instead of the higher-priced fresh milk.

By and large, consumers have made no united protest against fluid-milk prices, and hence they have been given only limited consideration either by milk-producer bargaining co-operatives or by the state milk control boards.

Where consumer interests have been injected into the scene, it has been more at the instance of certain local groups or leaders of political factions than by consumers per se. True, in one or two instances these groups representing, or purporting to represent, the consumers have made it known in a rather telling manner that they too should be considered in matters involving retail milk price and methods of handling fluid milk. However, the more general inclination on the part of consumers to acquiesce to price changes with no apparent resistance has led producers (mostly through their associations), distributors, and, all too often, public price-making agencies to presume that the problems of fluid milk were their concern and theirs alone. Accordingly, arrangements such as were agreeable to those parties were thereby presumed to be agreeable to all concerned. The voice of consumers, when heard, was usually welcomed but seldom followed. The situation may be likened to that of the parents deciding which of two eligibles the favored son should marry, as though he himself had no other interest or choice. Indeed, the son may have other desires and alternatives to which the parents had either remained blind or had been unwilling to acknowledge.

Both farm and resale price for milk delivered at the family doorstep or sold at retail to stores have been established largely upon the assumption that, since consumers ordinarily make no united protest against price increases, they will continue making rather constant purchases regardless of what prices are established; or, if consumers do reduce their purchases, the reduction is only for a relatively short time and, at most, involves a proportionately small decrease. It is not an uncommon practice for producers' associations and dealers to "build up" public sentiment through the press and other sources in anticipation that the consumer will acquiesce to the price increases with no appreciable change in the amounts taken. Such attempts at molding public sentiment doubtless do have the effect of maintaining fluid-milk consumption, at least temporarily, even at a new and higher price, but it will not remedy the shortage of the family budget or stop the attempt on the part of the family to adjust their purchases in such manner as to obtain what they believe to be greatest food returns for the money expended.

Distributors and possibly even a few producers are not entirely unaware that rivals of fluid milk are finding their way into the household, especially of those families whose incomes are low or moderately so. More specifically, some milk distributors are aware that evaporated milk and other food products may replace fluid milk if the price of the latter gets too far out of line with its rivals.

While the average housewife does not make rapid changes in her culinary operations, since she, like everyone else, is strongly influenced by habit, yet, when faced with a reduced family income, she makes every practical attempt to reduce expenses. As mentioned earlier, among other things, she decreases her purchases of fresh whole milk, replacing it with evaporated milk and to a lesser extent with other products in order to save the difference. The greater the price difference, the greater the inducement to make such replacements. Moreover, the reduced family income often results in the use of less refrigeration, thus perhaps lessening the purchase of fresh milk, since, without refrigeration, fresh milk is much more likely to deteriorate than is evaporated milk.

RESULTS SHOWN BY DETAILED SURVEY

For the purpose of obtaining specific information on the use of fresh and evaporated milk, 1,029 families (comprising 4,160 individuals) living in Milwaukee, Janesville, and Kenosha, Wisconsin, were interviewed under the supervision of the writer. Of these families, 7 per cent reported that they obtained an income of $400 or less per year.[1] Sixteen per cent received incomes of from $400 to $800 per year; 31 per cent from $800 to $1,200; 20 per cent from $1,200 to $1,600, and the balance of 25 per cent over $1,600 per year. Thus, briefly, 55 per cent received incomes of less than $1,200; 20 per cent received from $1,200 to $1,600; and the other 25 per cent received over $1,600. This is

[1] A considerable portion of these families were on relief, although it was difficult to obtain the exact information as to their status.

probably a rather typical cross-section of not only those cities but of the urban population of the country.[2]

Of the 1,029 families included in the survey, 970, or 95 per cent, used fresh fluid milk as part of their regular diet. The amount of the consumption increased directly, although not in a pronounced manner, with the increase of family income. Of the 970 families who consumed fresh fluid milk, the daily per capita consumption was 0.32 quart for those below incomes of $800 as compared with 0.44 quart for those of $2,000 or more.

Those using no fresh milk were largely in the low-income brackets. Accordingly, when all 1,029 families were included, those whose incomes were $800 or less reported a daily per capita consumption of only 0.28 quart (1.1 quarts per family of four) as compared with 0.42 quart for those over $2,000—an increase of 50 per cent.

Evaporated milk was used by slightly less than half (47 per cent) of the families included in the survey, but those who used it consumed a rather surprisingly large quantity. The low-income families used decidedly more than did those of higher incomes. The weekly per capita consumption of families with incomes below $400 was 1.2 large cans ($14\frac{1}{2}$ oz.) as compared with 0.85 can for those in the $400–$800 income class, 0.73 can for the $800–$1,200 group, and 0.55 can per week for those above $1,200.

The consumption of evaporated milk decreased continuously with an increase in family income. Fresh-milk consumption, on the other hand, increased continuously with each increase in family income. The lowest-income group used an average of 1.2 cans of evaporated milk per capita weekly and 2 quarts of fresh milk. The average per capita use for all families who used both kinds of milk was 0.77 can of evaporated milk and 2.5 quarts of fresh milk weekly.

Each type of analysis seems to indicate rather clearly that, in all income groups below $1,600, evaporated milk replaces fluid milk rather than serves as an addition to its use. In every income group up to and including the $2,000 income, those who used evaporated milk used less fluid milk than those who used no evaporated milk. Specifically, those with incomes of $400 or below using no evaporated milk consumed, on an average, 0.5 of a quart of fresh milk per person per day. In the same income group those who used evaporated milk reported a daily fresh-milk consumption of less than half this amount— 0.2 of a quart per capita.

In the next income bracket ($400–$800) the per capita fluid-milk consump-

[2] According to the 1930 census, of the 48,000,000 people gainfully employed in the United States, a total of over 58 per cent received incomes of less than $1,100 per year, assuming full-time employment (compared with 55 per cent receiving less than $1,200 in our study). Thirteen per cent received an average of around $1,400 per year (as compared with 20 per cent in our study), leaving 29 per cent of those gainfully employed with annual incomes above $1,400 (as compared with 25 per cent which we found to be receiving $1,600 or more).

tion was 36 per cent higher among the families using no evaporated milk than among those who purchased the canned product. The same general trend existed for those whose incomes ranged from $800 to $1,600.

The difficulty of establishing cause-and-effect relationships is to be recognized, yet it appears a significant fact that this same relationship held throughout the entire range of family incomes up to $1,600. Consistently, those who used evaporated milk consumed less fluid milk than did those who purchased no evaporated milk. The same type of analysis was attempted for the purpose of establishing the relationship between the amount of consumption of evaporated milk between those who did not use and those who did use fluid milk. The relationship here was clear and probably even more pronounced than was shown above. All those receiving incomes below $1,600 who used no fluid milk consistently used much more evaporated milk than those who purchased fluid milk. Those with annual incomes of $400 or below who purchased no fluid milk used, on an average, 2 cans of evaporated milk per week as compared with half that amount (exactly 1 can) for those who also purchased fresh milk.

The survey, while limited in the size of sample, seems to present clear evidence that for the lower-income groups the substitution of evaporated milk for cream is very common.

Those purchasing no evaporated milk use appreciably more cream (although a small total consumption) than those who use evaporated milk. The increase in the use of cream climbed rapidly as incomes increased. On an average, those receiving an income of $800–$1,200 used 0.05 pint of coffee cream per week, whereas those in the $1,200–$1,600 group consumed 0.25 of a pint per week, or five times as much. Cream consumption increased greatly for the higher-income groups, being over 0.5 pint a week for those with incomes over $2,400. It appeared that evaporated milk was serving to replace coffee cream in part or in full for all income groups up to those receiving about $2,400 annually. For those receiving $2,400 or above, the consumption of cream is substantially as large where evaporated milk was used as where it was not. This suggests that for those families evaporated milk may be used in addition to the fresh cream as contrasted with a replacement of it in the low-income groups.

TRENDS OF PRICES AND CONSUMPTION OF FRESH FLUID AND OF EVAPORATED MILK

The fact has been recognized though probably not stressed among fluid-milk producers and distributors that the difference in retail price between fresh fluid and evaporated milk has been increasing gradually during the last two decades.

Table D shows that the average United States price difference in 1919 between a quart of fresh milk and a 14½-ounce can of evaporated milk was 1 cent. At that time a quart of milk sold, on an average, for 1 cent more than did a can of evaporated milk. By 1926 this difference had increased to 3.6 cents, and by 1936 to 4.4 cents. The 1938 average was the highest on record—5.3 cents.

This widening of the price spread between the two products has furnished a stimulant to induce housewives to replace the more expensive product by that less expensive wherever possible.

TABLE D

AVERAGE RETAIL PRICE OF EVAPORATED AND FRESH MILK IN MILWAUKEE, CHICAGO, AND THE UNITED STATES, 1919–38, INCLUSIVE

YEAR	MILWAUKEE			CHICAGO			UNITED STATES		
	Evaporated Milk (Cents per 14½-Ounce Can)	Fresh Milk (Cents per Quart)	Diff. Fresh over Evaporated (Cents per Quart or Can)	Evaporated Milk (Cents per 14½-Ounce Can)	Fresh Milk (Cents per Quart)	Diff. Fresh over Evaporated (Cents per Quart or Can)	Evaporated Milk (Cents per 14½-Ounce Can)	Fresh Milk (Cents per Quart)	Diff. Fresh over Evaporated (Cents per Quart or Can)
1919....	14.9	12.6	−2.3	13.8	14.2	0.4	14.5	15.5	1.0
1920....	14.3	12.3	−2.0	13.1	14.8	1.7	14.0	16.7	2.7
1921....	12.8	9.4	−3.4	11.8	13.4	1.6	12.6	14.6	2.0
1922....	9.8	9.2	−0.6	9.3	12.0	2.7	10.2	13.1	2.9
1923....	10.5	10.5	0.0	10.3	13.5	3.2	11.1	13.8	2.7
1924....	10.2	10.8	0.6	9.9	14.0	4.6	10.4	13.8	3.4
1925....	10.1	10.0	−0.1	9.8	14.0	4.2	10.3	14.0	3.7
1926....	10.2	10.8	0.6	10.0	14.0	4.0	10.4	14.0	3.6
1927....	10.2	11.0	0.8	10.2	14.0	3.8	10.4	14.1	3.7
1928....	10.0	11.0	1.0	10.1	14.0	3.9	10.2	14.2	4.0
1929....	9.8	11.2	1.4	9.7	14.0	4.3	9.9	14.3	4.4
1930....	9.2	11.4	2.2	9.0	14.0	5.0	9.2	14.0	4.8
1931....	8.2	9.9	1.7	8.1	13.0	4.9	8.2	12.3	4.1
1932....	7.1	8.3	1.2	6.9	11.2	4.3	6.9	10.9	4.0
1933....	6.8	8.5	1.7	6.8	9.9	3.1	6.6	10.6	4.0
1934....	6.9	9.4	2.5	6.8	9.5	2.7	6.7	11.2	4.5
1935....	7.2	10.0	2.8	7.1	10.7	3.6	7.0	11.8	4.8
1936....	7.7	10.8	3.1	7.7	11.4	3.7	7.6	12.0	4.4
1937....	7.9	12.0	4.1	7.8	12.4	4.6	7.6	12.5	4.9
1938....	7.5	12.0	4.5	7.2	12.3	5.1	7.2	12.5	5.3

The fact that price was the most or among the most important considerations in purchasing evaporated milk was quite clearly brought out in the survey. Sixty per cent of the housewives answering the question gave price as the most important reason for its use. Aside from its use in infant feeding, convenience and flavor were listed as other important reasons. Many of those questioned indicated that they preferred cream to evaporated milk in coffee but that they preferred evaporated milk to fresh milk for this purpose.

Consumption of evaporated milk in the United States has increased rapidly during the past decade or more. The apparent consumption in 1936 was almost 40 per cent above that of 1923. During this same period fresh fluid milk had actually decreased about 2 per cent (see Table E).[3]

TABLE E*

ANNUAL PER CAPITA CONSUMPTION OF FLUID MILK EQUIVALENT
OF CONDENSED AND EVAPORATED WHOLE MILK

YEAR	CONDENSED AND EVAPORATED WHOLE MILK		MILK USED IN CITIES AND VILLAGES (LB.)	EVAPORATED AND CONDENSED AS A PERCENTAGE OF FLUID MILK
	Pounds (1)	Pounds Milk Equivalent (2)	(3)	(4)
1925.........	11.8	26.0	334.5	7.8
1926.........	11.9	26.2	338.0	7.8
1927.........	11.7	25.7	341.4	7.5
1928.........	12.3	27.1	342.3	7.9
1929.........	13.6	29.9	350.9	8.5
1930.........	13.6	29.9	344.9	8.7
1931.........	13.4	29.5	335.4	8.8
1932.........	14.0	30.8	336.3	9.2
1933.........	13.8	30.4	332.0	9.2
1934.........	15.0	33.0	310.5	10.6
1935.........	16.1	35.4	315.6	11.2
1936.........	15.9	35.0	328.5	10.7
1937.........	16.4	36.1	†	†
1938.........	16.9	37.1	†	†

* Source: Estimates of United States Department of Agriculture, Bureau of Agricultural Economics.
† Comparable data not available for 1937 and 1938.

The increased replacement of fresh milk by evaporated milk during the past several years has apparently taken place primarily because of the gradually widening of the retail price difference between the two products, partly as the

[3] The improvement in scientific methods of food preparation make it increasingly more easy to substitute various food products for fresh milk. Taste for a food or a user's judgment of its relative utility does not remain fixed and unchanged. The psychology of taste is too subtle to lend itself to specific measurement even by the taster himself. Furthermore, tastes are influenced not only by the actual flavor or the commodity but also by the creation of impressions through advertising and educational influences of users or potential users.

result of changes in taste of consumers for evaporated milk, and partly as a result of an actual change in the quality and taste of the product itself—the result of improved techniques of manufacture. The lower the purchasing power of the individual, the more carefully he will canvass the alternatives to find substitutes for a food product which, though desired, is so expensive as to be, in the mind of the buyer, a heavy drain on the family budget.

In the case of such products as fruits or vegetables, where substitution of one product for another can be made quickly and easily, the response of the housewife to changes in price relationships is often almost instantaneous. Here, the shifting from one to the other requires no pronounced change in the culinary operations. As an example, peas can be substituted for carrots or cauliflower and prunes for grapefruit or oranges without disturbing the housewife's regular routine of cooking operations. But attempts to substitute evaporated for fresh milk in a cake, pie, or pudding recipe disturbs not only the culinary operation but the resultant product may not meet with the entire approval of the family. Whether that variation be real or imaginary is a matter of indifference as far as psychic reaction is concerned. For those reasons, changes in the uses of fresh milk, or the replacement of fresh by evaporated milk, come slowly; but, once such replacements are made, they have an aspect of permanency and are not intermittent as in the case of substituting oranges for grapefruit or carrots for cauliflower.

The demand for fluid milk has been considered to be relatively inelastic, and, when regarded from the point of view of a short-time period, that supposition is correct. However, when a longer time is involved, there may be a decided replacement of fresh milk and cream by evaporated milk and other products. Studies showing relationships between the price and the consumption of fluid milk have been, no doubt, accurate in both fact and reason, and we should in vain attempt to demonstrate the falsehood of the facts, analysis, or conclusions. It may, however, be worthy of our curiosity to inquire as to what the nature of the evidence is when price-consumption relationships are analyzed, taking into consideration a period not of several weeks but of several years. From studies on short-time relationships it is not to be assumed that the same relationships hold also when a longer time is involved. Quite to the contrary, broad generalization based upon findings covering short-time periods may be quite unwarranted when longer spans of time are involved. The price-quantity relationships over a long time may be vastly different from those over a short time. There are forceful suggestions that they are.

The data from this study should by no means be looked upon as ample to prove conclusively that we know how consumers react toward demand influences. While certain things are clearly suggestive, the study probably shows more conclusively than anything else that there is a pronounced lack of understanding concerning the nature of demand for fluid milk and its rivals. There is a real need for such facts as will provide a general body of knowledge on consumer preferences, tastes, and desires, and the manner in which these are or may be influenced, as well as the method by which and the extent to which they are now being changed. Demand studies to date, for the most part, have not been taken with a high degree of seriousness by those who determine the price and market policies. If agricultural economists and fluid-milk producers and distributors continue to underestimate the importance of long-time price relationships to consumption, it may easily happen that distributors will discover only too late that the sales which they anticipated regaining are in the permanent hands of those who are supplying not fresh fluid milk but instead other products, especially evaporated milk.[4]

From the point of view of those concerned with marketing fluid milk, results of this type of study prompt one to raise the broad question as to whether the fluid-milk policies followed in many cities give adequate consideration to consumer responses.

The findings of this, and other studies, serve as a clear warning that, if the retail price differential between fresh and evaporated milk is permitted continually to widen, or even is held at its present variation, there will continue to be an increased use of evaporated milk and likely a lessened use of fluid milk. Fluid-milk producers cannot afford to ignore the fact that fluid-milk consumption in cities and villages is apparently not even holding its own, to say nothing about increasing (Table E, col. 3), whereas evaporated consumption is increasing rapidly. Moreover, producers in self-interest cannot afford to ignore giving attention to such adjustments in the methods of processing and distributing fluid milk that will make for narrower margins of distribution, with its resultant lower consumer price (without reducing the farm price), and the consequent tendency of increased fluid-milk consumption.

[4] For a discussion of manufacturing and marketing evaporated milk see Henry H. Bakken, *The Cost of Manufacturing and Marketing Evaporated Milk* (Rio, Wis.: Rio Journal, 1938).

BIBLIOGRAPHY

BIBLIOGRAPHY

AGRICULTURAL ADJUSTMENT ADMINISTRATION. *A Survey of Milk Marketing in Milwaukee.* "U.S.D.A., Marketing Information Series," DM-1. Washington, 1937.

BARTLETT, R. W. *Prices and Consumption of Milk in Specific Cities.* University of Illinois Bull. 397. Urbana, 1932.

BLANFORD, CHARLES. *An Economic Study of the Costs of Selling and Delivering Milk in the New York Market.* Cornell University Agricultural Experiment Station Bull. 686. Ithaca, 1938.

BROWN, C. A. *Margins and Other Related Factors in the Distributing of Fluid Milk in Four Illinois Market Areas.* University of Illinois Bull. 318. Urbana, 1928.

BUCKINGHAM, S. McLEAN. "Dealers' Spread in Connecticut." Hartford, 1938. (Mimeographed.)

CASSELS, J. M. "Excess Capacity and Monopolistic Competition," *Quarterly Journal of Economics,* LI (1937), 426–43.

———. *Study of Fluid Milk Prices.* Cambridge: Harvard University Press, 1937.

CASSELS, J. M., and SORENSON, HELEN. "The English Milk Market," *Quarterly Journal of Economics,* L (1936), 275–96.

DOW, GEORGE L. "Ways of Reducing Cost of Distributing Milk in Maine," *Journal of Farm Economics,* Vol. XXI (February, 1939).

ERDMAN, HENRY E. *The Marketing of Fluid Milk.* New York: Macmillan Co., 1921.

FEDERAL TRADE COMMISSION. *Distribution and Sale of Milk and Milk Products (Boston, Baltimore, Cincinnati, and St. Louis).* House Doc. 501. 74th Cong.; 2d sess. Washington, 1936.

———. *Distribution and Sale of Milk and Milk Products: Chicago Sales Area.* House Doc. 451. 74th Cong.; 2d sess. Washington, 1936.

———. *Distribution and Sale of Milk and Milk Products: Philadelphia and Connecticut Milksheds.* House Doc. 152. 74th Cong.; 2d sess. Washington, 1935.

———. *Distribution and Sale of Milk and Milk Products: Philadelphia and Connecticut Milksheds.* House Doc. 381. 74th Cong.; 2d sess. Washington, 1936.

———. *Distribution and Sale of Milk and Milk Products: New York Sales Area.* House Doc. 95. 75th Cong.; 1st sess. Washington, 1937.

———. *Distribution and Sale of Milk and Milk Products: Twin City Sales Area.* House Doc. 506. 74th Cong.; 2d sess. Washington, 1936.

FEDERAL TRADE COMMISSION. *Summary Report of Conditions with Respect to the Sale and Distribution of Milk and Dairy Products.* House Doc 94. 75th Cong.; 1st sess. Washington, 1937.

———. *Cooperative Marketing.* Senate Doc. 95. 70th Cong.; 1st sess. Washington, 1928.

GAUMNITZ, E. W., and REED, O. M. *Some Problems Involved in Establishing Milk Prices.* "A.A.A., U.S.D.A., Marketing Information Series," DM-2. Washington, 1937.

HARROD, R. F. "The Law of Decreasing Costs," *Economic Journal,* XLI (1931), 566.

———. "A Further Note on Decreasing Costs," *ibid.,* XLIII (1933), 337.

HIBBARD, B. H., and ERDMAN, H. E. *Marketing Wisconsin Milk.* University of Wisconsin Bull. 285. Madison, 1917.

KALDOR, N. "Market Imperfection and Excess Capacity," *Economica,* II (new ser., 1935), 33.

KING, CLYDE L. *The Price of Milk.* Philadelphia: John C. Winston Co., 1920.

MARSHALL, JOHN, Jr. "Cost of Distributing Market Milk in San Francisco." Sacramento: Division of Markets, California Department of Agriculture, 1932. (Mimeographed.)

METZGER, HUTZEL. *Cooperative Marketing of Fluid Milk.* U.S.D.A. Technical Bull. 179. Washington, 1930.

MORTENSON, W. P. *An Economic Study of the Milwaukee Milk Market.* University of Wisconsin Research Bull. 113. Madison, 1932.

———. "Distribution of Milk under Public Utility Regulation," *American Economic Review,* XXVI, No. 1 (March, 1936), 23–40.

———. *Economic Considerations in Marketing Fluid Milk.* University of Wisconsin Research Bull. 125. Madison, 1934.

PIERCE, C. W. "Survey of Milk Routes in New York City," *Farm Economics,* XVII February, 1935), 2131–33.

QUINTUS, PAUL E., and STITTS, T. G. *Cooperative Fluid Milk Associations in Iowa.* Farm Credit Administration Cooperative Circ. C-105. Washington, 1937.

RITTENHOUSE, CHARLES F., *et al. Summary Report on Cost of Distributing Milk in the Boston Market.* Prepared for Massachusetts Milk Control Board. Boston, 1936.

ROBINSON, JOAN. "Imperfect Competition and Falling Supply Price," *Economic Journal,* XLII (1932), 544.

ROSS, H. A. *The Marketing of Milk in the Chicago Dairy District.* University of Illinois Bull. 269. Urbana, 1925.

SHOVE, G. F. "The Representative Firm and Increasing Returns," *Economic Journal,* XL (1930), 94.

SPENCER, LELAND. "Costs and Profits of Milk Dealers in New York City, August, 1933." Report to the Division of Milk Control, New York State Department of Agriculture and Markets, April 16, 1934. (Mimeographed.)

———. "Costs and Profits of Milk Dealers in Up-State Cities, August, 1933." Report to the New York State Milk Control Board, March 24, 1934. (Mimeographed.)

———. "Milk Distribution a Public Utility," *American Produce Review*, October 26, 1938, pp. 774–75.

———. "Milk Distributors' Costs and Profits." Preliminary Report to the New York Milk Control Board, October 17, 1933. (Mimeographed).

———. "Practice and Theory of Market Exclusion within the United States," *Journal of Farm Economics*, XV (January, 1933), 141–58.

SRAFFA, P. "The Laws of Returns under Competitive Conditions," *Economic Journal*, XXXVI (1926), 535.

STELZER, R. O., and THURSTON, L. M. *Milk Distribution Costs in West Virginia*. West Virginia Bull. 266. Morgantown, 1935.

TINLEY, J. M. *Public Regulation of Milk Marketing in California*. Berkeley: University of California Press, 1938.

WELDEN, WILLIAM C., and STITTS, T. G. *Milk Cooperatives in Four Ohio Markets*. Farm Credit Administration Bull. 16. Washington, 1937.

WILLIAMS, JOHN R. "The Economic Problems of Milk Distribution in Their Relation to Public Health," in *Transactions of the Fifteenth International Congress on Hygiene and Demography*, V, 128–40. Washington, 1913.

INDEX

INDEX

Accounting: errors in, 34; systems of, 34

Accounts: collection of, 48; method of collecting, 57; past due, 41, 89

Adjustments, regulation, 11; advantages of public control, 16

Advertising, 31, 36, 39, 189, 196; cost of, 77; savings through unification in, 76

Affected with a public interest, 8, 126

Agricultural commission, 152

All other costs, 80–85

Analysis: adequacy of, 34; operating costs and profit, 132; purposes of, 26

Apartment-house districts, delivery to, 59

Associations; *see* Co-operatives

Automatic features, for processing, 42, 72

Bad debts, 25, 31, 36, 39, 78–79, 189, 196; savings through unification in, 82, 85

Bang's disease, 108

Bargaining associations, 163, 185; influence of, 175, 176

Beard, Charles A., 133, 134

Bibliography, 211

Bigham, Truman, 139

Blanford, Charles, 49

Bonds, 141; revenue, 142

Bordon Co. v. *Ten Eyck*, 115

Bottle caps, 80

Bottle fillers, 69

Bottle losses, 41

Bottles, 80

Bottling, 32

Brandeis, Mr. Justice, 133

Brands of milk, special, 43, 52, 53

Buildings: capital investment in, 100; depreciation of, 71–72, 74; repairs of, 76; savings through unification in, 71

Capacity: bottle-filling machine, 69; existing operating, 68; ideal, 68; pasteurizer, 69; plant, 68

Capital: borrowed, 92; cost of, 141; defined, 93; fixed and movable, 70; fixed and required, 67; investment, 100

Cardozo, Justice, 113

Cases, 80

Changes, in present system, 24

Class I milk, 5, 174, 175, 176, 177, 178, 179

Class II milk, 174, 175, 176, 177, 178, 179

Clayton Act, 4

Cleaning: methods, 67; of plant, 42

Clothed with a public interest, 14

Collection: of accounts, 48; methods of, 57; for milk, 47, 48; time spent for, 49

Collective action, 4

Commissions, 163, 164; agricultural, 152; enforcement by, 11; orders of, 11; price-control, 7; public utility, 152

Companies: large and small compared, 41, 42; low-cost, 38; milk-distributing, 154

Competition, 91, 120, 177; freedom of, 3; regulated, 131; wastes in, 131

Competitive system, 136, 140, 141; time required to serve customers under, 56

Consolidation, 90

Constitution: interpretation of, 132–36; rights of, 14; validity of, 106

Consumers: benefits to, under unification, 80; convenience of, 88; gains to, under unification, 166, 173; influence of, on prices, 164; protest of, 202; service desired by, 42, 87–89

Consumption, 91; effect of consumer incomes on, 183; of fluid milk and cream, 177; of fresh and evaporated milk, 201; increase of, 178; per capita of evaporated milk, 206; substitution in, 207

Control, 150; boards, 164; measures, 7; obstruction to, 10; progress of, 9; purpose of, 8; trends of future, 11

Conveyors, 43

Cooler space, 43

Co-operatives: bargaining, 185; milk-distributing, 154; producer, 23

Costs, 33; advertising, 77; all other, 80; bottles, 80; of capital, 141; cases, 80; delivery, 41, 45, 198; division of, 189; feed, 80; general survey of, 23; insurance, 79; light, 79–80; milk distribution, 189; operating, 35, 93, 198; original, 156, 157; power, 79–80; repairs, 76;